1835

1835

**THE FOUNDING OF MELBOURNE
& THE CONQUEST OF AUSTRALIA**

James Boyce

Black Inc.

Published by Black Inc.,
an imprint of Schwartz Media Pty Ltd
37–39 Langridge Street
Collingwood VIC 3066 Australia
email: enquiries@blackincbooks.com
http://www.blackincbooks.com

Map of the Aboriginal languages of Victoria (p.7) © Victorian Aboriginal Corporation for
Languages, based on the work of Ian Clark. Map of pastoral expansion in Victoria (p.ix) is
adapted from *The Public Lands of Australia Felix* by J.M. Powell, Oxford University Press,
1970. Map of pastoral settlement in Australia (p.viii) is adapted from *The Oxford History of the
British Empire*, Oxford University Press, 1999.

Every effort has been made to contact the copyright holders of material in this book.
However, where an omission has occurred, the publisher will gladly include
acknowledgment in any future edition.

The National Library of Australia Cataloguing-in-Publication entry:

    Boyce, James.

    1835 : the founding of Melbourne & the conquest of Australia / James Boyce.

    3rd ed.

    9781863956000 (pbk.)

    Includes bibliographical references and index.

    Melbourne (Vic.)--History.
    Australia--History.
    Australia--Colonization.

    994.51

Text design: Thomas Deverall
Index: Michael Ramsden

Printed in Australia by Griffin Press.
The paper this book is printed on is
certified against the Forest Stewardship
Council® Standards. Griffin Press holds
FSC chain of custody certification
SGS-COC-005088. FSC promotes
environmentally responsible, socially
beneficial and economically viable
management of the world's forests.

Australian Government

This project has been assisted by the Australian Government through the Australia Council,
its arts funding and advisory body.

Contents

To Julie Pender and Terry Burke,
heroes of Port Phillip

∾

Map of pastoral settlement of Australia

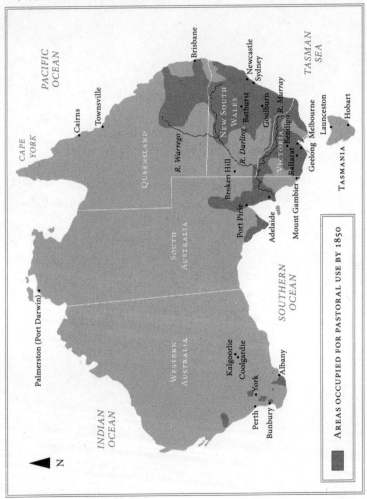

AREAS OCCUPIED FOR PASTORAL USE BY 1850

Map of pastoral settlement of Victoria

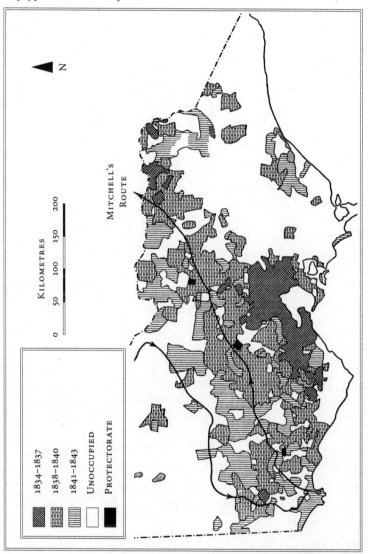

One cannot complain of what cannot be otherwise.
—ISAIAH BERLIN, 1954

PREFACE

In 1835 an illegal squatter camp was established on the banks of the Yarra River. This brazen act would shape the history of Australia as much as would the arrival of the First Fleet in 1788, because it was now that the continent was fully opened to conquest. No more was settlement to be restricted to defined boundaries: within twelve months the British government would allow settlers to go where they pleased.

Melbourne's birth, not Sydney's settlement, signalled the emergence of European control over Australia. Britons had, of course, never been wholly confined within the official 'limits of location' (which by 1835 extended about 120 miles inland from Sydney),[1] but it was only after the abandonment of the long-established policy of concentrated settlement that exclusive territorial claims beyond defined borders were made, perfect sovereignty over Aboriginal country was asserted, and the continental land rush began.

Between 1835 and 1838 alone, more land and more people were conquered than in the preceding half-century. By the end of the 1840s, squatters had seized nearly twenty million hectares of the most productive and best-watered Aboriginal homelands, comprising most of the grasslands in what are now Victoria, New South Wales, South Australia and southern Queensland. It was 'one of the fastest land occupations in the history of empires.'[2] In little more than a decade, the continental pinpricks which represented the totality of British occupation in 1835 became a sea of red.

The catalyst for this momentous change in settlement policy was the founding of Melbourne, the only major Australian city established without government sanction. The movement of men and sheep across Bass Strait from Van Diemen's Land, as Tasmania was then known, was a private and highly speculative investment. No one was in any doubt that it was also trespass. Consequently, the pioneers' principal challenge was not to subdue the physical environment – this was benign grassland country – but to achieve a change in law and policy.

The principal obstacle to achieving a political decision favourable to the squatters' cause was the Aborigines. After the abolition of slavery throughout the British Empire in 1833, energised evangelical reformers had turned their attention to the plight of the empire's native peoples. In 1835 a Whig government led by Lord Melbourne came to power, and evangelical activism permeated the highest offices of the land.

One of the most important questions of Australian history is why, at the apex of imperial concern for the rights of indigenous people, an evangelical Secretary of State for the Colonies, Lord Glenelg, responded as he did to the challenge posed by the ambitious property speculators of Van Diemen's Land. Why did he decide to end the policy of restricted settlement and allow the sheep barons to send their men and flocks anywhere they chose? How did he and other evangelical political leaders of London (and indeed Sydney and Hobart) come to promote a legal and policy change that saw colonisation degenerate into a frenzied land grab?

To understand how the floodgates were opened to the continent's vast pastures, it is necessary to travel far from the Port Phillip district, as Victoria was then called. In 1835, in Hobart, Sydney and London, the inter-related questions of the Aborigines and colonisation were being considered by bureaucrats, politicians and activists.

It will be seen that the squatters themselves were far from passive agents: through their famous treaty with the Aborigines and their careful lobbying, conducted all the way from remote grasslands to the offices of Westminster, the well-connected gentlemen of Van Diemen's Land pursued their profitable cause. The squatters did not win private title, but the open access conceded by the government had more dramatic consequences than even their ambitious scheming could have anticipated. The tsunami generated by the change in government policy in 1835–36 was such that almost every resident of Australia, black and white, was swept up in its tide.

After the founding of Melbourne, colonial ambition, regulation and law finally came into alignment. So strong was the new consensus (despite endless dispute over detail) that the right of settlers to live where they chose soon became taken for granted. What had been one position (albeit the dominant local one) in a complex debate was now taken to be common sense. Indeed, the ridicule of the previous policy of concentrated and restricted settlement was so effective and long-lasting that the most important question of all seems to have disappeared: could it have been different? Did the continent have to be colonised this way?

I set out to write a book about the founding of Melbourne. Only full immersion in the Yarra's murky waters led me to understand that the policy turmoil which followed the establishment of a squatters' camp in 1835 had a significance far beyond the baptism of a great city. In this place, at this time, 'Australia' was born.

PART I

SETTING THE SCENE

1.

THE YARRA 1835

ABOUT FORTY MILLION YEARS AGO volcanoes began erupting in what is now Victoria. As Tim Flannery recounts, in time the resulting basalt rock 'would break down to form the largest area of rich soils in Australia ... [and] one of the continent's most productive regions.' The lava flow and the basalt plains were concentrated in the west, with the Yarra River sitting astride the soil divide.[1] Under Aboriginal land management, through what has become known as fire-stick farming,[2] much of the country to the west and north of Melbourne became open grassland. It was these hunting grounds that would eventually be the focus of British ambitions, although equally characteristic of the lower Yarra were the oft-forgotten swamps.

So widespread were these wetlands that Flannery imagines Melbourne in 1830 'as a sort of temperate Kakadu.'[3] The heart of the lakes, marshlands and billabongs was the Yarra River, but it was a radically different watercourse from the one bearing that name today, which from the present-day Botanic Gardens to Port Phillip Bay now 'flows through an almost totally artificial channel.'[4] The river was tidal up to a rocky basalt ledge (where Queens Bridge now stands), at which point it was as much as ninety metres wide.[5] What the British would call 'the falls' acted as a barrier to the saline tidal flows, ensuring that upstream of the rocks could be found a permanent source of fresh water.

This natural bridge, where salt water met fresh, was also where geology and botany divided in an apex of ecological encounter. Within an easy walk could be found grasslands, various woodlands, as well as, in almost every direction, mud. On the northern side of the river, stretching three kilometres to the north-west, 'was a wide expanse of flat, boggy land, greater than 1000 acres ... in extent.' In the middle of this was a permanent lagoon, which one early settler recalled as 'a beautiful blue lake ... intensely blue, nearly oval and full of the clearest salt water; but this by no means deep.' On the southern side of the Yarra, between the river and the edge of the bay, swampy land stretched for about six and a half kilometres and included a number of permanent lagoons, including what was to become (with more than a little taming) Albert Park Lake. There were also extensive lagoons in the region of what is now Port Melbourne.[6] By contrast, much of today's central business district was well-drained grasslands, framed by gentle and lightly wooded hills, such as Batman's Hill, where Southern Cross Station now stands, and the pastoral plains stretched far to the north and west.

Of all Australia's major cities, the natural environment of Melbourne before British settlement is perhaps the most difficult now to imagine. This is in part a product of the city's size and flat topography, but it also reflects the extent to which the region was dominated by swamps and grasslands – the two ecosystems that were most comprehensively transformed by conquest.

The draining of wetlands has been a northern European obsession for centuries. The ordered agricultural lands of England's East Anglia region, for instance, are so different from the lost wilderness they replaced (where the people once roamed almost as freely as the animals) that cultural memory has been unable to retain a picture of the vanished landscape, even though the most intense drainage occurred only in the nineteenth century. At the time of Melbourne's founding, the focus of Australian farming had shifted from cropping to sheep, and most of the wetlands were left alone for twenty years, allowing them to fulfil, to some extent, their ancient British purpose of providing a refuge for the landless and poor. However, once property speculation began in earnest, the marshes were drained with ruthless efficiency, and only very pale reflections of their lost splendour now remain.

Even more difficult to imagine are the vanished grasslands. Here language misleads – the native grassland of the Melbourne region was as different from contemporary pastureland as an old-growth forest is from a tree plantation. Port Phillip's once-vast temperate grasslands have almost completely vanished, with the remnant pockets that survive able to support only a fraction of the original ecological diversity.[7] The extinct pasture abounded in diverse herbs, flowers and orchids, as well as grasses. According to Gary Presland in his revealing history, *The Place for a Village: How Nature Has Shaped the City of Melbourne*, the plant communities of the grasslands close to Merri Creek alone 'contained at least 156 species, including 31 different grass species … 24 species of Rush or Sedge, and a wide range of herbaceous species.'[8]

Although it is often assumed that British settlers couldn't appreciate the Australian landscape, almost all visitors were astounded by the beauty and wealth of these grasslands. The 1836 observations of John Norcock, an officer on HMS *Rattlesnake*, the vessel that transported the first government officials from Sydney to Port Phillip, are typical:

> The country here is enchantingly beautiful – extensive rich plains all round with gently sloping hills in the distance, all thinly wooded and having the appearance of an immense park. The grasses, flowers and herbs that cover the plains are of every variety that can be imagined, and present a lovely picture of what is evidently intended by Nature to be one of the richest pastoral countries in the world.[9]

The fauna, too, was magnificently diverse, especially the bird life. One early observer listed more than 180 bird species within a one-mile radius of Melbourne, including the ground birds of the open grasslands such as the emu, Australian bustard, plains wanderer and brush turkey.[10] The wetlands provided the richest concentration, including swans, ducks, brolgas, magpie-geese, Cape Barren geese and over twenty migratory species.

There were also at least twenty species of fish in the rivers, creeks and marshes, including two types of eel. The Aborigines gathered annually to harvest the shortfinned eel (*Anguilla australis*), which each year moved up the rivers and creeks into the Yarra wetlands (eventually migrating downstream again on sexual maturity, beginning an extraordinary journey to the Coral Sea to breed and die). In places the Aborigines 'devised earthworks and stoneworks' to catch the well-travelled eels, constructions which, as Geoffrey Blainey notes, 'when we think of their simple equipment, quite take the breath away.'[11] The so-called 'founder of Melbourne,' John Batman, observed such eel traps in creeks near Melbourne on his first visit in 1835: 'The walls were built of stones about four feet high, and well done and well planned out. Two or three of these places following each other down the stream with gates to them.'[12] Good eating river blackfish and bream were abundant in the waterways, as were the local yabby (*Cherax destructor*) and the Yarra spiny crayfish (*Euastacus armatus*).[13]

As Presland points out, the creek valleys were also human transport corridors, traversing ecological and political boundaries (a role he observes they have to some extent maintained, with highways and railways often constructed over these creek beds). The Moonee Ponds Creek valley, along which much of the Tullamarine Freeway now runs, was a major highway to the north, particularly to Mount William, where greenstone (metabasalt) was mined and used in making hatchet heads.[14]

Given its rich soils, abundant water and diverse food, it is not surprising that the area around Port Phillip was one of the more heavily populated regions of Australia (although it is likely that by 1835 the population had already been reduced by introduced disease).[15] There were two groups whose territories directly bordered Port Phillip Bay. On the western side were the Watha wurrung,

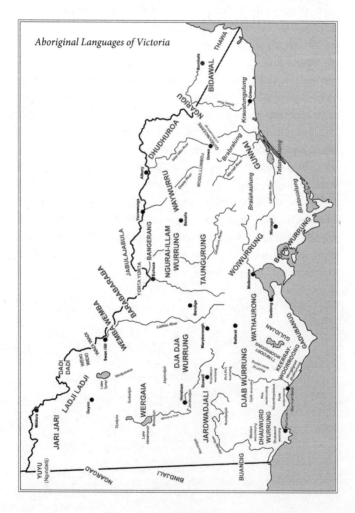

whose lands stretched from the Otway Ranges to the Werribee River. To the east of the Mornington Peninsula, the area around Westernport and the southern Dandenongs was the home of the Boon wurrung-speaking people. The Woi wurrung homeland composed the area drained by the Yarra River and its tributaries. Two other peoples, the Daung wurrung and Djadja wurrung, whose territory was to the north of Port Phillip Bay, completed the Kulin federation, which shared language and cultural ties.[16]

Within Kulin country, what is now central Melbourne was a hub of meetings and movement. The basalt ledge (Queens Bridge) provided a convenient crossing point to diverse ecological regions that contained seasonal food supplies capable of feeding large gatherings of people. Many of the creek highways meandered their way to the Yarra, and what better place for different language groups to meet for ceremony and business than in the bounteous grass next to the large pond where the fresh water began?

In 1835 the British did not chance upon an unknown place. The advantages of the Melbourne region had been known for millennia. John Batman and the other would-be founders of Melbourne merely recognised what had long been obvious: this was a place where *homo sapiens* might thrive.

2.

BASS STRAIT 1835

LONG BEFORE THE FIRST TENTS WERE PITCHED on the banks of the Yarra and the first sheep were let loose on the vast hunting grounds of the Kulin, a motley collection of Britons lived in Victoria.[17]

The Bass Strait region was first colonised by the British only a decade after the arrival of the First Fleet in 1788, and some five years before the official settlement of Van Diemen's Land. The motives for the movement south, far from the centre of British power, were both profit and freedom, with the immediate source of these being the hundreds of thousands of resident seals. These defenceless animals, having never known humans (the Furneaux Group of islands had been unpopulated for thousands of years), were clubbed easily and mercilessly to their death, with the skins largely exported to China. The sealers soon pushed beyond the Bass Strait along the southern coast of the Australian mainland in pursuit of more such game. Official exploration parties regularly came across evidence of the resulting contact with the Aborigines. An officer with an 1803 expedition reported, after two hostile encounters with the Aborigines in Port Phillip Bay, that 'In both instances they signified their knowledge and fear of the effect of firearms.'[18]

Such was the ease with which seals could be bludgeoned that, in spite of the incessant search for new colonies, yields soon declined. More lasting than the vulnerable animals were the human communities that developed around them. Men, especially former convicts, lived for months, sometimes years, at a time in these remote regions, and gradually began to form permanent settlements. They killed remnant seals and kangaroos, sold the skins, ate the meat from these and other animals, and even had gardens and small farms with crops and goats. The *Sydney Gazette* reported on Captain Hammond's experience of meeting Europeans and Aboriginal women living on Kangaroo Island in a 'curious state of independence' in 1817:

> They are complete savages, living in bark huts like the natives, not cultivating anything, but living entirely on kangaroos, emus and small porcupines, and getting spirits and tobacco in barter for the skins which they capture during the sealing season. They dress in kangaroo skin without linen and wear sandals made of seal skin. They smell like foxes.[19]

Phillip Island was another such base. The seal colony at Seal Rocks had been discovered by James Grant as early as 1801,[20] and the officers who founded a short-lived military outpost at Westernport during 1826 reported that sealers from Port Dalrymple (Launceston) were already in permanent residence on the island, with a couple of acres of wheat and some maize growing well.[21]

Attempts were made to bring these communities and the resources they plundered under imperial control. This was one of the reasons Governor King gave for the official colonisation of Van Diemen's Land in September 1803, but little authority could in practice be exercised, and the two streams of British colonisation proceeded largely independently of each other.

Nor were sealers the only unofficial colonisers. Whales had been hunted in southern Australian waters since 1775, when three vessels of the whaling house Enderby pioneered the pursuit in the South Seas, and their crews spent extended periods ashore gathering food, fuel and water.[22] During the 1820s, bay whaling, conducted in small boats from semi-permanent stations along the south coast of mainland Australia, became widespread.[23] For four or five months each year, the migration patterns of the Southern Right Whale took them on a predictable route close to the coast, making them vulnerable to the whalers who took up residence in favoured bays and estuaries.

Although the bay whalers concentrated first on what is now the South Australian coast, from the early 1830s parts of what is now Victoria were the centre of their enterprise. The largest such concern, conducted by the Launceston Fishing Company, had its main base at Portland Bay. Shipping records show a steady stream of vessels sailing across Bass Strait by the mid-1830s, delivering men and stores, picking up oil and assisting the whaling operations.[24]

From the 1830s, too, easily accessible supplies of wattle bark were exported to Britain, where they were used to tan leather. This was an industry that needed no capital investment to enter, and for the predominantly emancipist (former convict) white residents, bark supplemented animal skins and seasonal wage labour to ensure a steady supply of tobacco, tea, rum, sugar and other provisions from the merchant traders plying the coast.

For both the commercial interests and the self-employed workers themselves, work and residence could shift easily. Sealers and whalers regularly moved between the Port Phillip coast, the Bass Strait islands and the mainland of Van Diemen's Land, hunting, working on whaling stations and collecting bark in the off-season.

The cash profit from these diverse enterprises was concentrated in the hands of a small number of absentee investors, and for most resident-emancipists capital accumulation was neither possible nor their principal object. The abundant 'free' resources enabled these men to pursue a way of life in which isolation and material deprivation were traded for independence from magistrates and masters.

The documented adventures of John Boultbee, resident at Phillip Island in the summer of 1824–25, provide an insight into the 'sealer' way of life (all Britons resident in the Bass Strait region before 1835 were somewhat misleadingly described as sealers and historians have generally followed suit). Boultbee, unhappy with conditions on board the trader *Sally*, requested that he be left on the island. The lure was the diverse and plentiful food: muttonbirds, shellfish and fairy penguins. Boultbee lived on Phillip Island for some months and met men who had come to shoot swans (whose feathers were another saleable commodity). Eventually he joined a group of hunters living largely off seal carcasses. When a schooner arrived to trade the skins for provisions, Boultbee departed, but his companions stayed on, in what was to them home territory.[25]

Unlike the land grabbers to come, the sealers' territorial claims were provisional, and their comparative vulnerability and desire for skins, food and company fostered trade and cultural ties with the Aborigines. Indeed, the unfree labour of Aboriginal women – skilled in hunting animals, obtaining food, building shelters, travelling the country and facilitating land access – was essential to the success of the enterprise, and as integral to their relations with white men as sexual exploitation. Slavery was not officially abolished in the British Empire until 1833, and so many sealers brought the mindset of slavery to their relations with the Aboriginal women they 'acquired.'[26] Edward Henty, who settled Portland Bay in 1834, used the usual idiom when he wrote in his journal on 5 January 1835 of the 'Black Woman belonging to Wm Dutton.'[27] From the late 1820s dramatic changes in Van Diemen's Land – the privatisation of profitable resources, the removal of the Aborigines (including the women) and the extension of government authority as far as the Furneaux Group – meant that many sealers migrated permanently across the strait. One such left a note to this effect for George Augustus Robinson, the government's 'conciliator' of the Aborigines, when he visited the Kent Group in 1831: 'Gone to Western Port.'[28] The result was that the boundary of the Van Diemonian frontier (or the line of official control) shifted north, and former convicts seeking the freedom and resources of the 'common' arrived in the Port Phillip District in ever-increasing numbers.

During the early 1830s conflict with Aborigines, often arising from the abduction of women, increased in all of the sealer-populated regions. This intensifying violence was a product of the growing white population, shifts in the balance of power, more intense exploitation of resources, growing Aboriginal resistance and the regional fall-out from the fighting engulfing Van Diemen's Land.

Robinson documented typical examples of sealer violence in his journal. On 15 October 1830, he 'Asked Bull.rer alias Jumbo who took her from her people. Said Munro [a leading member of the sealing community] and others rushed them at their fires and took six, that she was a little girl and could just crawl; said she had been with Munro ever since. Said the white men tie the black women to trees and stretch out their arms (showed me the way they tied them) and then they flog them very much, plenty much blood, plenty cry – this they do if they take biscuit or sugar.'[29]

In 1836 the Van Diemen's Land government was asked to return women 'who have been forcibly taken from their husbands and families, from the southern coast of New Holland, by some employed in sealing, and who frequent the islands in Bass Strait.'[30] It was also advised of a recent bloody attack on young women and children by sealers, and heard that 'about a year and a half ago a similar attack was made upon the natives and four of their women were taken from them,' and that 'like outrages have been committed upon the Aborigines at Portland Bay and other whaling stations.'[31]

Blame for one of these incidents was attributed by the investigating magistrate to 'a half caste named Tomlins at present employed in a whaling establishment at Portland Bay' but who was then 'collecting mimosa bark.'[32] Edward (or Ned) Tomlins seems to have been the leader of a gang securing women before the new whaling season commenced. On 29 March 1836, just a few weeks after the attack 'on young women' at Westernport, Edward Henty noted in his journal: 'Arrived the schooner Thistle … Passengers E. Tomlins & 8 Men for Whaling Company, also one woman kept and stowed away.'[33] The presence of Tomlins, a second-generation sealer (his mother was a Tasmanian Aborigine known to the British as 'Bullrub') who had moved from his former base in north-west Tasmania where Robinson had first met him in 1830,[34] was a testament to how entrenched the Van Diemonian community was across the Bass Strait region by 1835.

Henty, who is often called the 'first' settler of Victoria (the poor don't count: class distinctions still resonate), provides more evidence of the conflict between sealers and Aborigines before Melbourne was founded. He had little contact with the Aborigines, even though the country inland from Portland Bay seems to have been thickly populated (one village Henty saw had fifty huts).[35] It is not surprising the Aborigines kept their distance. Shortly after he arrived in December 1834, Henty set off with some resident whalers, Dutton's Aboriginal woman and fourteen dogs on an exploratory trip. Only one Aborigine was seen, and as soon as he was spotted, 'the Men set the Dogs on' him[36] (these were the formidable hunting dogs, a cross between wolfhounds and greyhounds, which accompanied Van Diemonian Britons everywhere and made a formidable first-strike force in raids on Aboriginal camps). Henty also consistently referred to one stretch of the local coast as the 'Convincing ground'[37], named for reasons he later revealed to Robinson: this was where whalers had 'let fly … right and left upon the natives.'[38] Henty claimed the fight had started over whale meat, but one of the headsmen at Port Fairy would later tell Robinson that it had also related to the abduction of women.

Given the conflict between Europeans and Aborigines at Port Phillip before 1835, it is not surprising that the legendary 'white Aborigine,' William Buckley, claimed to have long 'avoided going to Westernport' because the sealers 'ill-treated the blacks and were attacked and ill-treated in their turn.'[39] Buckley, a convict, had escaped from the short-lived penal outpost established in 1803 near present-day Sorrento by David Collins (who soon decided to relocate to Hobart). Buckley lived with Aboriginal people from early 1804 until 1835, avoiding all contact with whites in the interim.

Such was the impact of white incursions in the early 1830s, according to Buckley, that some Aboriginal people came to believe there was a danger the sky would fall in. He recalled that 'just before the settlers came to Port Phillip' in 1835, the spirit in charge of the pillar which supported the sky had ordered that tomahawks be sent 'to enable him to repair a new prop for the sky, as the present [one] had become rotten and their destruction was inevitable should the sky fall upon them.' But where were the goods to be obtained 'to prevent so dreadful a catastrophe, and to supply the offering of tomahawks as speedily as possible'? Already the complexity of resistance was evident: 'some of the blacks repaired to Westernport and stole the iron work from settlers' carts left there.'[40]

The 'founders' of Melbourne, then, did not encounter Aborigines unfamiliar with British ways. Misunderstanding and conflict might have been rife, but the 1835 encounter would not be a 'dancing with strangers' as at Port Jackson fifty years before.[41] The Aborigines of Port Phillip already understood both the utility of British goods and the threat posed by British power, and it is thus not surprising that some of their number would prove both ready and able to negotiate.

VAN DIEMEN'S LAND 1835

MELBOURNE WAS NOT FOUNDED, like every other Australian capital city, by government-sanctioned settlement parties sent from London or Sydney, but instead by private adventurers from the notorious penal colony of Van Diemen's Land. Just as the founding of Sydney in 1788 must be seen in the context of developments in Britain, the establishment of the camp on the Yarra can only be understood with reference to Van Diemen's Land. Melbourne, too, has her mother island.

There was much more to the infamous society to the south than Port Arthur, road gangs and a harsh penal apparatus. In 1835 the island was a thriving centre for investors and speculators. James Bellich points out that from 1827 Van Diemen's Land experienced the 'world's first Anglo boom outside North America.' By 1835 the population had increased to about forty thousand (about seventeen thousand of whom were convicts still under sentence), roughly one-third of the European population of Australia.[42] Well before 1820 the island was home to the majority of Australia's sheep – in that year Van Diemen's Land had twice as many as New South Wales. Although these animals were initially kept for meat, by the early 1830s Van Diemen's Land was also Australia's leading wool exporter. The colony's economic output was larger than that of New South Wales on a per capita basis and during the early 1830s it threatened to overtake the mother colony even in absolute terms. The chair of the Colonization Commission for South Australia, who was keen to emulate Van Diemen's Land's success, believed that in 1835 Van Diemen's Land, 'in proportion to her population, has a commerce nearly six times greater than that of the Canadas; five times greater than that of Nova Scotia; [and] four and a half times greater than that of the Cape Colony.'[43]

Political stability contributed to the island's prosperity. Lieutenant Governor George Arthur was, in 1835, enjoying the last full year of his reign. One of the most powerful and capable political leaders in Australia's history, this hard-working technocrat had, after eleven years of imperial service, transformed the disordered society he inherited in 1824. Van Diemen's Land now presented two faces to the world. For the empire's poor it was a byword for terror, while for free immigrants from Britain it was a respectable and profitable enclave that reproduced the social and economic order of rural England.

The engine of economic growth was the rapidly expanding pastoral industry, but the success of this enterprise was not so much due to Arthur's policies as to Aboriginal land management. The easily accessed and well-watered native grasslands which stretched from Launceston to Hobart had been created and managed by the Aborigines as their principal hunting grounds over thousands of years. Here was to be found prime sheep country which needed no clearing and little capital investment. With minimal threat from native predators (the island was dingo-free), the only serious obstacle to landowners' quest for profits was 'other people,' both white and black.

As I documented in my book *Van Diemen's Land*, convicts and former convicts, who represented the large majority of the colony's population, had been living independent lives in the grasslands since about 1805, and they proved surprisingly difficult to evict. Throughout the open midland country they had become accustomed to obtaining food, clothing and shelter directly from the land with the aid of nothing more than a kangaroo dog. By the 1820s their environmental knowledge was considerable, and even though by 1830 Arthur's gallows, chain gangs and penal fortresses ensured that the grasslands had been securely privatised, and former convicts seeking to live independent lives had retreated to less sheep-friendly country, this expertise remained. It would prove very useful when the landowners of Van Diemen's Land decided to move men and sheep across Bass Strait.

While Arthur's achievements in controlling the convicts were acknowledged even by his political enemies, even more widely celebrated (locally at least) was his success, which culminated in 1835, in ridding the island of Aborigines. Removal of the remnant population to a designated place of exile, Flinders Island, was seen as the surest guarantee of a permanent peace. The view that Van Diemen's Land had been blessed by the removal of its 30,000-year-old custodian culture was near universal, shared by public evangelicals and private pagans alike. Few disagreed with the observation made by Charles Darwin, who visited in February 1836, that 'Van Diemen's Land enjoys the great advantage of being free from a native population.'[44]

It had taken Arthur's agent, George Augustus Robinson, five years to accomplish the removal, during which time his strategy had changed from one of friendly mission and political negotiations to deceit and force. Robinson and Arthur advised London that the removal had been undertaken with the consent of the removed, who, as British subjects, could not otherwise be indefinitely detained. If it were not for Robinson's private journal, we would still not know that the large majority of Aborigines never consented to even short-term removal, and that none agreed to permanent exile. Less imperially sensitive was the removal team's belief that exile provided a providential opportunity for the Aborigines to be civilised and converted, and to be safe from settlers' guns. Nor was there any dispute or embarrassment about the fact that a land free of Aborigines would mean higher land prices and increased profits. In 1835 Arthur informed the Secretary of State for the Colonies, Lord Glenelg, that the removal was 'one of the most influential causes of the present prosperity of the Colony, and the high prices brought by the waste lands of the Crown.'[45]

Control over white and black threats to land and property, a newly subservient labour force and a rapidly increasing demand for wool from the industrial mills of Yorkshire – all were conducive to an explosion in land prices. Free settlers who had been given their land for nothing under the extraordinarily generous policies in place until 1831 made enormous capital gains, but for those wanting to buy into the boom, or expand their holdings, property inflation was now causing major problems.

Ultimately the biggest problem facing aspiring landowners was limited supply. While Tasmania has some of Australia's richest grazing country, most of the island was too wet or too wooded to be of much use for pastoral pursuits. Few settlers were prepared to embark on capital-intensive land clearing, and by the mid-1830s 'all the open grazing lands' had, as Arthur informed the Secretary of State in May 1835, 'with perhaps the exception of a few small isolated tracts … long been occupied.'[46] The shortage of unalienated grazing land had a number of grave implications. Not only was development constrained, but revenue from land sales – the most significant source of colonial revenue after the duty on imported liquor – declined from 1834. Furthermore, as Arthur noted, land shortages meant that the settler 'demand for convicts' – the foundation of his reformed penal system – 'was not so great,' at the very time when increasing social discontent in the United Kingdom was causing a rise in transportation.[47]

It is therefore not surprising that from 1833 the Lieutenant Governor looked to the vast 'empty' grasslands across Bass Strait to be the new Van Diemonian frontier. His aim was to persuade London to extend the jurisdiction of Van Diemen's Land so as to include the southern coast of New Holland, as mainland Australia was still commonly called.

There was a powerful logic to Arthur's territorial pretensions. In the age of sea travel, Port Phillip was much closer to Van Diemen's Land than was Sydney and so, as he advised London, 'the forming of an outstation ... might easily be accomplished ... while the expense attendant upon it would be trifling from its very inconsiderable distance from Launceston.'[48] Arthur recommended that the new settlement be 'protected by a small military party detached from this colony' and that he assume personal command for the first few weeks, the period he considered most critical to establishing peaceful relations with the Aborigines, noting that 'nothing would individually afford me greater gratification than being instrumental in aiding in the occupation of that part of the coast by means which might tend to secure the protection and promote the civilization of the Aborigines.'

He also emphasised the material benefits of colonising Port Phillip: 'once New Holland is fully stocked with improved sheep, Great Britain will thenceforth be little dependent upon the [European] Continent for wool, and in the promotion of this speculation the land on the Southern Coast might be sold and the proceeds applied to emigration.' Such a scheme would also allow for an increase in transportation: convicts with a ticket of leave could be deemed eligible for pardon 'on condition of residing in Southern Australia, a measure which would be advantageous in drawing off part of our convict population and thereby making room for the usual succession of transported felons to be certainly punished and probably reformed in Van Diemen's Land.'[49]

Arthur's vision for the future of Port Phillip was grounded in his view of Van Diemen's Land's past. In a somewhat contradictory narrative, he broke the otherwise obvious connection between the suffering of the Tasmanian Aborigines and the conquest of their land, explaining to the Secretary of State in 1835 that 'On the first occupation of the colony it was a great oversight that a treaty was not, at that time, made with the natives, and such compensation given to the chiefs as they would have deemed a fair equivalent for what they surrendered; a mere trifle would have satisfied them, and that feeling of injustice which I am persuaded they always have entertained would have had no existence.'[50]

What Arthur meant by a 'treaty' was not what is usually understood by this term. In Arthur's view, the prime purpose of a treaty was to achieve *successful* rather than *just* colonisation. In this (as will be explored in more detail later), Arthur differed from other evangelicals who questioned the morality of annexing land without real compensation or genuine agreement.

Arthur frequently drew on Van Diemen's Land's past in contemplating the future settlement of mainland Australia. In January 1832, commenting on the intensified conflict with Aborigines in Western Australia, which had required troop reinforcements to be sent from Hobart, he suggested that 'the utmost care should be taken' to give the Aborigines 'presents (the most trifling will satisfy them)' in return 'for whatever land is taken possession of,' because if 'this system been early adopted in Van Diemen's Land, many deplorable consequences, I have no doubt, would have been averted.'[51] Arthur was equally 'very confident the Aborigines of Southern Australia may be saved from the like destructive calamity, if prudent measures are adopted *from the commencement.*'[52]

Arthur's counter-history challenged the generally accepted narrative. It was a much-discussed fact within Van Diemen's Land that the outbreak of sustained hostility with the Aborigines had actually occurred twenty years *after* first settlement and was contemporaneous with the granting of the Aborigines' main hunting grounds to the free settlers. Indeed, as late as January 1828 Arthur had himself argued that the recent upsurge in violence had resulted from 'the white people' having 'taken possession of their country, encroached upon their hunting grounds, and destroyed their natural food, the kangaroo.'[53]

In Arthur's attempts to divorce the policies of his own administration from the origins of the increasingly disastrous conflict, much more than his reputation and career prospects was at stake. Unlike in New South Wales, there had never been 'limits of location' (the boundary beyond which no land could be claimed) in Van Diemen's Land. Rather, during the 1820s free settlers had been allowed to claim 'crown' land wherever they wished in what was generally acknowledged to have been a chaotic and lax regulatory regime. If the notorious bloody fighting that occurred after 1824 was thought to have been caused by this unfettered land policy, extending this practice to mainland Australia was likely to face rigorous questioning. On the other hand, if peaceful colonisation could be achieved simply by reaching an early understanding with the Aborigines, then the settlers' desire for land, the government's ambitions and humanitarian sentiment could all be conveniently reconciled.

In early 1835 Arthur put a new proposal to London, extending his argument that by applying the lessons learnt in Van Diemen's Land, the peaceful and beneficial colonisation of southern Australia could be achieved. He suggested that his own emissary to the Aborigines, George Augustus Robinson (whose work in Van Diemen's Land was nearing completion), be sent to New Holland to 'open communication' with the natives. Furthermore, he recommended that Robinson take with him 'the Aborigines from Flinders Island' to assist him in the conciliation endeavour.[54]

Arthur dropped this plan once he was sure that London and Sydney opposed it, but on the eve of Arthur's recall to London in October 1836, Robinson made a further appeal that the Aborigines of Van Diemen's Land be employed in 'the work of Christian instruction and civilization.' Robinson's persistence probably arose from a desire to honour his original promise to the Aborigines that their removal to Flinders Island would be temporary (while bearing in mind that there was near-universal resistance among the settlers to bringing them home). He now proposed that 'a principal station be formed on a central part of the South Coast of New Holland' and that 'other stations ... be opened at every available spot that might be occupied by European colonists, and at which an Agent with Aboriginal assistance should be placed.' As will be considered in more detail later, in broad terms this was the proposal that Arthur would put with such effect to a House of Commons Select Committee on Aborigines, which in turn led to the establishment of the Aboriginal Protectorate in Port Phillip, with Robinson the first Chief Protector, in 1839.[55]

Thus it was that a number of factors – the requirements of the penal system, the lure and ideals of colonisation, the hunger for land, the need to redeem and explain the tragic decline of the Tasmanian Aborigines and the deal done to facilitate their removal – became intermixed with Arthur's own values and ambitions to create sustained support from the Lieutenant Governor of Van Diemen's Land for the colonisation of Port Phillip.

Arthur's preferences would have been common knowledge within Van Diemen's Land's small and close-knit establishment, and they must have played a critical role in fuelling settler schemes for colonisation. It would not be surprising if the landowners of Van Diemen's Land also assumed that their Lieutenant Governor's power to promote the project was greater than it was. Within their world, Arthur had almost unlimited power: even the Colonial Office rarely overruled him, and his patronage directly influenced balance sheets. For those weighing up the high risks and the vast potential rewards of the proposed property speculation, Arthur's advocacy fuelled the dream.

As talk raged, a considerable number of settlers unsuccessfully petitioned London directly. One such group was the eight Launceston settlers who informed the Secretary of State in 1834 that 'in consequence of the great difficulty of now obtaining any extent of tolerably good land in this colony, we are desirous of forming a settlement on the southern coast of New Holland.' These men were willing to pay five shillings per acre, the minimum price for sale of crown land after free land grants ended in 1831, and noted that: 'We are aware that other individuals of respectability have made similar proposals to our own, with whom we are prepared to co-operate in forming a free colony.'[56]

Despite the widespread interest, only one aspiring landlord, the Henty family, actually took the gamble and crossed the strait during 1834. Their estate at Portland Bay included a productive farm, but the number of sheep transported and the quantity of land occupied was limited. Their core businesses from 1834 to 1836 were whaling and supplying other whalers with goods and services. As Portland Bay was an established whaling centre with a resident white population before the Hentys arrived, this new enterprise was more an extension of what was already in place than the first wave of a new pastoral invasion.

Although the Lieutenant Governor's support reduced the risk involved in any private colonisation scheme, it could not remove it. Significant uncertainty remained because, despite claims by Arthur to the contrary, it was known that the territory did *not* come under his jurisdiction. Arthur pretended that this was a matter for the British government to decide, but his own attorney-general had provided straightforward advice that Port Phillip was part of New South Wales in 1834.[57]

In the new year of 1835, it was not economic, environmental or technical considerations that held back the many would-be colonisers of Port Phillip. Rather it was uncertainty about the likely response of both London and Sydney to trespassers. If the British or New South Wales governments were to order that action be taken against unauthorised land access, the significant investment involved in moving sheep and men across the strait would be forfeited. Even prosecution was possible. This was not much of a problem for the vagabond former convicts who made up the majority of the sealers and whalers already in residence around Westernport,

Port Fairy and Portland Bay – they had no property or reputation to lose – but it was a major risk for respectable men with capital. Given this political and legal reality, it is not surprising that there remained a widespread reluctance to sail.

4.

SYDNEY 1835

ALTHOUGH SPECULATION ABOUT THE colonisation of Port Phillip was fervent in Van Diemen's Land in the new year of 1835, few in New South Wales knew of the islanders' dreams. Arthur's practice of bypassing Sydney when promoting the colonisation of Port Phillip had achieved its desired object: the government with territorial jurisdiction over the 'empty' grasslands remained ignorant of Van Diemonian plans to conquer them. When Governor Bourke sent his surveyor-general, Thomas Mitchell, on a journey to explore new pastures, Mitchell was astounded to find the Hentys and other Europeans already in residence at Portland Bay.[58] Given that the country was at least four days' sailing time from Sydney and, until Mitchell returned, inaccessible overland, the fact that Port Phillip remained an unknown wilderness in New South Wales is not altogether surprising.

If there was little interest in Port Phillip until Mitchell publicised his excitement at 'discovering' what he termed 'Australia Felix,' there was already wide interest in colonising other grasslands. Among the Sydney establishment, dissatisfaction with the British government's policy of concentrated settlement had become rife.

As noted, since 1788 government policy and practice had so successfully restricted settlement that by 1835, while the commission of the Governor of New South Wales extended over the eastern two-thirds of the continent, only a tiny portion of this vast territorial claim was occupied. New settlements within the region had been established as government-sponsored outposts, most for penal or strategic purposes, and had little geographical reach. Around Sydney itself land grants and leases were only made within defined territorial limits. Until 1820 grants were mostly small, and the primary object was to build a society of emancipist farmers on small holdings. As Richard Waterhouse notes, even though the crossing of the Blue Mountains in 1813 'was subsequently mythologised as a feat that allowed the transformation of the colony ... the reality was that the expedition did not lead to a massive population exodus westwards.'[59]

In 1820 a commission of inquiry, conducted for the British government by Thomas Bigge, decided that pastoralism based on large estates employing assigned convicts and emancipist workers was the key to both prosperity and penal reform, and recommended that small grants to former convicts cease. Competition for grassland intensified as increasing demand from England pushed up wool prices in the late 1820s. The limits of location, beyond which no land was to be 'located' (possessed), were now formally delineated. In 1829 these limits were extended and surveyed into nineteen counties (by 1835 they included a twentieth, the district of Port Macquarie).[60] After land grants ceased in 1831, only these 'crown' lands were available for sale or lease.

The expanded limits of location was no small area in English terms, but puny on an Australian scale. Comprising a semicircle of about 120 miles' diameter out from Sydney, they extended from the Manning River in the north, past Orange in the west, and south of Bateman's Bay to the Murrumbidgee River in the south. In an administrative and even legal sense, this line on the map represented the effective boundary of New South Wales. As Alan Atkinson notes, 'Mitchell, as surveyor-general ... filled in the space with the cartographic symptoms of civilisation – counties, parishes, roads and towns. So the line became "the limits of the Colony."'[61]

27

During 1834 these 'limits' became increasingly porous as land-owners placed sheep and shepherds outside them. The novelty was not the movement of animals or people per se, but the participation of the landowning class in the exodus. As in England itself, squatting on 'waste' lands was a long-established custom of the poor and landless. Most of the early squatters were ex-convicts, and by 1835 they were forming permanent communities: 'In every part of the country,' a newspaper editor lamented that year, 'squatters … have formed stations,' and worse, 'have reared families.'[62] However, the wealthy men who financed and organised the second wave of squatting were a very different breed. While most personally stayed within the secured borders of the colony, they armed their servants (both paid employees and assigned convicts) to do whatever was necessary to assert exclusive land claims in the grass-lands beyond.

Squatting outside the nineteen counties was not as expensive as moving men and sheep across Bass Strait, but it nevertheless in theory carried significant risk. These men, too, were trespassers on crown land, and if the government chose, it could have treated them as such. As will be explored in more detail later, Bourke's argu-ment that he was powerless to evict the squatters was flimsy. It was admittedly difficult to evict poor whites without capital or land, but expelling the second wave of unauthorised intruders was not a ques-tion of policing but of political will. This second group of squatters was more receptive to government action, not because they were more law-abiding but because they had more at stake. Such men sought two privileges that the government had the immediate power to assign: secure land rights and convict labour. A proclamation advising that trespassers on crown land would be permanently barred from the right to purchase or lease such land or to obtain convict labour – the latter a discretionary power the government regularly exercised – would have brought most squatters into line. Alternatively, the example of even a single prosecution would have disciplined the majority of this select mob. In fact, it was only *after* it became evident that Bourke's administration not only tolerated but welcomed respectable trespass (no doubt aided by the fact that to a large degree the Sydney-based absentee 'squatters' *were* the government) that the illegal land rush accelerated. Far from the government being a powerless force desperately trying to keep up with enterprising adventurers (as is usually portrayed), the second wave of the squatting invasion was directly fostered by government policy and practice.

Bourke was not the most obvious candidate to promote a squatter-led invasion of the grasslands of New Holland. An Irish landowner related to Edmund Burke (whose letters he was to edit in retirement), and a hero of the wars with France, Bourke's six-year tenure as Governor of New South Wales from December 1831 is justly regarded as a landmark period of liberal reform. In South Africa, Bourke's three years as acting Governor of the Cape Colony between 1825 and 1828 are equally well remembered for the progress he made in promoting the rights of indigenous people.

What can be confusing for contemporary progressives is that far from acting as a constraint on colonisation, Bourke's liberal sentiments were central to his defence of the squatters' cause. Like most reformers in the 1830s, Bourke's politics and policies were grounded in his faith in the inherent goodness of private enterprise. Unlike his conservative predecessor, Governor Darling, Bourke believed that it was not the business of government to contain the divinely inspired force that motivated the colonisation of the grasslands. As Bourke's record in South Africa testifies, he believed that even the rights of indigenous people were best served when this principle was upheld.

As acting Lieutenant Governor of the Cape Colony, Bourke brought in the celebrated Ordinance 50 in 1828. This decree gave the indigenous people, the Khoikhoi, equality before the law, including freedom from forced labour and the right to own property.[63] The reforms, however, were not motivated by human-rights concerns alone, but were part of a broader agenda. It was hoped that the former beneficiaries of unfree Khoikhoi labour, the settlers of Dutch descent, would become proper capitalists, and the Khoikhoi industrious workers.[64] Land issues were not totally ignored – a significant Khoikhoi settlement at Kat River was established in 1829 – but this was totally inadequate for the number of dispossessed people, and both on and off the reserve the future of the native people was seen to lie primarily in their participation in the market economy.

The primary problem Bourke perceived in the Cape was not the far-reaching private appropriation of grasslands, but that this had led to the crown's rights being overlooked and much revenue being lost. It was out of concern that this could also occur in New South Wales that Bourke passed an act in 1833 to 'prevent the unauthorised occupation' of crown lands 'being considered as giving any legal title thereto.'[65]

Despite clarity on this legal point, the immediate practical issues resulting from government-sponsored squatting had become pressing by 1835. What was the New South Wales government to do about law and order in these frontier lands? This 'problem' paradoxically provided Bourke with his best hope of achieving the changes he sought in British government land policy. In a stratagem common to most illegal colonisation schemes, the cause of the problem was presented as a matter of 'history,' with the only practical solution to accept 'reality' and authorise an extension of government authority.

The problem from Bourke's perspective was not the illegal occupation of land per se, but *who* was occupying it. Bourke, like all governors in the convict era, was particularly concerned with establishing social and economic order, as the challenge of constructing a society on a foundation of convicted criminals could not be met solely by building gaols or constructing a penal apparatus. Due deference and willingness to work relied, as it did in England, on the lower classes' dependence upon their social superiors for the everyday essentials of life. This was threatened by the existence of 'free' land and resources beyond the limits of location. Bourke's promotion of 'respectable' squatters was one means of countering unauthorised occupation by the poor, which was perceived to be the foundation of social and economic disorder and lawlessness. Even the Aborigines were seen to be far more vulnerable to unrestrained convict passions than to an upper-class land grab.

While the language could be contradictory (the rapid change in meaning of the word 'squatter' caused confusion even at the time), there was no doubt about what Bourke wanted to achieve: a change in land policy that would allow respectable settlers legally to occupy land beyond the limits of location. The problem was similarly straightforward: his superior, the Secretary of State for the Colonies, strongly supported the existing policy and saw no need for change.

In 1834 Bourke was approached by the settler James Atkinson, who was keen to purchase a large tract of land at Twofold Bay, about ninety miles south of the existing limit of location. Bourke endorsed the venture to London and strongly suggested that the British government change its policy of concentrated settlement. However, the Conservative Secretary of State, Lord Aberdeen, not only rejected Bourke's proposal, but reasserted the existing policy and instructed the New South Wales government to uphold it. On Christmas Day 1834, Aberdeen signed a dispatch to Bourke that was destined to arrive in Sydney just before the squatter invasion of Port Phillip commenced:

> Adverting to the general question to which you call my attention ... the expediency of extending the location of Settlers beyond the present authorised limits ... I have to acquaint you that, notwithstanding the advantages which you have pointed out in your dispatch as likely to result from to the grazing and other Agricultural Interests of the Colony, His Majesty's Government are not prepared to authorise a measure, the consequence of which would be to spread over a still further extent of

Territory, a Population which it was the object of the late Land
Regulations to concentrate ... I am glad however of the opportunity, which you have thus afforded me of expressing my sentiments upon this point; and you will not fail to discountenance
any plans, which may hereafter be proposed to you for settling
the Territory beyond the present limits to which the location of
Settlers is restricted ...[66]

Bourke now had unambiguous instructions to contain settlement within the limits of location, but despite this he did not – and
thus had now even more vigorously to claim he *could* not – act
against the trespassers, with the predictable result that they continued to increase in number as more 'respectable' men rushed to share
in free land and easy profits.

Bourke was in effect buying time, allowing the facts on the
ground to evolve, presumably aware that the political situation in
Britain was tumultuous and that he was likely to get a more favourable reception from a liberally inclined Whig administration, with
which he would also have strong personal ties. Thus it was not surprising that when Bourke belatedly heard that the squatters had
committed their most brazen act of trespass yet – the colonisation of
Port Phillip – the Governor viewed this as a strategic opportunity to
break the impasse with London and let loose the benign spirit of
private enterprise upon the vast wastelands of the continent.

5.

LONDON 1835

IN 1835 BRITAIN WAS A NATION IN TRANSITION – from a pre-industrial agricultural society to an urban industrialised one, from autocracy to democracy, from old empire to new. The familiar, self-assured imperial culture of mid-Victorian England was yet to emerge. Instead social, economic and political turbulence was making it as hard for many individuals, as for the nation itself, to 'settle down.'

Accelerating urbanisation and industrialisation were not yet accompanied by any consistent rise in living standards, and large groups were stuck in desperate poverty. Most policy-makers saw the rapidly growing population as the primary cause of the widespread hunger, homelessness, disease, malnutrition and, above all, social disorder and crime. Informed by the thinking of Thomas Malthus, who had published his *Essay on the Principle of Population* in 1798, the population debate was in full swing: how to prevent the population increasing beyond what Malthus had termed the 'means of subsistence'? Across the political spectrum this was widely seen as the most pressing policy question of the age – perhaps not surprisingly given the doubling in the English population from 1800 to 1850, and the even more phenomenal growth of cities; during the 1830s, the biggest metropolis in the world, London, reached a population of two million people.

The problem of subsistence was not confined to the cities. In rural areas the population also continued to increase, even as, in the aftermath of the final enclosures of common land, millions of people became wholly dependent on poorly paid and frequently scarce seasonal labour to survive. Hundreds of thousands of landless poor hit the road to get by, with many resorting to petty crime along the way. The elite, frightened by the effects of the industrialisation, urbanisation and enclosure from which they were also profiting, assumed that there existed a criminal class which had been encouraged in a life of sloth and crime by indiscriminate charity. The result was the New Poor Law of 1834, which greatly restricted relief and sought to instill a work ethic in those receiving assistance through the harsh regime of the workhouse.

Social and economic turbulence was reflected in political activism. Arguably no period in British history has been richer in movements for radical reform than the two decades following 1830. Chartism, trade unionism, factory reform, Owenite socialism, co-operation, anti-Poor Law agitation, secularism, the struggle for an unstamped press, the Anti-Corn Law League, anti-state church campaign, millenarianism, machine-breaking and agricultural riots all co-existed in a motley subculture of protest and discontent.[67]

In part this activism reflected the fact that most people remained disenfranchised. The passing in 1832 of the Reform Bill, which increased the number of people eligible to vote and redistributed seats, had been preceded by mass demonstrations, riots and a genuine fear of revolution, and while further reform was felt to be necessary, few in the upper classes supported extending democratic rights too far down the social order. Parliamentary politics was increasingly organised around the two main groupings of the Whigs and the Conservatives (Tories), although they were not yet political parties in the modern sense of the word. The Whigs had returned to office following the first general election under the reformed system held in December 1832, but King William, fearful they might press for further changes, dismissed this ministry in late 1834. The general election that followed, held in January 1835, did see Tory gains, but not enough for Robert Peel, the King's choice, to survive as prime minister beyond April 1835. The leader of the Whigs, Lord Melbourne, became prime minister, leading an administration that was to extend its reformist liberal agenda to Britain's expanding empire.[68]

After the loss of most of its North American territories following American independence, Britain once again had sizeable colonial possessions. The main political focus in the mid-1830s was not what was to become 'the jewel in the crown,' India, but the Cape Colony of Southern Africa and to a lesser extent the colonies in Canada and Australia. Imperial issues were seen through the lens of the economic and social transition underway in Britain. The empire was part market and supplier of raw materials to the new factories, particularly the textile industry, and part safety valve where surplus population could be productively disposed of. Transportation was one component of this – a way of ridding the nation of a fraction of its criminal class and controlling the mob through the dread of a similar fate.

The empire was also the context for a wider philosophical debate on the question of what Britain stood for (akin in this respect to the contemporary 'culture wars'). As Alan Lester has highlighted, this debate was not about 'the necessity for British colonialism, but [rather] … the nature of that colonialism, its ultimate purpose and, perhaps above all, over the imagined characteristics of Britishness which was its expression.'[69]

Despite the eighteenth-century Enlightenment, Christianity continued to provide a common language and conceptual foundation for questions about national identity and values. The evangelical revival of the late eighteenth and early nineteenth century, in which the Methodists played an important role, had long since permeated the Church of England, and led to the formation of influential missionary societies to convert and civilise the empire's native people. The revival led to Christian activism reaching not only into the industrial cities and outward to the empire, but also to the centre of political power at Westminster. The loosely aligned, religiously inspired politicians, bureaucrats and lobbyists are usually known as 'evangelicals,' although this is a somewhat misleading term, both because personal religious practices and affiliations were more diverse than the grouping implies,[70] and also because they differed considerably from 21st-century 'evangelicals,' most of whom now broadly belong to an American fundamentalist tradition. The term is nevertheless retained here because the alternative, 'humanitarian,' has even more limited utility – in the political climate of the mid-1830s almost every public official claimed to be so inclined.

The evangelicals played a critical role in re-imagining Empire. While the questioning of the imperial project was not new, the evangelicals brought to the debate a concentrated focus on the *moral purpose* of colonisation, and a determination to link their vision to political change. 'Colonization is an imperative duty on Great Britain,' argued Samuel Taylor Coleridge in 1834. 'God seems to hold out His fingers to us over the sea. But it must be a colonization of hope; not, as has happened, of despair.'[71] The British Empire, the Select Committee on Aborigines concluded in 1837, existed 'for some higher purpose than commercial prosperity and military renown.' It was called 'to carry civilization and humanity, peace and good government, and, above all, the knowledge of our true God, to the uttermost ends of the earth.'[72]

By 1835 the evangelicals were proclaiming their vision in the joyful aftermath of their greatest victory: the outlawing of slavery across the British Empire in 1833 – a political achievement which is justly recognised as a defining juncture in human history. Slavery had been a widespread and highly profitable system of labour across diverse societies for millennia, and it had taken decades of struggle to achieve prohibition. The momentum generated enabled the victorious campaigners to turn their attention to what they saw as the next (and related) moral imperative of empire: the physical treatment and spiritual care of native peoples. Thomas Fowell Buxton, who had inherited the parliamentary leadership of the anti-slavery campaign from William Wilberforce during the 1820s, successfully moved for the establishment of a 'Parliamentary Select Committee on the Aboriginal Tribes (British Settlements)' to 'consider what measures ought to be adopted with regard to the native inhabitants of countries where British settlements are made ... in order to secure to them the due observance of justice and the protection of their rights; to promote the spread of civilization among them, and to lead them to peaceful and voluntary reception of the Christian religion.' This Committee became the focus of evangelical activism between 1835 and 1837.

Of equal importance was the make-up of Lord Melbourne's government, which took office in April 1835. Both the Parliamentary Under Secretary for the Colonies, Sir George Grey, and the Secretary of State for the Colonies, Charles Grant (who was quickly elevated to the House of Lords to become Lord Glenelg), were active in evangelical circles. With the assistance of their fellow evangelical James Stephen, soon to become the permanent head of the Colonial Office, the British government became focused on the physical and moral welfare of indigenous people to an extent unknown before or, for the most part, since.

The overlapping personnel, ideals and organisations of the anti-slavery campaign and the new cause is obvious enough. However, the links between the two movements can obscure equally significant differences. As Elizabeth Elbourne has shown, the political influence of the campaign for the rights of native people did not last more than a few years, and its influence was largely confined to a small elite.[73] However, the relatively short and concentrated nature of evangelical political influence on this issue need not concern us here. The peak period of their action and concern, between 1835 and 1839, directly corresponds with the founding of Melbourne. Indeed, the incoming Whig administration, the formation of the Select Committee on Aborigines and the colonisation of Port Phillip are almost exactly contemporaneous.

Buxton and his allies were not opposed to colonial expansion per se; rather they were focused on the imperial duty of protecting, civilising and converting native peoples. While drawing moral comparisons with the anti-slavery campaign, Buxton himself emphasised the different assumptions underpinning the two crusades. In the case of slavery, the reformers recognised that they had fought 'great interests,' but Buxton argued that when it came to the suffering of native peoples:

> no vested rights are associated with it, and we have not the poor excuse that it contributes to any interest of the state. On the contrary, in point of economy, of security, of commerce, or reputation, it is a short-sighted and disastrous policy. As far as it has prevailed, it has been a burden on the empire. It has thrown impediments in the way of successful colonization; it has engendered wars, in which great expenses were necessarily incurred, and no reputation could be won; and it has banished from our confines, or exterminated, the natives, who might have been profitable workmen, good customers, and good neighbours.[74]

Rather than private and national interests being understood as formidable *obstacles* to overcome, as in the anti-slavery campaign, commerce and colonisation were seen to be the primary *means* of achieving Aboriginal protection and progress. The problem in this instance was 'the sinfulness of (mostly lower-class) settlers, traders, and sailors across the British world,'[75] who were commonly perceived to be only marginally more civilised than the 'savages' with whom they came into disastrous contact. Government control, along with support for enterprising 'respectable' settlers, was urgently needed to counteract the harm done to natives by lower-class Europeans. In Australia, a society peopled largely by convicted criminals, the perceived necessity to control the poor was exaggerated even further.

The evangelical view on how best to assist Aborigines was equally fraught. Their faith in enterprise, order and the virtues of respectability crossed cultural divides. Civilisation and Christianity were seen to be so closely intermeshed that vigorous debate raged about which should come first for productive missionary endeavour.

Alan Atkinson is one of the few Australian historians to emphasise the downside of the resurgent evangelical concern for native peoples. Atkinson sees a change for the worse with the decline in influence of the older policy perspective, which was 'anchored in a secular frame of mind and utilitarian understanding of the duties of government.' The rise of evangelical certainties meant that the British government was 'more absolute in their dealings with the rest of the world and less interested in the mental universe of those they governed.'[76]

It is important to acknowledge, however, that evangelicals did approach the question of native rights to land from a perspective which often brought them into direct conflict with settlers. The simple fact that evangelicals accepted that people had rights based on prior possession set them apart from the dominant settler discourse, which argued that the right to land arose from using it for farming (although just where this left land speculators or even pastoral operations in which no land was 'improved' was never clear). Furthermore, the foundation of the evangelicals' disagreement with other settlers was genuine outrage. For example, in *Humane Policy; or, Justice to the Aborigines of New Settlements* (1830), the former attorney-general of New South Wales, Saxe Bannister, concluded that European colonial rule had 'crushed irretrievably many millions of unoffending men ... Outraged affections, the greatest physical wants, and often cruel inflictions of bodily pain, mark his tedious decay.' Bannister considered the Aborigines 'in the highest degree oppressed, through the founding of a convict colony among them, and through their utter destitution of property.' Robert Dawson in *The Present State of Australia* (1830) argued that should Aborigines continue to be exposed to convict influence without protection or assistance, they would be 'debased and ultimately destroyed.' William Howitt's *Colonization and Christianity*, published in 1838, described the European presence in Australia as a 'fearful curse.'

The difficulty is that it was *because* of these concerns, not in spite of them, that men like Bannister and Howitt could also countenance European colonisation, on the basis that the assimilation of native peoples into the liberal economic and social order was not only good in itself, but was the primary means of ensuring that Aborigines were not degraded or killed by the lower order of Europeans.[77]

The divine judgment on which the evangelicals ultimately relied for their critique of British colonisation thus proved a mixed blessing. On the one hand, it ensured that projects which didn't pay due regard to native peoples were opposed with deep moral conviction; on the other, those that were perceived as doing so were supported with an equivalent missionary fervour. At times it seemed that the possibility of converting the natives, even to a nominal Christianity, could justify all. Stephen believed that 'he who should induce any heathen people to adopt the mere ceremonial of the Church ... and to recognize the authority of its Divine head would confer on them a blessing exceeding all which mere philanthropy has ever accomplished.'[78]

The complexities and contradictions of the evangelical view of colonisation are most clearly seen in the two 'SAs' – South Africa and South Australia. The Cape Colony was the principal site of evangelical and government concern in 1835. In response to escalating border skirmishes, Governor D'Urban had sent troops into Xhosa territory and annexed some seven thousand square miles of their land. This annexation became the subject of political action that culminated in a remarkable dispatch from Glenelg to D'Urban on 26 December 1835, which both returned the conquered country to the Xhosa and recalled the Governor.

This dispatch would be hailed by the newly founded Aborigines Protection Society in their first Annual Report as 'the most comprehensive, the most statesmanlike, the most British, the most Christian document of all on this great subject,' and there is no doubt that such a rapid withdrawal from conquered lands on moral grounds alone has few parallels in the long history of the British Empire (or any other). However, it is important to put this landmark 1835 intervention in context before making a premature comparison with the contemporaneous expansion in Port Phillip. First, the territory was returned to an agricultural people with a political authority and national borders that were recognised by the British. Even D'Urban had acknowledged the national status of the Xhosa through the treaty he obtained to end the war and take possession of much of their territory, and Glenelg's intervention was based on his conviction that this treaty was fraudulently obtained. Second, the intervention did not change policy or restore land to the indigenous Khoikhoi who, in British eyes, had a similar apolitical status to that of the Aborigines. In general Glenelg was strongly opposed to land grants to indigenous people, and acted to ensure no more were made. Soon after taking office, he advised that 'settling Hottentots on lands of their own' would merely 'perpetuate their poverty and their depression in the social state,' and that to induce them 'to work for wages as labourers' was in the 'interests of all classes.'[79] As Bourke did when he was acting Governor of the Cape, Glenelg believed that the future for the Khoikhoi lay in them selling their labour, not in the indiscriminate provision of land that he believed would inhibit their cultural and moral development.

It is also important to recognise that the South African intervention only came about because of the activism of the superintendent of the London Missionary Society, Dr John Philip, who knew Buxton and other prominent evangelicals. Philip personally gave evidence to the Select Committee on Aborigines and met with Glenelg and other officials, and it was on the basis of information he provided that government action was taken.

While the evangelical missionary societies were also present in the Australian colonies, there was no equivalent to the London Missionary Society presence and its public activism in the Cape, with the greater distance from London also not helping with the flow of information. The LMS had only ever had an 'extremely limited' role in Australia, and its most effective missionary, Lancelot Threkeld, had been recalled in the late 1820s after confronting the local establishment with a catalogue of abuses against the Aborigines.[80] After his departure there was no prominent Christian voice sufficiently courageous to sacrifice social standing by publicly defending Aboriginal interests against the landed elite.

The small, interconnected evangelical networks could facilitate action when a cause was pushed and pursued, but they could equally inhibit scrutiny or intervention when there was no such advocacy, or, more seriously, when false reassurance was received from trusted sources. This meant that in 1835 the politically active evangelical circle centred on London knew much about the Cape Colony, but remained remarkably poorly informed about the condition of the Australian Aborigines. In the Select Committee Report, the section covering the Cape is far longer and more detailed than that concerning New South Wales, and only a couple of paragraphs are given to Van Diemen's Land. The Committee evidently knew almost nothing about the impact on the Aborigines of the squatter invasion already gathering pace, the new Port Phillip settlement, the forced removal of the Aborigines of Van Diemen's Land, or the high death toll at the government-run Aborigines Establishment on Flinders Island. Indeed, in the absence of an independent missionary voice, much of the information provided (for example, the numbers of

Aborigines removed from Van Diemen's Land) was empirically incorrect.

As its dispatches of 1833–35 highlight, the British government was remarkably ignorant, too, of the frontier reality associated with the rapid expansion of pastoralism in the Australian colonies. This was probably in part because the tumultuous political events in Britain itself were too much of a distraction to continually changing ministers of mixed ability and the very small number of officials running the Colonial Office. The result was that when the 1834 South Australia Bill came before parliament, 'all the Lands of the said Province or Provinces (excepting only portions which may be reserved Roads and Footpaths)' were deemed 'to be Public Lands open to Purchase by British subjects,' and not even cursory mention was made of the Aborigines.[81]

Consistent with this neglect, when the chairman of the Colonization Commission for South Australia, Robert Torrens, developed the case for the new colony in 1835, he ignored evangelical discourse in favour of espousing an 'art' of colonisation 'based upon the science of wealth,' which was centred on the sale of 'waste' land.'[82] Settlement was to be concentrated and carefully regulated, but the justification for this was provided by colonisation theorists such as Edward Gibbon Wakefield – who abhorred the consequences of uncontrolled dispersion on colonial society – rather than humanitarian concern for the Aborigines. Indeed, Torrens managed to discuss the colonisation of an 'empty' land for close on two hundred pages without a single reference to the Aborigines. Once the new Whig administration turned its attention to South Australia in late 1835, this blindness to the Aborigines was to change dramatically. Henry Reynolds notes that before granting the Letters Patent to the new venture (which amounted to final approval), 'Lord Glenelg informed the head of the Colonization Commission that the would-be colonists would have to make arrangements to buy the land from the Aborigines.'[83] The change in political mood was reflected in the first report of the Colonization Commission of South Australia, which now promised to protect the Aborigines 'in the undisturbed enjoyment of their proprietary right to the soil, wherever such right may be found to exist; to make it an invariable and cardinal condition in all bargains and treaties made with the natives for the cession of lands possessed by them, in occupation or enjoyment, that permanent subsistence shall be supplied to them from some other source.'[84]

By the end of 1835 it had obviously become clear even to Torrens that new colonisation projects would need to be seen to acknowledge Aboriginal interests, and to assist in civilising and converting Aboriginal people, if they were to gain government sanction. Provided this acknowledgment was made – and words could be cheap – evangelical influence arguably increased the possibility of new conquests receiving imperial blessing, in the name of both Christian virtue and private profit. The evangelicals looked favourably on respectable Christian invaders motivated by a spirit of enterprise and benevolence. This was a political and policy context which the gentlemen of the newly formed Port Phillip Association in Hobart Town and Launceston, as well as the governors of New South Wales and Van Diemen's Land, were to show that they understood very well.

PART II

SETTING SAIL

6.

THE PORT PHILLIP ASSOCIATION

While political circumstances in 1835 were conducive to the private conquest of Port Phillip's grasslands, and the dream of crossing Bass Strait and claiming possession had never seemed closer to fulfilment, it was still far from inevitable that this would occur. Considerable risks remained under the existing law, and sensible landowners preferred to wait for others to make the first move. A bold or reckless individual was needed to take the plunge. It is hard to imagine anyone better suited to the task than John Batman.

The endless dispute about the validity of Batman's status as the founder of Melbourne has obscured the true significance of his actions. To settle Port Phillip was to trespass on crown land and commit a crime. Batman's risk-taking was the catalyst for breaking down the inertia associated with this well-known and indisputable fact. Furthermore, he was one of the very few landowners with sufficient experience of the Australian environment or Aboriginal people to undertake the necessary negotiations. Other free settlers, highly conscious of their social status and largely removed from the realities of the land and its people, lacked the nerve or the capacity, while convicts (even when their terms had expired) were precluded by their dubious respectability.

John Batman was one of a select breed of local capitalists who were born in Australia and of convict descent. His father, William, sentenced to fourteen years' transportation in 1796 for stealing saltpetre, an essential ingredient of gunpowder, was fortunate to be accompanied to New South Wales by his wife, Mary. By 1799 the growing family was living in Parramatta, where John was born in 1801. William would eventually become a devout Wesleyan.[1] One of the benefits of Methodist membership was contact with Aboriginal people, who were encouraged to come into Parramatta for education and charity; in 1818 the Wesleyan Sunday School included nineteen Aborigines. By the time John left for Van Diemen's Land in November 1821 – three days after the Parramatta Orphan School committee had met to consider his responsibility for the pregnancy of an unfortunate resident[2] – John had both a familial ease with the evangelical world view and knew many Aborigines, a patrimony that would profit his future career.

It was a fortuitous time for an ambitious young working-class man to make the move south. In the early 1820s Van Diemen's Land's boom times were still to come, and the number of respectable free immigrants remained low. Furthermore, the grasslands of Van Diemen's Land were a largely lawless frontier, in which independent bushmen and stockmen (only some of whom were bushrangers) exercised a greater degree of day-to-day control than the government. In this world, stock-owners who could negotiate frontier power relations, and thus protect their animals from theft, enjoyed a competitive advantage over their more conventional and respectable competitors. Lieutenant Governor Arthur's wide-ranging and ruthless assertion of order during the late 1820s largely closed down this opportunity for the native-born and former convicts to accumulate land and capital, but by then a few bush-wise entrepreneurs, such as Batman, had profited from their environmental experience and diverse cultural affinities. With the aid of his partner Eliza, an Irish convict absconder who found refuge at Batman's estate near Ben Lomond, this convict's son had prospered and found some degree of acceptance in the upper echelons of Van Diemen's Land society.

Batman's status and prosperity were confirmed under Arthur through his active government service in the campaigns against both bushrangers (he was central to the capture of the infamous Mathew Brady) and Aborigines. In September 1829 Batman reported to Arthur on the actions of his roving party, which had so successfully attacked a large group of Aborigines that the survivors had told him that '10 men were wounded in the body which they gave us to understand were dead or would die, and two women in the same state had crawled away, besides a number that was shot in the legs.' He further reported that the next morning he had been 'obliged to shoot' two of these captives because they couldn't walk. Another captive, a small child, survived to become John Allen, one of the forgotten founders of Melbourne, and was with Batman until the latter's death.[3] However, Batman's service in the Black War involved far more than slaughter. From 1830 to 1832 he was seen by the colonial government as almost as central to the conciliation work – which operated in parallel with the military campaign – as George Augustus Robinson.

In all his work for the government, Batman employed Aborigines. While not unknown in Van Diemen's Land, this strategy had not been widely employed before Batman used contacts from his Parramatta days to bring down Aborigines from Sydney. Batman developed close working ties with some of these men over a long period of time, and seven of them, known to the British as Pigeon, Jo the Marine, Old Bull, Bungett, Bullett, Jacky or Joe King, and Stewart, proved critical to the success of various ventures.

Savvy in both bush-lore and political relations, Batman was well suited to pursue the colonisation of the extensive southern Australian grasslands which he had been told about by a childhood friend, the explorer Hamilton Hume. Nevertheless, effective action depended on him securing project partners. One of the Van Diemen's Land government surveyors, John Helder Wedge, was a critical early ally. Wedge recalled that when they first met in 1825, 'the subject of an

exploring expedition into the interior of New Holland was …
mooted, and its practicability discussed; and we seldom, if ever,
met afterwards without adverting to the subject.'⁴ In 1827 the pair
unsuccessfully sought land at Westernport, where the short-lived
military outpost had been established the previous year, but by the
early 1830s they seemed to be aware that better land lay around Port
Phillip Bay. In 1833 Thomas Henty wrote of 'a surveyor (Mr John
Wedge) who is anxious to explore not only that coast ['nearly opposite us on the western side of New South Wales'], but to proceed on
to the eastern side, a new country …'⁵

In December 1834 Wedge, and three other men, all of whom
would soon become partners in the Port Phillip Association, joined
Batman on a three-day excursion to the summit of Ben Lomond,
the peak that dominates the skyline of north-east Tasmania and
which abutted Batman's estate. The nineteenth-century historian
James Bonwick records that one of these men, William Sams, told
him that:

> It was then that I first heard Port Phillip spoken of as a desirable
> place for a settlement, Batman telling me that when he was in
> Sydney he had heard from a schoolfellow (Hamilton Hume,
> who with Captain Hovell, had explored the neighbourhood of
> Port Phillip) that the country there was of the finest description,
> and that this information had dwelt in his mind, and made him
> anxious to verify the truth or otherwise of the report. It then
> occurred to me to suggest the formation of a company, in order
> that the expenses incidental to the exploration should be light
> when borne by a number. The idea was at once agreed upon and
> forthwith proceeded with.⁶

Through the early months of 1835 Batman and his allies actively
sought the money and political support to put their plan into action.
A further spur for action over prudence might have been provided

by the fact that Batman was afflicted with syphilis, which was to claim his life just four years later. As Alistair Campbell has pointed out, 'Cerebral syphilis in its early phase has a stimulating effect, and some artists, explorers and others have realized their greatest achievement under its influence.' Cecil Rhodes, for example, had the same condition.[7] Perhaps more pertinently, by 1835 Batman's disease was far enough progressed for him to know that if he was to fulfill his long-held dream of colonising the new country, there was no time to waste.

The visible symptoms of venereal disease – already Batman's nose was being eaten away, and within a few years he would scarcely be able to walk unaided – as well as his convict ancestry, fuelled negative opinions of Batman's moral worth. Robinson condemned him as 'a bad and dangerous character. He married a prison woman. He recently lost part of his nose from the bad disease.' The eminent gentleman artist and Batman's near-neighbour, John Glover, was still more succinct, describing the future founder of Melbourne as 'a rogue, thief, cheat, liar, a murderer of blacks and the vilest man I have ever known.'[8] However, Batman also had his admirers – including the wealthy Launceston merchant and occasional Wesleyan missionary Henry Reed and, on other occasions, Robinson himself! – and historians ever since have been tempted, largely unproductively, to adjudicate on the matter. Batman deserves both his defenders and detractors, but what ultimately cannot be disputed is how central he was to the colonisation of Port Phillip. The respectable landowners of Van Diemen's Land needed a John Batman to stake a claim on the sheep country across the water as much as Batman needed a broad coalition of support if his land grab was not to be seen as the action of a socially suspect, disease-ridden trespasser. While it took some time for what would become known as the Port Phillip Association[9] to be publicly identified, from the beginning Batman worked in partnership with Wedge, Sams and other landowners and government officials (most were in fact both). In the first six months of 1835 it was not a formal association with a clear hierarchy or organisational structure, but rather an informal alliance of well-connected property speculators.

Nor was the alliance just a random assembly of rich men. The skills and contacts of the group were carefully chosen. While every dubious property speculation needs a competent surveyor (as Wedge was), a good lawyer is equally critical to success. The Association's so-called 'treaty' with the Aborigines (the subject of the following chapter) that Batman carried with him to Port Phillip in May 1835 was drafted by one of Van Diemen's Land's leading lawyers, Joseph Tice Gellibrand, a former Attorney-General. Gellibrand was particularly attuned to legal questions concerning Aborigines; it was a matter in which he had shown interest since the Black War of 1824–31, although, having been dismissed by Arthur in 1826 in acrimonious circumstances, it was thought best that Gellibrand do the Association's legal work behind the scenes. In any case, a number of other partners in the Port Phillip project were better placed to handle relations with Arthur.

The most obvious of these was the Lieutenant Governor's nephew, Henry Arthur, another of the Ben Lomond climbers. This young man brought the added advantage of being the Collector of Customs at Launceston, which greatly assisted planning since vessels were only meant to be cleared to designated ports, of which Port Phillip was not one. However, familial loyalties aside, Henry Arthur carried less weight with his uncle than other members of the partnership. James Simpson, the influential Commissioner of the Land Board and a police magistrate, was particularly close to the Lieutenant Governor. William Sams, the aforementioned Under Sheriff and Notary Public for Launceston; John Collicott, Postmaster General; John Sinclair, Superintendent of Convicts in Launceston; and Anthony Cottrell, Superintendent of Roads and Bridges (and a former leader of conciliation expeditions to the Aborigines) all also enjoyed good relations with him.

Other than Batman, however, no one was so critical to the venture as Charles Swanston, member of the Legislative Council, ally of Arthur and, most significant of all, a leading banker. In November 1831 Swanston had been appointed managing director of the Derwent Bank, and he soon assumed full personal control. By 1835 Swanston dominated the local banking sector, with a business model that relied on attracting overseas capital – particularly from India, where Swanston had extensive networks – by offering high interest rates, and then lending the capital to local land speculators. The largest single investor in the Derwent Bank was George Mercer of Edinburgh, who would also become a member of the Port Phillip Association and its chief lobbyist with the British government.

Swanston's role as lead financier was as important as Batman's on-the-ground actions. While there was a solid economic foundation to the project through the high demand for wool, the largest profits were expected to come from an appreciation in land value, as had occurred in Van Diemen's Land. The colonisation of Port Phillip was fundamentally a grand property speculation financed on borrowed money. The risks were high, but the potential profits almost limitless.

As will be seen, this debt-fuelled business model is critical to subsequent events – and not just to the depth of the crash that came when the boom ended in the early 1840s. It was a very different mode of land settlement from the free hand-outs of the decade before in Van Diemen's Land, which required little upfront investment in land or labour. With so many Port Phillip squatters deep in debt to Swanston and other financiers, and locked into high interest rates and equally high stock, transport and labour prices, many operations would prove to be marginal concerns. This fuelled the impatience with anyone or anything that inhibited their enterprise, most particularly the Aborigines, who in both perception and reality posed the gravest risks to stock and profit.

There has long been speculation as to whether Arthur himself was a silent partner in the Port Phillip Association. He was undoubtedly well informed of its plans through Swanston and a multitude of other closely involved government officials and establishment figures, and probably no member of the Association was in any doubt, as Wedge told his father, that 'Col. Arthur is favourable to this P.P colonization and is doing all he can to support it.'[10] Yet it is equally certain that the Lieutenant Governor was too politically savvy and mindful of his relations with London to become directly involved before settlement had been authorised by the British government. The situation, however, was quite different once permission was granted and in 1838 Arthur became a significant absentee investor in Port Phillip and possibly even a member of the Association.[11]

It is often forgotten that Arthur was not only an evangelical colonial administrator but also a seasoned property speculator, who made considerably more money from land deals than from his generous salary. As Arthur's biographer, A.G.L. Shaw, has noted, Arthur became 'extremely wealthy' during his tenure in Van Diemen's Land. He purchased over fifteen thousand acres between 1828 and 1836, and in 1833 'lent £14,000 on mortgage to settlers and officials such as John Burnett, Matthew Forster and John Montagu,' profiting both 'from a normal rate of interest exceeding 10 per cent and the enormous rise in land value.' The total value of Arthur's Van Diemen's Land investments in 1839 was nearly £50,000, and he thought he could safely rely on an annual income of £5000 from the colony, which was more than three times his annual salary. There has always been, as Shaw notes, a suspicion that Arthur's property was 'improperly acquired,' but both standards and judgments have varied. Perhaps the fairest assessment was that of the distinguished nineteenth-century historian John West, who concluded that the 'moral weight of government was compromised ... by the air of mystery' around the Lieutenant Governor's land dealings, and that 'Arthur benefited by his foreknowledge.'[12] The pertinent point here is that Arthur was sympathetic to speculation in property, had business ties with a number of the chief protagonists, and saw these men as trusted political *and* commercial partners.

Other members of the Port Phillip Association had solid connections with the evangelical movement and their circles of influence in London. Foremost among these was Thomas Bannister, the brother of Saxe Bannister, the former Attorney-General of New South Wales. Saxe Bannister had published his text *Humane Policy: or Justice to the Aborigines* in 1830, given evidence to the House of Commons Select Committee and was a founder of the Aborigines Protection Society. Both brothers were supporters of treaties, and Thomas copied relevant sections of his brother's book for fellow Association members to read.[13]

While never a member of the Port Phillip Association, the Attorney-General of Van Diemen's Land, Alfred Stephen, also provided a bridge between its members and evangelical circles in London. A cousin of the head of the Colonial Office, James Stephen, he knew various members of the anti-slavery group known as the Clapham Sect (as did Arthur). It was because of a letter of support from James Stephen that Arthur had appointed Alfred Stephen to the post of Solicitor-General in 1825. The latter also borrowed money from Arthur to buy real estate before being confirmed as Attorney-General in 1832. Stephen was to provide legal advice to Arthur as early as 1834 on the validity of private treaties with Aborigines and the extent of the Lieutenant Governor's jurisdiction outside Van Diemen's Land.

In short, the Port Phillip Association was a bastion of respectability, whose political and economic influence went to the heart of the small ruling elite of Van Diemen's Land and extended to evangelical circles in London. Apart from Batman, only one other member had a questionable social status. One of Batman's shares was secretly held for a Launceston merchant, Joseph Solomon, who as a former convict could not be publicly associated with the Association given their explicit determination to write convicts out of Melbourne's founding story before it even began.

When the rules of the fledgling Association were drawn up in February 1835, there were two guiding principles. The first was that it was to proceed on the basis of an agreement with Aborigines that would be conducive to their civilisation and welfare, and the second that no convicts would be allowed in the new settlement (care was made to avoid any reference to *former* convicts, who by necessity made up the majority of the labour force). The two criteria were linked by the idea, as commonly expressed in political and evangelical circles in London and Sydney as in Hobart, that it was the moral degradation of convict settlers, not the land grab itself, which had led to hostilities with the Aborigines.

During the first six months of 1835 this coalition did not have a monopoly on interest in Port Phillip. With all the good sheep country claimed, and Van Diemen's Land awash with capital, talk of colonising the southern coast of New Holland was commonplace. However, these plans were being pursued by the conventional means of letters and lobbying, seeking government *permission* to possess the 'empty' grasslands. What ultimately set the Port Phillip Association apart was that John Batman was not prepared to wait.

Not all of the shareholders of the new Association were formally signed up when Batman crossed the strait to meet with the Aborigines in May 1835. However, when he returned triumphant in June and proclaimed himself in John Fawkner's Launceston hotel to be 'the greatest landowner in the world,'[14] the worth of the treaty he boasted of to the bar might have been doubted and mocked by some, but without being assertively disallowed by Arthur, it provided enough surety for Swanston, Gellibrand and Wedge to persuade nine more men to join the Association, and for other adventurers to make their own moves.[15] How was it that this anomalous document in Australian history, a purported 'treaty' with the Aborigines, came to be so central to the founding of Melbourne?

7.

THE TREATY

It was in early June 1835 that John Batman met with a group of Kulin elders to negotiate land access. Little is known of what transpired, as the only direct record of the encounter, Batman's private journal, was written to provide supporting documentation for the Port Phillip Association's subsequent land claim. Batman was not writing a personal diary but a government submission. Nevertheless it is clear that this was considered a serious meeting by both sides. Batman was accompanied by a highly experienced conciliation team made up of seven of his Aboriginal and three of his white employees, while the Kulin representatives included a number of senior men from different clans.[16]

The essence of Batman's story as told to colonial and imperial governments is expressed in the 'treaty' drafted by Gellibrand which Batman carried with him to Port Phillip. This purported to prove that the Aborigines had consented to transfer hundreds of thousands of acres of their land in return for 'the yearly rent or tribute of one hundred pair of blankets one hundred knives one hundred tomahawks fifty suits of clothing fifty looking glasses fifty pair scissors and five tons flour.'[17] Clearly this was a lie. There was no possibility that the Aborigines had consented to the incomprehensible concept of selling their land by signing a written treaty. The more interesting question is this: why did the Port Phillip Association believe that this claim could further their cause?

Consent to dispossession was the ultimate legal and ethical fantasy for both land grabbers and philanthropists (and many government officials were both). The treaty story was intended to provide backing for a land claim within the confused narrative of benevolent colonisation. Furthermore, Batman (and, to be fair, his intended audience) knew that his version of events could not be disproved, since the dispossessed party lacked English language, writing skills and access to the corridors of power.

The idea of a written agreement with the Aborigines seems strange to contemporary Australians only because of our unusual treaty-free history. However, those running the British Empire in the 1830s knew that Batman's treaty had a long colonial pedigree. In his comprehensive book *Possession: Batman's Treaty and the Matter of History*, Bain Attwood emphasises the influence of North American precursors, particularly 'that of the Quaker William Penn's legendary treaty of 1683' (on his return to Van Diemen's Land Batman was hailed as the 'Tasmanian Penn').[18] However, the central place of treaties in the history of Van Diemen's Land (also considered by Attwood) was probably of more immediate importance. Government policy there had generally favoured a treaty with the Aborigines between about 1827 and 1830, although policy was never consistent. But it was not so much this precursor as the revisionist history promulgated by Lieutenant Governor Arthur which underpinned the Port Phillip Association's approach. As discussed earlier, from around 1830 Arthur began to emphasise the lack of an initial treaty rather than the occupation of the main Aboriginal hunting grounds as the primary cause of conflict in Van Diemen's Land. He did not see the purpose of a treaty as being to provide fair compensation or arrive at genuine legal agreement; rather, the handing over of 'mere trifles' was meant to facilitate peaceful first settlement. The Association's 'treaty' was entirely consistent with this 'peace without justice' approach to land occupation.

The legal situation in the 1830s was also less straightforward than is assumed by those whose perspective has been determined by subsequent nineteenth- and twentieth-century Australian history. As in the post-*Mabo* world of the twenty-first century, in 1835 it was not clear that the crown's claim to Australia had extinguished native title – that is, the rights of the Aborigines 'to their traditional land and waters recognised at common law.'[19] The argument of the Port Phillip Association – that 'It is undoubted fact, that these Tribes are the actual possessors of the soil, and that although the land is situated within the limits of the British Territory of New Holland, yet it is without the jurisdiction of New South Wales, or any other British settlement' – had considerable legal backing at a time when the notion that the crown could claim 'perfect' (that is, one which acknowledged no other) sovereignty over unoccupied lands was contested.[20]

The legal ambiguity was acknowledged in the advice given by Attorney-General Alfred Stephen to Lieutenant Governor Arthur in November 1834. Stephen, who was to become Chief Justice of New South Wales and ultimately a Privy Councillor, left open the question of whether the Aborigines could dispose of their lands by means of treaties:

> It is a matter of history that the English Government has possessed itself of the whole of New Holland … How far this possession may be insisted on, to deprive the Aboriginal Inhabitants of the power of selling any part of the Territory, I need not probably now inquire. If any such transaction shall really have taken place, it may be fit to institute a previous inquiry – whether or not it had been, in truth and in fact, a fair and bona fide purchase, or a simulated and cunningly devised contrivance, intended only to evade the claims of the British Crown.[21]

Legal opinion in London also generally recognised that Aborigines had rights in common law based on their possession of the land. The opinion of the prominent lawyer William Burge was that 'the right to the soil is vested in the Crown [but] ... This principle was reconciled with humanity and justice towards the Aborigines, because the dominion was qualified by allowing them to retain, not only the rights of occupancy, but also a restricted power of alienating those parts of the territory which they occupied.'[22]

The Port Phillip Association's promotion of its 'treaty' with the Aborigines was thus designed to progress its land claim within the legal and policy context of the time. However, it is also true that some Association members seem genuinely to have believed that the treaty provided the best means of protecting the Aborigines' interests. Gellibrand – ironically, the one Association member to be killed by the Aborigines – was reported by another Association member, James Simpson, to have 'taken up the case [for a treaty] with the additional impetus of religious zeal.' Simpson viewed with cynicism Gellibrand's claim that 'We attempt to colonize not by knocking the Aborigines on the head but by buying their property and endeavouring to induce industrious habits,' arguing that this is what 'Little George [Arthur] may like to hear ... but [he] is not likely to be gulled by it either.' Opinions were divided on this. Thomas Bannister was another who seems to have had a serious commitment to upholding Aboriginal rights:

> The only chance for the natives is [for officials] to listen favourably to our proposition, our principle once introduced into N Holland would rescue the British name from reproach ... it is new to English history to seize distant countries as has been done in Australia without at least pretending to compensate the natives – and it well becomes the advanced spirit of the times, to substitute real benefits for them, in place of the verbal benevolence heretofore bestowed ...[23]

What is easily overlooked, however, is that the debate about the treaty's purpose, legality and integrity is a quite separate matter from consideration of the real-life negotiations conducted on that early winter's day in 1835. While the written treaty was a propaganda document for *government* consumption and provides no credible evidence as to the nature of any actual agreement with the *Kulin*, this does not mean that no agreement was reached. Batman's separate report to Arthur on his meeting with the Aborigines provides a potentially more revealing account of what may have transpired:

> I fully explained to them that the object of my visit was to purchase from them a tract of their Country, that I intended to settle among them with my wife and seven daughters, and that I intended to bring to this Country, sheep and cattle. I also explained my wish to protect them in every way, to employ them the same as my own natives, and also to clothe and feed them, and I also proposed to pay them an annual Tribute in necessaries, as a compensation for the enjoyment of the Land – The Chiefs appeared most fully to comprehend my proposals, and much delighted with the prospect of having me to live amongst them … my object has not been possession and expulsion, or, what is worse, extermination, but, possession and civilization, and the reservation of the annual tribute to those who are the real owners of the soil.[24]

There are three reasons to give credence to Batman's claim that some Kulin leaders agreed that a small group of Britons could access the grasslands of Port Phillip in exchange for goods and protection. First, both parties had a strong motive to make such a deal; second, both had a greater capacity to cross the cultural divide than is usually assumed; and third, the subsequent actions of both parties suggest that an agreement involving some degree of mutual understanding had in fact been reached.

In considering motive, it is important to remember that Batman needed to broker an understanding with the Kulin not only because it was what officials in London, Hobart or Sydney required (which was where the spin came in), but also because the security of stock and shepherds demanded it. In November 1803 the missionary accompanying David Collins in his aborted attempt to colonise Port Phillip, Samuel Crook, had observed that the objection against permanently settling Port Phillip was 'the number of natives and the small number of marines we have.'[25] The capacity of the Aborigines to prevent white settlement in remote regions, or at least impose very heavy costs upon it, had become even better understood since then. The recently concluded Black War in Van Diemen's Land had exposed the vulnerability of the European pastoral project and the enormous costs involved in securing private property claims over prime Aboriginal hunting grounds. Nearly two hundred whites had died during the seven-year war, and significant regions of the colony had to be temporarily evacuated. The fear of the Aborigines had been intensified by their use of fire – burnt-out huts, farms and crops stood as stark testament to the capacity of the Aborigines to defend their home territory even when their numbers had been much depleted. Therefore, in considering a costly private scheme which involved the colonisation of some of the most heavily populated grasslands in Australia by a small group of hopelessly outnumbered whites without military support or official backing, the practical necessity of a negotiated agreement with the Aborigines was paramount. It might be easy enough to secure a whaling station or a confined coastal farm, as the British had done in the Port Phillip District up to that time, but it was another matter to move sheep deep into Aboriginal hunting grounds where the valuable animals and their shepherds would be highly vulnerable to attack. And, to add a final incentive for negotiation, nothing would undermine the Association's cause with the authorities more than the outbreak of war.

Not only did the Europeans have a motive to negotiate, they also had a greater capacity to cross the cultural divide than is usually recognised. During 1835 the government conciliation mission in

Van Diemen's Land was in its fifth and final year, and the team which went to Port Phillip had extensive experience in this 'embassy,' as it was widely called. As noted, Batman had become an important figure in the conciliation work, and he was present at the critical talks between the Aboriginal leadership and Lieutenant Governor Arthur in October 1831 near Launceston, in which the basic terms of a settlement seem to have been agreed to. The essence of this agreement was recorded by Robinson in his journal: the Aborigines 'would be allowed to remain in their respective districts and would have flour, tea and sugar, clothes &c given them; that a good white man would dwell with them who would take care of them and would not allow any bad white man to shoot them.'[26]

The seven Aborigines who accompanied Batman to Port Phillip in 1835 were as experienced in the work of conciliation as their employer, if not more so. Among these so-called 'Sydney' Aborigines, the two men usually called John Pigeon (Warrora from Shoalhaven) and Tommy or John Crook (Johninbia or Yunbai from near Five Islands, Wollongong) had provided the longest service, accompanying both Batman and Robinson on various journeys since 1829.[27] In January 1832 Pigeon was severely wounded while undertaking this work (he was shot by a shepherd who was probably overly keen to collect the government bounty) and was one of the Aborigines who were approved for 100-acre land grants in recognition of their service. Pigeon had also spent time with the sealers and is thus likely to have already met Port Phillip Aborigines. When their diverse and difficult life experience in New South Wales is also recalled, these men can be justly acknowledged as experienced veterans in mediating the brutal cross-cultural encounter in Australia.

The New South Wales Aborigines' critical role in facilitating an understanding with the Kulin was recognised by others at the time. Batman wrote to Wedge on 18 June 1835 that on his recent return to Launceston, '[John] Fawkner called on me ... He was going to settle near Point Nepean [outside the Port Phillip Association claim] and wishing to purchase land off the natives, he asked for the assistance of the Sydney blacks to conduct negotiations.'[28]

Batman's white servants should also not be forgotten. Robinson's obsessive concern to ensure that he received sole credit for the 'success' of the conciliation project in Van Diemen's Land meant that the convicts who shared in the work were written out of the story. James Gumm, who was part of the Port Phillip party, was one of the convicts who played an important role. Between June and August 1829 Gumm took personal charge of a conciliation expedition, and in 1832 received a conditional pardon because of his extensive service.[29]

The group taken to Port Phillip was a carefully selected and highly experienced team. It is therefore unsurprising that, as Batman recorded, they used techniques that had already proved successful in Van Diemen's Land. It was the Aboriginal members ('stripped off and ... quite naked') who arranged the first meeting, a day before any white man approached. A range of goods was handed over and the group joined in dancing and singing: 'My natives gave the chiefs and their tribe a grand corroboree tonight.'[30]

The proposal put to the Aborigines also seems to have echoed the Van Diemen's Land agreement, in which 'a good white man would dwell with them' and provide protection and supplies. Batman gives us a strong hint of this when he writes that the Aborigines were 'much delighted with the prospect of having me to live amongst them,' a phrase with a very different emphasis from the formal language of ownership contained in the treaty, but almost exactly that used by Robinson to describe the earlier deal.[31]

What of the Aboriginal side? Did they also have the motive and the capacity to reach an agreement with Batman's party?

While nothing can be known with certainty about why the Kulin elders met with Batman, or what they agreed to, their incentive to strike a deal and their capacity to bridge the cultural divide were also greater than is usually assumed. The view that the Aborigines of the Port Phillip district were unfamiliar with white people and thus separated from them by an impenetrable cultural gulf relies on an analysis that has been seriously distorted by ignorance of the sealers, whalers and wattle-bark collectors, the first European colonisers of Port Phillip. As described, sealers had relations with the Aborigines stretching back over thirty years – remember that the Aborigines had 'signified their knowledge and fear of the effect of firearms' as early as 1803[32] – and violence and the abduction of women had increased dramatically since the late 1820s. Indeed, the first group of Aborigines Batman encountered in Port Phillip was 'afraid I should take them by force and ill-use them, as some of their tribe had been already.'[33]

The impact of the two previous if short-lived official British settlements in 1803–04 and 1826–28, a number of exploratory parties, decades of visits by off-shore whalers and, not least, having a white man, William Buckley, in permanent residence since 1803 should also not be underestimated. Buckley recalled how the people 'would listen with the greatest interest while I talked to them about the English people, their firearms, cannons and great ships, and also about the fighting in Holland in which I had a part.'[34]

On the question of the cultural divide, Robert Kenny has even suggested that what is likely to have been transacted was not 'mutual incomprehension between the Port Phillip Association and the Kulin,' but 'mutual interest.' He argues that 'the clan-heads may have made a very informed decision' to 'limit the number of settlers in Port Phillip' to Batman and his associates in an attempt 'to at least curtail the destruction they heard had happened elsewhere.' His argument becomes still stronger when the destruction wrought by sealer settlement within the Kulin's own territory is recognised.[35]

Similarly, Richard Broome has noted that while the Kulin 'may appear to us as victims of a poor deal,' they knew the value of flour, mirrors, beads and metal hatchets and blades. Broome points out that:

they recognised the efficiency of the latter instantly. Indeed, a week earlier Batman had peered into a woman's string bag and found a sharpened piece of iron hoop [in fact 'several pieces'[36]], obviously traded hundreds of kilometres from New South Wales.

These goods were well known and valued, but why imagine they had originated in New South Wales? The more likely trade route was from the adjacent Port Phillip coast. Furthermore, is it not feasible that, as trading relations broke down with the abductions and fighting of the early 1830s, an agreement with Batman might have been intended to procure a secure alternative supply of such familiar and already desired European goods?[37]

The possibility that even the ceremonies enacted in June 1835 might have been mutually meaningful was first highlighted by Diane Barwick, who pointed out the similarities between the ritual of feoffment, the traditional English form of conveying freehold estate which Batman claimed to have carried out, and the Tanderrum, the means by which the rights of other peoples to access Kulin land and resources was granted.[38] Feoffment (not legally abolished in Victoria until the 1920s) included a requirement that the feofforer (vendor) pass to the feoffee (purchaser) a twig, some grass or something else growing on the land being conveyed. The 'Ceremony of Tanderrum or Freedom of the Bush,' meanwhile, was described by a Protector of the Aborigines, William Thomas, in the following terms:

> There is not, perhaps, a more pleasing sight in a native encampment than when strange blacks arrive who have never been in the country before. Each comes with fire in hand (always bark), which is supposed to purify the air ... They are ushered in generally by some of the intermediate tribe, who are friends of both parties ... the aged are brought forward and introduced.

The ceremony of Tanderrum is commenced; the tribe visited may be seen lopping boughs from one tree and another, as varied as possible of each tree with leaves; each family has a separate seat, raised about 8 or 10 inches from the ground … Two fires are made, one for the males and the other for the females. The visitors are attended on the first day by those whose country they are come to visit, and are not allowed to do anything for themselves; water is brought them which is carefully stirred by the attendant with a reed, and then given them to drink (males attend males and females female); victuals are then brought and laid before them, consisting of as great a variety as the bush in the new country affords … during this ceremony the greatest silence prevails … You may sometimes perceive an aged man seated, the tear of gratitude stealing down his murky, wrinkled face. At night their mia-mias [huts] are made for them; conversation, &c. ensue. The meaning of this is a hearty welcome. As the boughs on which they sit are from various trees, so they are welcome to every tree in the forest. The water stirred with a reed means that no weapon shall ever be raised against them.[39]

Bain Attwood suggests that Batman's performance of feoffment and the Kulin's performance of the Tanderrum might 'have suggested to each party that the other understood their particular ceremony, and thus enabled the two groups, who were strangers to one another, to mime an agreement, albeit one they understood in radically different ways.'[40] (And a crude version of this custom seems to have been practised in Port Phillip after 1835. There are several accounts of British and Aboriginal people waving a green bough of peace – which also had a customary meaning in England – to strangers they saw in the distance.)[41]

There is no doubt that the Aborigines could have had no concept of land transfer as understood in English law, or of the reality of white settlement as it was to occur in Port Phillip; nevertheless, the initial ceremony need not have been 'understood in radically different ways.' Batman and his negotiating team, who had been exposed to similar customs elsewhere, were too experienced in cross-cultural contact to have been in any doubt that the ceremony only concerned land *access*, regardless of what they told London. Furthermore, Batman did not envisage the uncontrolled invasion of white people that was soon to follow – indeed, his express purpose was to exclude other Britons from making land claims. Batman only sought permission for a comparatively small party of Europeans to live on Aboriginal land. He didn't expect the Aborigines to leave the land, or imagine that his possession would end theirs; he was hoping for profitable co-existence, and maybe, after forty years of raids and forays (as well as the benefits brought by the visitors), the Kulin were too. Perhaps it is our difficulty in imagining such a scenario, rather than the obvious cultural divide, which explains our reluctance to allow that there might have been a genuine understanding reached in June 1835. At the very least it is worth remembering that if the Port Phillip Association's exclusive right to colonise had been upheld, the Kulin's decision to negotiate with Batman would now be celebrated as an act of political genius.

Perhaps the strongest evidence that an understanding about land access was reached comes from the subsequent actions of the two parties. On the British side, the Port Phillip Association accepted an obligation to hand over goods and provide protection to Aborigines. Within days of the ceremonies being concluded, a ration station was established at Indented Head on the Bellarine Peninsula (even though Batman himself returned to Launceston). In depicting life at Indented Head, emphasis is usually given to the white men, James Gumm and the diarist William Todd, but the main players in the continuing cross-cultural encounter which occurred there were undoubtedly the five Aboriginal members of the conciliation party, the men Batman called 'Bullet, Bungett, old Bull, Pigeon and Joe the

Marine.'[42] The Launceston paper, the *Cornwall Chronicle* (whose informant was Batman himself), went so far as to suggest that 'Mr Batman has left Mr Pigeon, commander of the Sydney Blacks (who acted under Black Robinson in catching the Blacks here) in possession of the territory.'[43] Certainly, when it came to the central matter of negotiating with the Aborigines, Todd's journal makes it clear that he and Gumm were little more than onlookers.

Todd documents extensive 'Corrobboring,' 'singing' and shared hunting parties that Todd himself but poorly understood and generally did not participate in. Todd recorded that all the local Aborigines 'seem to be much attached to Pigeon' and that 'the natives gave Pigeon &c [the other Sydney Aborigines] a young girl each for a wife.' Todd was perpetually nervous of the threat posed by the large numbers of locals moving in and out of the camp, but given that the Aborigines were prepared to leave their children there and to arrange marriages, their strategy at this time seems to have been to incorporate rather than evict the well-off newcomers.[44] Todd's fear was understandably heightened when the rations, which were being distributed on a regular basis, ran out. With hunting difficult – the kangaroo caught on 4 August was the first for a week, and a few 'flat head' could not feed everyone – supplies had been drawn down to the extent that by the 3rd or 4th of August Todd records that 'we are now without flour or meat.' Only the replenishment which came with the arrival of Henry Batman (John's brother) and Wedge in mid-August put Todd's anxieties to rest: on the 13 August 'natives corroberied for us; they are extremely quiet and well satisfied. Mr Batman allows them rations of potatoes and biscuit daily.'[45]

Wedge now asked William Buckley, who had come into the camp some time before, to tell the assembled Aborigines that ample food would be supplied and that the newcomers would help 'avenge any outrages' – in other words, Wedge restated the Association's commitment to the central planks of the agreement.[46] The Port Phillip Association continued to provide rations and some level of protection to the local people during the next year, including seeking the return of abducted women and the investigation of a sealer raid at Westernport,[47] and in May 1836, the first anniversary of the treaty, the designated goods were handed over.

It is true that handing over desired goods to Aborigines, including flour, sugar, tea, tobacco and blankets, was widespread on the Australian frontier. It had been established custom in Van Diemen's Land before the fierce fighting broke out, and similar practices were evident in New South Wales, where they were even reflected in government policy, such as the annual distribution of blankets which continued until 1844.[48] So the fact that goods were handed over is not in itself sufficient evidence that an agreement was being honoured. However, the language in which the supply was couched is here indicative of a prior agreement.

In August 1836 Wedge proposed to Sydney a scheme for the protection of Aborigines which included, along with financial incentives for shared land use, the establishment of 'three or four stations with daily ration and annual distribution of other items.' This, Wedge believed, 'would be observing the terms agreed upon by Mr Batman with the Native Tribes – and [the] fulfillment of which the Colonial Government took upon itself to perform ...'[49] Wedge's November 1836 claim that 'The Association has always fulfilled every promise made to the natives; in every communication they have kept faith with them' was undoubtedly exaggerated, but he did what he could to ensure that 'the pledge' was 'performed,' fearing that otherwise 'a permanent hostility will be engendered, the consequences of which it is unnecessary to remark upon.'[50]

Respect for the treaty was limited and local (concentrated around Melbourne and Geelong and restricted to some individuals), and its influence even within these limits declined once the New South Wales government assumed control of Port Phillip in the spring of 1836. However, even the New South Wales Executive Council initially accepted that the responsibilities of government included an obligation to pay the annual Port Phillip tribute and provide rations to Aborigines.[51] Consistent with this, the first government official in charge of the settlement, William Lonsdale, was supplied with provisions as 'presents for the natives at Port Phillip'[52], and these were regularly topped up until the arrival of Governor Bourke's replacement, George Gipps, who was determined to end the indiscriminate handover of goods. Under the new regime in place from 1837, the 'treaty' became irrelevant and government officials were ordered only to issue goods to the Aborigines 'for labour obtained ... services performed, or to conciliate adverse or strange tribes.'[53]

Some Aborigines were clearly not happy with the change. The Police Magistrate of the Geelong district, Foster Fyans, complained to Sydney in May 1838 that because he had so few blankets to distribute, the Aborigines 'left my place making use of many bad expressions' and that 'since this occurrence I regret to say they have continued a strain of abuse on me through the country.'[54] The following year Fyans appealed again for more supplies, as 'the tribe immediately at Geelong expect some gifts from me.'[55] The governor agreed to the request but reiterated that 'I attach very great importance indeed to the principle of giving these things only in return for services rendered.'[56]

It was not only the Aborigines who were angry at the government's change of policy. In July 1838 Wedge complained that:

The arrangement made by Sir Richard Bourke to relieve us from our engagements with the Natives, by the Government taking upon itself the fulfillment of the terms agreed upon, is also prejudicial to our interests, for the natives still expect to receive from our hands the fulfillment of the treaty – nor can they be made to understand the true bearing of Sir Richard Bourke's arrangement ... thus the onus of keeping up the friendly intercourse that was established by the treaty of 1835, [still] devolves upon us.[57]

The persistent references to obligations arising from the under-standing reached with the Aborigines – still usually termed a 'treaty' – make it unlikely that the rations distributed in the first years of settlement were merely familiar frontier stratagem. But perhaps stronger evidence still that a deal was reached in June 1835 is that when John Batman left Port Phillip after his fateful negotia-tions with the Kulin, he seems to have been genuinely delighted with what he had achieved. If the 'treaty' was nothing more than a ruse played on the British government, then there was no reason for him to be so excited by his discussions with the Aborigines. How likely is it that Batman could have sustained publicly and privately, with officials and friends alike, such a crude deception until his death four years later? Whatever transpired by that unknown creek bed, Batman clearly believed it had been more than idle chat. More-over, other adventurers initially gave it credence, even if the lure of land ultimately overrode all other concerns. John Fawkner went out of his way to reassure Batman on the latter's return to Launceston that his own territorial ambitions would be confined to Western-port – that is, outside of the Port Phillip Association's claim – and the first man to bring significant numbers of sheep to Port Phillip Bay, John Aitken, also initially stayed outside the treaty zone, land-ing near present-day Sorrento, although the search for grass soon pushed him north. The British government also accepted that some form of agreement with the Aborigines had been reached, even if its legal standing was a matter for dispute, and agreed to hefty compensation being paid to the Association in partial recognition of this.

In the intervening years, the significance of Batman's treaty with the Aborigines has come largely to lie in the realm of 'what might have been.' We are prone to see the treaty as a mere quirky footnote to the Melbourne story because we know that it was soon made redundant by events. But if we return to 1835, when the dramas in Hobart, Sydney and London converged on the main stage of the

Yarra River with the arrival of permanent British settlers, then the landmark agreement with the Kulin can take its rightful place as a defining juncture in Australian history – one which signposts the road not travelled.

8.

FIRST SETTLEMENT

FOR 175 YEARS THERE HAS BEEN DEBATE over whether John Batman or John Fawkner, whose small expedition was the first to establish a permanent camp on the Yarra, is the true founder of Melbourne. Whereas it is unsurprising that Fawkner, a convict's son who had no easy life (indeed, his own three-year sentence of transportation to the Newcastle penal station by a Hobart magistrate meant he himself was a former convict), should aggressively promote his founding rights in prosperous old age, the passion with which others have challenged or defended his cause is unsettling. How could this question have aroused more emotion than any other concerning the momentous encounter at the ancient camping ground?

The principal matter in dispute, who selected the village site, is, anyway, a misleading one. Batman's journal entry of 8 June 1835, in which he recorded that after going up 'the large river' for about six miles he found 'good water and very deep' and famously noted '*this will be the place for a village*,' was not an original insight (any more than was the accompanying observation of 'the natives on shore'). The combination of abundant fresh water and open pastures had long-standing cross-cultural appeal. Charles Grime, Surveyor-General of New South Wales, in the course of a survey of Port Phillip during February 1803, had rowed up the Yarra as far as Dight's Falls and come to the same conclusion as Batman. James Fleming, a member of his expedition, recorded that 'The most eligible place for a settlement that I have seen is on the Freshwater River' (the Yarra).[58] The camp-site abutting the basalt ledge or 'the falls' was the logical location for a British village for the same reasons that it was a favoured Aboriginal locale. As noted, the falls marked the divide between the tidal and saline reach and the all-important fresh drinking water above, and there were diverse food sources and extensive grasslands nearby. Furthermore, the falls acted as a barrier to sailing vessels going any further upstream even should they have wanted to, while the pool below served as a convenient harbour.

Any remaining doubt that Fawkner's settlement party, which had left Launceston on 21 July 1835, would disembark below the falls was removed by the informants available to them. On 16 August, Fawkner's expeditioners had a reportedly drunken ship-board rendezvous with Pigeon and others of the Sydney Aborigines and a local Aborigine resident at Indented Head. It is noteworthy that the visitors did not come into the camp and that Todd records that the meeting occurred 'entirely against Mr H. Batman's orders,' presumably because Batman knew that those on Fawkner's *Enterprize*, having already spent fruitless weeks sailing around Westernport and the eastern shore of Port Phillip Bay, would be seeking information about the best place to settle. At any rate Captain John Lancey recorded shortly after this encounter that they had 'found' the 'good stream of fresh water, and beautiful hills and plenty of good soil and excellent grass,' and on 23 August, 'at the commencement of the fresh water' (near present-day Market Street), they made camp.[59] It was nearly another week before the *Enterprize* was brought upstream, but on 29 August her chattels were unloaded and a village was born.

The final irony of the enduring founding-father debate is that Fawkner himself was not on board the *Enterprize*, having been prevented from leaving Launceston by his creditors. He was represented by three employees – Thomas Morgan, Charles Wise and the blacksmith James Gilbert. The latter was accompanied by his heavily pregnant wife, Mary, the only woman in the group – she would give birth to a boy before the year was out. Besides Captain Lancey, the other members of the expedition were William Jackson and Robert Marr, both carpenters, George Evans, a plasterer, and his servant, Evan Evans. Garryowen (the pen name of the nineteenth-century journalist Edmund Finn) was amused that the first settlers of Melbourne were made up of only 'five men, a woman, and the woman's cat'⁶⁰ – he continued the tradition of forgetting the servants – and indeed it was a peculiar demographic for a squatter camp. Following Fawkner's lead, these were artisans looking to build a town, not a pastoral empire – and of the paid-up settlers only George Evans and William Jackson, who both turned to squatting, seem to have stayed on. Perhaps, though, in the city's nativity can be glimpsed what remained a persistent feature of Melbourne – its tendency to stand somewhat apart from the countryside it served. What more appropriate founders of Melbourne could there be than carpenters and plasterers? From the outset there seems to have been a distinctively urban quality about the camp on the Yarra.

While the *Enterprize* was sailing up river, John Helder Wedge, the Port Phillip Association surveyor, was exploring the bay. As noted, he had arrived at Indented Head on 7 August with John Stewart and John Crook (Sydney Aborigines who had returned to Van Diemen's Land with Batman), John Allen (the child refugee from the Black War who lived with Batman), Henry Batman (John's brother) and Henry's wife and four children, even before Lancey and his party reached Port Phillip.

Wedge wrote in his *Narrative of an Excursion amongst the natives of Port Phillip and the south coast of New Holland* that there were seven families of local people resident around the huts at Indented Head, including the young women 'promised in marriage to the Sydney natives.' Wedge saw these Aborigines as both a financial burden and a strategic opportunity. To reduce the cost of supplying them with rations, he wrote to fellow Association member James Simpson that he had heard of 'damaged oatmeal' to be had cheap in Launceston, 'which would answer quite as well as the best wheat flour. Damaged rice, barley meal, pears, or any thing of that kind which can be got the cheapest will answer the purpose.' More significantly, Wedge saw the benefits of developing the ration station into an Aboriginal establishment that would facilitate Governor Arthur's desire to remove the Aborigines of Van Diemen's Land from Flinders Island to Port Phillip. Batman had asked Wedge in a letter of 18 June whether it would 'not be to our interest to give the Neck [the Bellarine Peninsular] of 100,000 acres to them?' and reminded the Surveyor that the Lieutenant Governor had mentioned this scheme 'to us when on the Coast with him.' Wedge now advised the Port Phillip Association that 'this Peninsula, or a part of it should be appropriated for an establishment for the civilization of the natives.' He further suggested that 'as the natives are at present so friendly disposed ... it would be well to invite the Government to send a person to witness the progress that has been made in leading them to civilization. I think this would tell well in strengthening our claim for the confirmation of the land.'[61]

Accompanied by experienced guides, Wedge soon left Indented Head for a seven-week survey of Port Phillip. It was towards the end of this ramble, on 2 September, that he came to the Yarra to mark out the new village.

On this matter Wedge's mind was already largely made up. Even before he left Van Diemen's Land, he had written that he was 'inclined to think the fresh water River mentioned by Mr Batman at the head of Port Phillip will be the best situation for the township'[62] and had drawn up a map showing a reserve for a 'Township and public purposes' on the southern banks of the Yarra. Indeed, the *Cornwall Chronicle* reported as early as 13 June that 'the site of the township has been marked off, to be called "Batmania" at the head of Port Phillip, well supplied with a running stream of fresh water.'

When Wedge found Lancey's party camped on the Yarra's banks, he asserted the Port Phillip Association's prior claim. However, with the legal status of the treaty unclear – Fawkner would even assert he had made his own treaty with the Aborigines – no one would budge. The matter was further complicated by the presence nearby of another small group of settlers, led by John Aitken, whose men had brought over the first flock of sheep to Port Phillip the previous month. Having failed to find the desired grasslands on the eastern side of the Bay, they had recently passed through Lancey's camp and established themselves about twenty miles to the north of it.

The urgent question faced by Wedge and the Port Phillip Association was what to do about the intruders, and on this opinions were divided. Gellibrand, Swanston and Batman advocated using their alliance with the Aborigines to drive them out – an action which would have been consistent with the settlement reached with the Kulin and have seemingly served the interests of both parties. Wedge strongly disagreed. On the day he arrived at the Yarra, he wrote to Batman:

> It is obvious, I think that if the residents get to loggerheads, the Government will interfere and dispossess both parties … I believe you are an advocate for using force or instigating the Natives to molest them. The former I think would be bad policy, because it would afford the Government a pretext for interfering, & of not confirming our arrangements with the Natives … Instigating the Natives might lead to the commencement of a career of bloodshed which no one could afterwards control. And if they afterwards took offence either at ourselves or at Servants we might feel the power that they had been taught to wield against others.[63]

However, Batman continued to believe that force was necessary to assert the claims arising from his treaty, and on 13 October Wedge wrote to all Association members that he had 'learnt from Mr Batman since my return from New Holland, that he is on the point of proceeding to Port Phillip with the intention of carrying into effect the recommendation of Mr Swanston and Mr Gellibrand, namely to remove Mr Fawkner and those connected with him, through the instrumentality of the natives.' Wedge continued to argue that this would 'lead to the most disastrous results ... It will at once open the eyes of the natives, and teach them their power, they will not fail to use it against us,' and went as far as to threaten to withdraw from the Association if the plan went ahead.

Batman, swayed by either the arguments or the threats of his old friend and key supporter, backed down: 'I have not the least doubt that Faulkner [*sic*] will see the necessity of crossing the River [the boundary of the Association's claim], as we shall over run the land at once with stock.'[64] This was a real threat. Fawkner, who had arrived in person at Port Phillip on 11 October, was almost unique in being more focused on crops than sheep – and as farmers from Van Diemen's Land well understood, in the absence of enforceable impounding laws agriculture was an impossible undertaking without the co-operation of stock-owners. Fawkner's vegetables and wheat crop, and even his pink-eye potatoes,[65] stood little chance should large numbers of cattle, pigs or sheep come their way.

There remained, however, the larger question of how the Kulin would respond to the influx of unauthorised arrivals. Immediately before Batman's return to Port Phillip – his first visit since the treaty-making – about four hundred Kulin from all five language groups gathered around the infant settlement. Fawkner recorded in his diary that on both 24 and 25 October 'the Blacks had a battle,' and Batman believed the Kulin had 'assembled for the purpose of settling some ancient quarrel.'[66] Was the dispute connected with different attitudes towards the unauthorised white presence? On 28 October Fawkner recorded that he had learnt that 'the Blacks ... intended to murder us for our goods.' In later life Fawkner was to elaborate on this brief statement, claiming that an Aborigine known as Derrimut,[67] a clan head of the Boon wurrung people, had warned him through William Watkins that the natives of the 'Goulburn and Barrabool tribes' (the Daung wurrung and Djadja wurrung) were plotting to kill all the whites, and that 'I took steps immediately to counteract them.'[68] Fawkner gave no indication in his journal (another 'private' document compiled to support land claims) as to what these steps were, but he would later claim that the settlers herded off the Aborigines by firing buckshot.[69]

Violence broke out again in mid-December. For three days running, Fawkner records that he used force to disperse Aborigines. On 13 December he 'chased the Blacks away some distance.' On the next day 'Charles and me mounted 2 of my horses and went out in search of the Blacks, each carrying one Pistol and a Sword, came upon them quite unawares and put them into great fear,' and on 15 December Fawkner 'knocked the men off work and took our pieces to chase the Blacks.' It was on this final day of conflict that 'Derramuck [Derrimut] changed names with me.'[70] Richard Broome notes that exchanging names was 'a key way of establishing kinship ties and of assimilating outsiders,' and that there seems to have been a division in strategy between 'the up-country Kulin,' who wished to attack, and 'the coastal Kulin,' who opted 'to befriend.'[71] The choice between evicting and incorporating invaders is one that is as old as conquest itself, but the different approaches probably also reflected the tumultuous change in established relations, land-access arrangements and traditional custom already caused by the white influx.

Batman, along with five hundred sheep, arrived in Port Phillip on 9 November in the middle of this unresolved situation. He had Buckley summon the Aborigines to a meeting, which many decades later was recalled by William Barak, the Kulin elder who was to lead his people through the difficult decades of the late nineteenth-century. In his short memoir, *My Words*, Barak recollected:

I … was about eleven years old when Batman visited Port Phillip Bay. I never forgot it … All the blacks camp at Muddy Creek. Next morning they all went to see Batman, old man and women and children, and they all went to Batman's house for rations, and killed some sheep by Batman's order. Buckley told the blacks to look at Batman's face. He looks very white. Any man that you see out in the bush not to touch him. When you see an empty hut not to touch the bread in it. Make a camp outside and wait till the man come home and finds everything safe in the house. They are good people. If you kill one white man white fellow will shoot you down like a kangaroo.[72]

Perhaps it was this timely combination of threats and provisions that helped to maintain, around Melbourne at least, an uneasy peace for the rest of 1835.

PART III

MELBOURNE'S FIRST YEAR

9.

A HIGHLY SUCCESSFUL CAMP

STORIES OF PIONEERING ADVERSITY are so dominant in Australian history that what stands out by contrast in Melbourne's first year is the ease with which the invaders negotiated a benign and familiar environment. These men and women did not see a barren or ugly land, but a bountiful and beautiful one. Perception was born of experience, as new settlers hunted, farmed and travelled across the country with remarkably little difficulty considering the remoteness of the locale. For many settlers, Port Phillip was, as John Pascoe Fawkner put it, 'a land flowing with milk and honey.'[1] By the time that Batman himself first visited the Yarra camp in November of 1835 he could report to Lieutenant Governor Arthur that:

I landed the cattle and sheep, and found everything progressing in a way beyond my most sanguine expectations; so favourable are the soil and climate to vegetation that we found the people well supplied with vegetables of the finest growth and quality, the produce of seeds sown only about ten weeks before, and they were able to supply the ship with potatoes and a variety of other vegetables for our return voyage. The wheat was looking most luxuriant, the people all well satisfied, and not one wishing to return. The country affords them an abundant supply of fish and wild fowl, and as regards the stock, all which were taken there ten or twelve weeks since had improved beyond description; and incredible as it may appear, the change for the better, which took place in the condition of the stock taken down by me, during the four or five days I remained, was so great that I must myself have witnessed it to have believed it.[2]

Batman's portrayal of fecundity was to be echoed by other visitors during Melbourne's first year. When Police Magistrate George Stewart visited in June 1836, he found that a population of fewer than two hundred Europeans had already spread over 'about 100 miles of country.'[3] The town which he termed 'Bearbrass' (although there was no consensus on this[4]) was still a humble settlement of '13 buildings, viz., three weather-boarded, two slab and eight turf huts,' but this was primarily because of the focus on settling the 'open grassy plains or downs.' So successful had been the pioneer colonisers that there were already eleven vessels 'employed in bringing stock from Van Diemen's Land.'[5]

Early Melbourne was also a remarkably healthy place. Fawkner claims that there were no deaths at all until 29 June 1836, when an infant boy passed away, and even if his claim of 'one death in just ten months' is difficult to verify, there is no doubt that mortality was very low.[6]

The success of the Port Phillip settlement had as much to do with the cultural background of the first settlers as with the geographical character of the region. It is a common mistake to assume that Australia's early settlers were homogenous in their knowledge and experience of the land, and hence to miss the significance of the fact that Melbourne was founded by Britons from Van Diemen's Land. The distinctiveness of the mother island underpinned the ease of the settlement, as compared to the genuine hardships experienced in the same era elsewhere, notably at Swan River in Western Australia, a settlement founded directly from Britain only six years before Melbourne. It obviously helped that Van Diemen's Land was close by, and that people, animals and supplies could be easily moved across a well-known trade route, but even more important was that by 1835 Van Diemonian Britons had been through three decades of environmental adaptation in a land with many similarities to Port Phillip.

The first residents of the camp on the Yarra (as opposed to those who funded them) were overwhelmingly former convicts. While the elite could legitimately claim that 'all our thoughts, feelings, habits, customs, and all our associations are English'[7], this seamless transfer of culture was not open to everyone. Wealthy immigrants and government officials were able to reproduce the society they had come from, but the poor often had no option but to adapt their diet, clothing, farming methods, hunting techniques and architecture if they were to obtain the essentials of life.[8]

Although convicts adapted to the New South Wales bush in similar ways to their southern brethren, Van Diemen's Land stood out because of the ready accessibility of well-watered grasslands to men on foot (horses were rarely available to the poor) and because of the transformative power of the dog. At the turn of the nineteenth-century Van Diemen's Land was one of the very few places of permanent human habitation where the dog was unknown: rising sea levels had closed the Bass Strait land bridge before the dingo arrived on the Australian mainland. When the British introduced to Van Diemen's Land what were commonly called kangaroo dogs – a cross between traditional hunting breeds such as the wolfhound and the greyhound – the rich bounty of the grasslands became available even to the poorest of the poor.[9] It was the dog that was at the centre of the encounter with this new world: guns were too inaccurate to rely on for kangaroo hunting until the mid-nineteenth century. Unlike in early Sydney, where the convict gamekeepers supplied kangaroo to the elite but the convicts themselves ate little fresh food, the possession of even a single dog allowed men to live in a state of complete independence in the bush, eating the flesh and selling the meat and skins of the plentiful native herbivores, which were un-adapted to their formidable new foe. From 1810 these men were also often stock-keepers (the term squatter was rarely used), and they became skilled in moving sheep and cattle through the native grasslands. Many lived semi-nomadic lives, wandering through the bush with little more than their canine companions and a knapsack and rug made from animal skins. Cross-cultural contact was probably less extensive than it is now fashionable to claim – both sides seem to have been as interested in avoiding contact as in facilitating it – but nevertheless the convict bushmen walked Aboriginal paths, copied Aboriginal architecture and occasionally formed relationships and alliances with Aboriginal people. They knew the reality, including the fear, of living in Aboriginal-owned and managed land, and from the mid-1820s they were also in the frontline of a ferocious conflict in which hundreds on both sides would die.

Even though this way of life was greatly disrupted after the best sheep country was granted to a select group of free settlers during the mid to late 1820s, the convict subculture of the bush was by then too well established and of too much utility to be completely suppressed. A Van Diemonian shepherd of the mid-1830s generally not only knew far more about obtaining indigenous foods than most Tasmanians today, but he could erect a rain-proof temporary shelter in a matter of hours – tents were rarely used by the poor because of their weight – or a semi-permanent hut split from local timber with nothing more than an axe in just a few days.

It was the formidable environmental knowledge of these men and (very few) women that explains the apparent speed and ease of Melbourne's settlement. Bush-wise emancipists like James Gumm are the true founding fathers of Melbourne. When Batman left this experienced operator behind at Indented Head, he set the pattern for the settlement of Port Phillip. Most early settler – and indeed later historical – accounts of early Melbourne gloss over the indisputable fact that almost none of the celebrated free-settler investors, including those who made up the Port Phillip Association, were resident in Port Phillip during 1835–36. Some Association members and Port Phillip squatters never visited at all, and those who did make sojourns rarely became permanent residents until their land had been secured. Even Batman did not permanently relocate until April 1836, although by this time he employed about thirty men. When the first resident government official, William Lonsdale, arrived in September 1836, Batman and Dr Alexander Thomson, who had been appointed as the Association's surgeon and 'catechist' (that is, the person designated to provide Christian instruction to the Aborigines), were the 'only persons of any respectability' present in the settlement. The census taken at this time might have showed forty-three proprietors of land (out of the total official population of 224), but almost all these men were absent, including the Association notaries Simpson and Wedge (who had stations on the Werribee River), Swanston and Gellibrand (whose sheep and men were on the Barwon and Werribee Rivers respectively), Sinclair (whose station was on the Moorabool) and Solomon (whose land was on the Maribyrnong). Fawkner himself had returned to Launceston for an extended period in August 1836. As late as February 1837 Lonsdale noted that even though 'Emigrants from Van Diemen's Land are constantly arriving ... scarcely any of them are persons of respectability' or would be considered 'desirable members of any community.' He was disappointed that 'the respectable portion of those who have stock in the district have not yet made this their residence.'[10] Even Gellibrand, one of the few squatters killed by Aborigines, was not permanently resident before he died in early 1837. His plan had been to 'settle for the summer months at Port Phillip' once his land 'was confirmed.'[11]

The dubious background of these first settlers may partially explain the peculiar fact that while the sheep belonging to the 'respectable portion' of the district have received much attention from historians, their shepherds have been all but forgotten. The attitude of one of the landed class of Van Diemen's Land, who wrote to her father on 31 October 1836 that 'I am delighted to find that my dear Alex is not going off to Port Phillip yet; but by all means let him *send some stock*,'[12] has remained far too widespread. Do stock look after themselves?

To the former convict, Port Phillip offered remoteness from official authority, a general shortage of labour, absentee employers and the rich natural resources of the common. Not surprisingly, it proved very difficult to exercise legal or social controls over such workers, and a number seem to have decided to take the opportunity to become independent of anyone. In April 1836 Fawkner reported that:

> the Men who are at large without any Masters have had a meeting with Batman's men and that they have come to the determination to resist being sent up [to Launceston], and one of the number has put up a written notice stating that he is independent of everybody in Port Phillip and several of them have been marking out land for themselves and have actually commenced building, and the whole of the men at the late meeting of the Convention, have agreed to stand by their order to resist oppression to the death …[13]

What happened to these rebellious souls is not clear, but it is unlikely that their employers would have been able to exercise the considerable coercive powers available to them in law. Fawkner chronicles employees illegally withholding labour and moving between employers (he himself poached James Gumm), and reported that in July 1836 the settlers couldn't find someone to dig two graves (a day's work) for 20 shillings – a fortnight's wage for a labourer in Van Diemen's Land.[14]

While he shared the frustration of employers, Fawkner, who was 'well read in radicalism,' also sympathised with the emancipist dream of independence. His three years in Newcastle penal station had been punishment for helping convicts escape and he often wrote of oppression by the ruling class. In the new colony he went so far as to draft a visionary constitution for a town republic that would be governed by all its men, with 'each individual acting as to him may seem just and conducive to his interest, comfort or whim.' Alan Atkinson suggests that Fawkner's scheme 'had some echoes on the ground in early Port Phillip,' as 'nowhere else in Australia was it so readily assumed that the pioneers would take charge and make what they could of the place.' Fawkner's proposed governing council, to be elected by universal male franchise, even met on one occasion, in May 1836, to settle a dispute between himself and Henry Batman. Ultimately, however, even Fawkner seems to have preferred to pursue the protection of His Majesty's Government than the vagaries of independence.[15]

With the usual instruments of coercion crippled by shortages of labour and the liberty of distance, workers had to be motivated in other ways. Henry Batman concentrated on the discretionary distribution of liquor, and this was no doubt a common stratagem. Another long-established technique was to provide particularly generous rations, while food that was not up to scratch could be rejected. For example, in May 1836 Fawkner reported that there were 'Plenty of blacks about, say 100 to 120' and John Batman gave them 'rice and bread made from the damaged flour the men at his work refused to eat.'[16] A more sophisticated approach was to give workers a share of the profits by paying piece rates (this was especially useful in bark collecting). Some shepherds were paid according to what was termed the 'thirds,' whereby they received one-third of the natural increase of stock as an incentive to protect and care for their charges.

While the background of the first colonisers goes far to explain the remarkable ease with which Port Phillip was first settled and the freedoms enjoyed in its society, the other factor, equally important, was the land itself. When Batman landed in May 1835, he walked into 'kangaroo grass two feet high, and as thick as it could stand.' It had no doubt benefited from an Aboriginal burn. Batman estimated that there were not more 'than six [trees] to the acre, and those small sheoak and wattle' and declared that he 'never saw anything equal to the land in my life.'[17] When George Russell arrived in Melbourne the following autumn, he similarly observed that 'the country immediately around at this time looked very pretty. The grass had all been burnt off by bush-fires and autumn rain had caused it to spring up again.'[18] Such grassland was the environment in which Britons, as a pastoral people, always felt most at home.

This does not mean that sheep and cattle provided the only industry. There was also significant investments in agriculture, hunting and, above all, wattle-bark collecting. From 1 December to 9 December Fawkner's three men were working full time 'stripping' and tying up bark, and then carting it to the beach.[19] One early settler claimed to have made £1000 from bark alone.[20] Nevertheless, pastoralism was the raison d'être of the Yarra camp, and underpinned both the movement of people and the investment of capital.

Despite the wealth of the grasslands, there were still distinct environmental challenges to confront. Principal of these was the need to secure permanent water for stock. Port Phillip was not a homogenous landscape which the British uniformly possessed as they expanded their frontier. Rather, the settlers seized grass *and* water, while landscapes that were devoid of either were initially avoided. Expansion progressed along permanent rivers and creeks, with infill around springs, lakes and inland swamps. Sometimes apparently good land would be 'discovered' only for the possessor to find, as George Augustus Robinson's son did, that it was a 'useless place' as there was 'no water in the summer hot weather.'[21] The geographically determined movement of stock and people heightened the cross-cultural contact – and, soon enough, the conflict – because permanent water was also the focus of Aboriginal settlement and land use. In Melbourne's first year settlers regularly sought Aboriginal guides, less to find grass (which was everywhere) than to reveal often-obscure springs and waterholes. When in December 1835 Fawkner reported that 'the Natives led us to a small spring ... of good cool water,' we can be sure that he was documenting a precursor to possession.[22]

Other environmental challenges of this generally benign country had been evident since John Batman first landed in May 1835. Within days of his arrival 'the founder of Melbourne' shot a dingo, searched in vain for timber 'fit for sawing or splitting' and set his dogs to chase 'some kangaroo' only to find they 'could not catch them.'[23] All three experiences were to be repeated over and over again. Although scant in detail, Batman's report pointed to significant differences between the country around Melbourne and the mother island to the south.

The presence of the dingo was important in a number of ways. Early reports leave no doubt that kangaroo and wallaby were both less common than in Van Diemen's Land and, being already adapted to dogs, more difficult to kill. Batman left six kangaroo dogs at Indented Head, and on the first day there and most days thereafter, residents of the camp went 'Cangarooing.' Despite extensive nearby grasslands, kangaroo proved to be neither easy to find nor straightforward to hunt. The first 'Forester' (the Van Diemonian idiom for the Eastern Grey Kangaroo) was killed on 13 June 1835, but this was after three unsuccessful forays.[24] Such intermittent success set the pattern for future British hunting parties, with the scale of plunder more akin to early Sydney than early Hobart, where fresh meat had soon become the staple ration. Given that this was ideal kangaroo habitat, it can only be assumed that the dingo, both as wild animal and Aboriginal hunting companion, was a major reason for the comparatively low density of herbivores.[25] A greater human population density was another reason suggested by Van Diemonian settlers at the time.[26]

Fawkner's journal documents the same pattern of regular hunting expeditions with only occasional success during Melbourne's first year, although late in life he claimed that the dogs he supplied to the expeditioners on the *Enterprize* had ensured that 'on the first day of landing a fine boomer was started not many yards from the vessel, driven into the river just above the site of the Princes Bridge.'[27]

The presence of the dingo also represented a significant threat to sheep and it was not long before the settlers went to war with the native carnivore. A public meeting of settlers on 1 June 1836 resolved to put a five-shilling bounty on wild dogs. It was the imported hunting dogs which proved to be the most effective weapon against the dingo. One early Van Diemonian squatter recorded that 'a fine kangaroo dog ... who has gained some celebrity as a destroyer of the wild dogs' had been purchased for 'only thirty shillings,' which was thought 'very cheap if he prove as good as he is reported.'[28] Yet these animals could cause still greater problems for stock when they went wild, as so many had done in Van Diemen's Land.

The difficulties caused by the dingo were to some extent made up for by the comparative abundance of fish and birds. Fishing is a form of hunting that greatly benefits from local knowledge, and thus friendly relations with the Kulin might have been as critical to the success of fishermen at Port Phillip as the bountiful waterways themselves. The rich birdlife of the swamps were another useful source of protein, and guns in this instance finally came into their own. Yet small animals such as fish and birds do not provide sufficient meat to live off unless an inordinate amount of time is spent hunting. Furthermore, while these foods were abundant around Melbourne, this was not typically the case in the adjacent pastoral country. The result was that almost all early settlers remained dependent to a large extent on imported supplies throughout 1835 and for some time after. James Willis might have exaggerated in claiming that 'Old Tom,' the shepherd he dined with soon after crossing the Strait, 'had tasted nothing but salt pork for twelve months,' but from a Van Diemonian perspective his judgment that 'all kinds of wild animals (save the wild dogs) [were] scarce' was fair.[29]

The comparative shortage of fresh food meant that even native plants were sometimes eaten. In almost every instance when this has occurred in Australia, it provides evidence of cross-cultural contact, or at least close observation of indigenous custom, as there was generally no other source of knowledge about plant foods.[30] At Indented Head, as supplies ran low and the daily hunting and fishing expeditions provided insufficient food to feed everyone, William Todd recorded that on 3 August 1835, 'We have commenced eating Roots the same as the Natives do.'[31] The roots in question were those of the murnong or yam daisy, *Microseris lanceolata*, a tufted perennial herb prevalent on the basalt plains that regenerated annually from a fleshy tuberous root.[32] This plant formed a staple of the Aboriginal diet and was also favoured by some of Port Phillip's early settlers. Alexander Mollison's men, 'having exhausted their stock of provisions, roasted and ate some of these roots.'[33]

During Melbourne's first year settlers were not only forced to eat imported food, but to reside in imported dwellings. Batman's first reference to the timber of the new land is significant here. As noted, by 1835 vernacular architecture in Van Diemen's Land (and in New South Wales) included a range of overnight, short-term and semi-permanent huts which had rendered tents virtually redundant. Their construction required no more than an axe because splittable timber was ready to hand. However, as the *Hobart Town Courier* of 28 October 1836 noted, there was 'a great deficiency of timber fit for building and fencing' around Melbourne. This meant that Todd's experience of being forced to pitch a 'temporary tent until such time as we can find timber to build with' would be repeated many times over.[34] Fawkner was constantly looking for suitable timber with limited success during the first months of settlement.[35] The census of 1836 revealed that there were very few log or slab huts, even in the country districts.[36] Batman's own house was brought over in pre-fabricated form from Van Diemen's Land and as late as 1837 Phillip King observed that 'the [timber] framed houses have all been sent from Sydney or Launceston.'[37] Even in 1840 Charles Griffiths reports that the roofs of Melbourne houses were made 'principally, I might almost say, entirely, with shingles, which are imported from Van Diemen's Land.'[38]

The result was that cumbersome tents had to be employed for short-term accommodation, and the labour-intensive traditional British building technique known as 'wattle and daub' often resorted to for more permanent dwellings. At least, as the missionary George Langhorne recalled, 'The tea-tree with which the south bank of the Yarra was lined afforded a welcome supply of poles, and the wattle for the wattle and daub huts.'[39] And the abundance of horses, which could easily carry tents, meant that the difficulties in constructing shelters did not pose the usual barrier to movement. Eventually territorial expansion ensured a supply of palings and shingles for the usual variety of hut designs.

Ultimately, however, whatever challenges the new land posed, there is no doubt that they were not sufficient to affect the success of settlement. At Port Phillip a benign environment combined with settler expertise made for a remarkably straightforward colonisation, and it would only be the Aborigines who presented any serious barrier to conquest.

10.

CAMPING IN KULIN COUNTRY

THE CHALLENGE OF SETTLING ONE OF the most densely populated regions of Australia defined the settler experience of early
Melbourne. A small group of dispersed Europeans was now occupying prime ceremonial and hunting grounds without military protection, and this shaped not just policy and lobbying efforts, but
daily life. The Yarra camp was not a secured beachhead like early
Sydney or Hobart, but a vulnerable outpost in the centre of Kulin
territory. Given the balance of power, and the delicate political situation vis-à-vis the British government (a public slaughter would be
disastrous to the squatter cause), the incentive to keep the peace was
unusually strong.

Town-centred cross-cultural contact was not an unusual experience in early Australia – Aborigines resided in most British outposts, motivated initially by curiosity, rations and trade, and later as
refugees dispossessed from their homelands. Inga Clendinnen has
memorably depicted the first encounters at Port Jackson in *Dancing
with Strangers*, while Grace Karskens in *The Colony* has shown how
Sydney remained for so long also an Aboriginal town.[40] Nevertheless, the intensity of cross-cultural life at the Yarra in the first months
of settlement is almost without parallel. Throughout Melbourne's
first year it was less a case of Aborigines 'coming in' to the British
camp than of a small group of Britons 'coming in' to Kulin country.
During 1835 and 1836 Britons had little alternative but to fit in with

the Aborigines and provide them with a liberal supply of provisions – a significant cost given that the black population often outnumbered the white. Confusion, misunderstandings and conflict were never absent, but overall the Aborigines' expertise was successfully enlisted in the colonisation project, especially as guides and guarantors of safe passage into the grasslands beyond.

The men who belonged in neither camp – the so-called Sydney Aborigines – continued to be central to cross-cultural relations. By the time Pigeon and his colleagues permanently relocated from Indented Head in November 1835, they had experienced many months of travelling the local country with local people. Fawkner describes Pigeon as 'a very good guide in the bush' and records others in the group also performing this work.[41] The Sydney Aborigines also helped with hunting and trade. On 23 December Fawkner reported that 'me & Chas with Mr Batman & 4 Sydney Blacks' went 'to the Bay & caught four swans, and shot 3 ducks & 1 teal.'[42] Such was their general utility that Fawkner was wont to complain that Henry Batman 'monopolizes the Sydney Blacks.'[43]

This was not a straightforward partnership, as the relations between John Batman and the Sydney men had been transformed by their relocation to Aboriginal-controlled territory. Their independent actions at Port Phillip, often in cohort with the local people, suggest they recognised that their relationship with the Kulin conferred both responsibility and power. For example, on 8 January 1836 Fawkner reported that 'Batman's Sydney Blacks absconded last night & took all the Blacks about here away, except Dr Cottar's boy.'[44]

William Buckley, who had lived for so long with the Aborigines that he is perhaps most accurately seen as a Watha wurrung Briton, occupied an equally complex position between the new and old worlds. The usefulness of his work as translator and mediator was widely acknowledged during Melbourne's first year, when he was employed by the Port Phillip Association. Fawkner regularly complained about Buckley, both because of his work for the Batmans –

in April 1836 he noted in his journal that Buckley and Batman 'ordered the Blacks not to sell us any squirrels [possums] or baskets'[45] – and suspicions about where his primary racial loyalties lay. As the white population increased, these suspicions became widespread. In 1837 the missionary George Langhorne observed that Buckley appeared 'always disconnected and dissatisfied, and I believe it would have been a great relief to him had the settlement been abandoned and he left alone with his sable friends ...'[46]

What of the locals? How did they respond to the British presence? People came to the Yarra and other camps to obtain food and supplies – even guns were regularly lent to the Aborigines at this time – and some embraced the wider possibilities created by the still manageable British presence and sought to incorporate the newcomers into the existing political and social order. Large gatherings of Kulin were summoned for significant meetings with influential Britons. A few hundred were present when Batman returned in November, and a large group met with Police Magistrate George Stewart in May 1836. Other visits reflected customary movements. As William Thomas wrote in 1840:

> Long ere the settlement was formed, the spot where Melbourne now stands and the flat on which we are now camped [near the present day Royal Botanic Gardens] was the regular rendezvous ... [occurring] twice a year or as often as circumstances and emergencies required to settle their grievances, revenge, deaths, etc.[47]

A small but significant group of Kulin, including a Woi wurrung man, Billibellary, the pre-eminent Kulin clan head,[48] was more or less based in Melbourne and sometimes lived with the settlers. In October 1836 Fawkner claimed to the New South Wales government that:

I have kept from four to twenty of the Aborigines constantly at my house and have taught them to row my boat, which they frequently do, fourteen miles in a day, viz, from the Township to the Anchorage and back. I have caused a youth in my employ to devote his time to learning the native language which he has very successfully accomplished. The Natives also hunt and fish for me, and in order to impress upon their minds, the great power and kindness of the English, I have at my own cost and charges brought over from Port Phillip to Van Diemen's Land, three of the Natives.[49]

While Fawkner was undoubtedly exaggerating his hospitality, even Lonsdale's rebuttal confirmed how common it was for Aborigines to live with the whites:

I cannot ascertain what was expended on the blacks by Mr F. but I have no doubt he did to some extent as did most others, either from a feeling of humanity or to ensure their own safety by making friends with the blacks ... I do not perceive that the blacks are more domesticated by Mr F. than in most other families. There are commonly some who attach themselves to particular people and some appear to have done so with Mr. F., but I cannot perceive they are more useful than others ... There is a lad with Mr F. who can speak something of the native language and he took two of the blacks to Van Diemen's Land in his schooner and brought them back since I have been here.[50]

What is clear is that the settler relationship with domiciled Aborigines was not a straightforward labour exchange. While the Aborigines frequently acted as guides, often hunted for settlers (especially with the borrowed guns) and on occasion performed an array of menial tasks, this was still done on Aboriginal terms, and the work was often interrupted. For example, on 14 April 1836

Fawkner reported that 'Nearly all the blacks left the settlement this day. Hunting and fishing &c. Bait-Bainger & Derrah-Mert [two men who resided with Fawkner] went also although we wanted them to go Kangarooing.'[51]

As in other regions of Australia, many of the Aborigines who visited the British camp were intensely curious. The Wesleyan missionary Joseph Orton raised the oft-expressed possibility that this related to a belief in reincarnation. When he visited the Yarra in April 1836 and conducted the first service by an ordained minister, he found the Aborigines:

> anxious to obtain information on all points which were suggested to their minds, and they are equally disposed to communicate ... they decidedly hold the doctrine of transmigration, and since Europeans have settled among them they seem to have imbibed the ludicrous notion that the white people are their ancestors returned to them – and that after they die they will 'jump up white man.' One of the most interesting opportunities that I had was when performing Divine Service with the Europeans on the settlement, on which occasion a considerable number of natives assembled together and surrounded the shed under which the service was performed. Some apprehension was excited lest our devotions would be interrupted by their noise and restlessness, for they are usually exceedingly loquacious and in their social intercourse maintain a constant jabber and confusion. But contrary to our expectations the reverse was the case, and though the nature of our performance could not be comprehended by them, they were apparently remarkably attentive and quiet all the time; especially during singing they appeared to be struck with silent admiration ... On the eve of my departure I had all the natives who were on the spot collected together, and through the medium of Buckley, who acted as my interpreter, I addressed this interesting audience.[52]

Trade was another aspect of cross-cultural relations, with fresh meat, skins and baskets exchanged for British goods. Fawkner, always a merchant at heart, was regularly buying from and selling to the Aborigines and confronting cartels. On 21 February he noted, 'Mr Hy Batman sent Blacks out to get Parrots, got Buckley to abuse W.W. [William Watkins] for buying squirrel skins for me, and I find that he is forbidding the natives to sell us any skins or birds. He wants them all for himself.' Fawkner had more luck on 7 March: 'A number of Blacks came in this day and their wives, got 3 kangaroo tails from them and two fine baskets.'[53] Wedge made much of the supposedly civilising benefits of trade, reporting that he 'commenced a barter trade with the Natives receiving in exchange for tea, sugar, bread etc, articles [they] manufactured themselves, such as baskets, spears, and other implements – fish and kangaroo – and in fact anything which involved the necessity of employment and a communication with ourselves.'[54]

Wedge argued that this exchange was 'observing the terms agreed upon by Mr Batman with the Native Tribes,' and although this was a dubious interpretation of the treaty, it is true that peaceful relations with the Kulin were now largely based on the British providing food and supplies. Even though the May 1835 understanding had been grossly violated by the size of the unauthorised white presence, the protection tenets of the agreement had been strongly reinforced by Batman when he returned in November 1835. Batman informed Governor Arthur that 'During my stay there Buckley explained to the several chiefs our motives and intentions in settling amongst them and the consequences which might arise from any aggression on their part. He also explained that any ill-treatment on the part of white men towards them, if reported to the heads of the establishment, would meet with its proper punishment. With this understanding they were perfectly well pleased, and promised to act in conformity with it.'[55]

Furthermore, the Port Phillip Association *did* follow up complaints made by Aborigines. On 15 March 1836 Wedge advised government officials of an attack at Westernport:

> Since my late arrival at this place I have learned that a flagrant outrage has been committed upon the natives at Westernport by a party of men employed in collecting mimosa bark ... A few weeks since, William Buckley heard that the men employed in collecting bark had attacked the natives and wounded several of them, but doubts being entertained by some of the correctness of the report, Buckley despatched messengers to request that the wounded natives might be brought to this place, and on the 11th instant the families arrived, and on visiting their huts I found that four individuals had received gunshot wounds. It appears that the natives were fired upon soon after sunrise, whilst lying in their huts, and one young girl about thirteen years of age was wounded in both her thighs, the ball passing through one into the other, grazing the bone in its passage, which has so far disabled her at the present moment that her parents were obliged to carry her on their backs from Westernport to this place – a distance of about 30 miles – and it is apprehended that she will not recover the use of her legs. To rescue this poor girl the mother took her in her arms, and in carrying her away was fired at and wounded in her arm and shoulder with buckshot.[56]

The protection clauses underpinning Batman's agreement with the Aborigines were given further expression when action was taken against two shepherds who were accused by the Aborigines of rape. The men were sent back to Van Diemen's Land, although the reality of the Port Phillip frontier is highlighted by the fact that this incident is almost the sole instance in which *any* action was taken against rapists, and that no thought was given to prosecuting the offenders.

Such actions, and the philanthropic sentiments which accompanied them, are confusing for those who seek to separate the colonists into those who defended Aborigines and those who would kill them. The reality is that humanitarian interventions and sentiments co-existed with a near-universal belief in the necessity of teaching a lesson to, and 'striking terror' into the hearts of, those Aborigines who threatened sheep or shepherds. While the balance of power and political realities generally dictated restraint, before Melbourne's first year was out, the most philanthropic leaders of the Port Phillip Association would prove that they were as committed to the necessity of occasionally launching indiscriminate vigilante raids against whole tribal groups as were their shepherds in the front line.

EARLY CONFLICT

CHARLES SWANSTON WAS STILL living the banker's life in Hobart Town when two of his shepherds were speared in March 1836 and he lost about £2000 in stock.[57] Such resistance by Aborigines was seen to threaten the whole colonisation project, both because of the level of investment involved in purchasing and transporting ewes, and because even battle-hardened Van Diemonian shepherds were not willing to live in remote grasslands without protection. Fawkner noted that after the March attack, 'all Mr Swanston's men are coming in to the township, they are afraid to live in the bush for fear of the Blacks.' Fawkner was angry that Henry Batman (John was again absent) had not immediately sent a reprisal party, and he sympathised with the shepherds: they 'reason we may all be served the same way if this is all the notice the Companys agent takes of the news of men being speared.'[58] Wedge wondered if the Van Diemen's Land solution of exiling the Aborigines should be applied and sheep stealers sent to Kings Island, as 'a little promptitude in meeting those outrages in the commencement will save a deal of blood as it respects both the Europeans and the blacks.'[59]

Nevertheless, in defiance of popular opinion and frontier imperatives, the Port Phillip Association did not act in March 1836. Although its military capacity was still too limited for effective protection of remote runs should the conflict escalate, it was the politics of the situation that primarily impelled restraint. The Association was aware that a reprisal raid would undermine its claim that the illegal land grab was designed to benefit the Aborigines too. And while the British government's response to the land occupation was uncertain, this risk was significant. Nevertheless, when news came a few months later that Aborigines had now killed one of the squatters' own, Charles Franks, along with an unnamed shepherd, there seems to have been a general acceptance that the time for caution was over.

Franks's station had been on the Werribee River near Mt Cottrell, and when his dead body and that of his employee were discovered in early July 1836, parties were quickly organised to punish the perpetrators. Almost immediately after Franks was laid to rest in the new public cemetery, men on horseback rode west to convey a clear message to the supposedly guilty tribe.

Fawkner presented the expedition as consistent with the wider understanding that had been reached with the Aborigines: 'we enlisted as many Natives as would consent to go and agreed to send them out to deal with the Murderers as they think according to their Rules.'[60] However, it is clear that this was no more than an old-fashioned reprisal, which sought to exploit traditional tribal animosities to achieve its grisly purpose (although in this respect at least it had limited success: only a single local Aborigine accompanied the avenging party). Gellibrand wrote matter-of-factly on 7 August that 'Several parties are now after the natives and I have no doubt many will be shot and a stop put to this system of killing for bread.'[61] William Buckley seems to have sympathised with the Aborigines: according to Bonwick's informants, 'when the body [of Franks] was being carried in solemn possession past Buckley's hut, he laughed aloud. He refused to allow the body to rest in his hut, refused to attend the funeral and took no part in the search for the guilty Aborigines.'[62] This was despite the fact that, the foray being into his home country, his services as scout and guide would have been highly desired.

The *Cornwall Chronicle* recorded the success of Henry Batman's party: 'The avenging party fell upon the guilty tribe about daylight in the morning, having watched them the previous night, and putting into effect a preconcerted plan of attack, succeeded in annihilating them – This tribe, which we now presume to be no longer troublesome, were it appears, a particularly treacherous people – less numerous than any of the others, and despised by all.'[63]

Wedge was acutely aware of both the political opportunities and dangers created by the massacre. He expressed his concern to Swanston that it was important not to 'afford General Bourke a pretext, which he is most anxiously looking for, to interfere with our occupation of the land' and urged that 'the circumstances should be immediately made known to the Sydney Government, and again urge the appointment of a Magistrate and the establishment of a constabulary.'[64]

Most likely it was through Swanston acting on this advice that Lieutenant Governor Arthur in Hobart was able to send the following information to Sydney in August 1836:

From the account received it appears that … the whites assembled to the number of eight, with four Sydney natives and five domesticated natives of the Port Phillip, all armed, it is represented, with muskets. They proceeded in search of the natives whom they supposed to be the murderers … They came up with a tribe, consisting of men, women, and children, to the number of from fifty to one hundred, and perceiving upon the persons of some of them articles which were recognized as having belonged to Mr Franks, a recontre followed. It is not stated however what resistance the natives made, but none of the opposing party were injured, although it is feared that there can be little or no doubt that ten of the tribe of Port Phillip natives were killed.[65]

In reporting the killings, Swanston provided Sydney with a second opportunity to intervene in the affairs of the Port Phillip settlement, as Arthur's offer to investigate left Bourke little option but to send down a magistrate even if he was not already so inclined.

This inquiry, conducted by William Lonsdale, provided a template for future Port Phillip investigations conducted by governments and courts. Henry Batman testified that he went 'in search of the blacks who had murdered Mr Franks and his shepherd ... in company with William Winberry, George Hollins, Michael Leonard and the native of Port Phillip named Benbow, and three Sydney natives, Bullett, Stewart and Joe the Marine' at the request of John Batman and Gellibrand, and that:

> On the 13th I reached the River Werribee where I fell in with Mr John Wood who had a party also going for the same purpose ... We continued following up the track till the evening of Friday the 15th instant, when we saw a smoke ... On Saturday morning we pursued the tracks till we could hear voices; we went on till we came in sight of some natives by their huts. We here divided our party. When we came up to them there were more than I expected. There were nine large huts and about 70 or 80 natives ... Finding the noise I made did not intimidate them I fired my gun, which was loaded with shot, above their heads, for the same purpose of making them run. It had the effect I wished, for they ran off immediately. Some other shots were fired by some of the party but I know not by whom ... When I came up to the huts I found the property was there and I stopped to secure it. The rest of the party were running after the blacks ... In about a quarter of an hour the whole party was collected together and we returned with such of the property as was worth bringing in; the remainder we burnt ... I do not know if any of the blacks were killed or hurt during this transaction. I did not see any that were.[66]

Henry Batman's claim that *I do not know if any of the blacks were killed or hurt during this transaction* almost certainly amounted to perjury. Even if we accept that Batman was not among them, how likely is it that the mounted men 'running after the blacks' neither confirmed nor denied having killed any Aborigines on their return, given that the avowed purpose of the expedition was to inflict punishment? What had been the basis of the estimate of casualties Batman had recently provided to his Association employers and Arthur had passed on to Sydney? Lonsdale's decision to accept Batman's testimony and focus his recommendations on the crimes of the *Aborigines* provided an early indication of what justice on the Port Phillip frontier would mean in practice: 'I shall endeavour to take the two blacks who committed the murder and send them to Sydney.'[67]

This was not the only killing of Aborigines investigated by the judicial system during the latter part of 1836.[68] By year's end the generally peaceful cross-cultural encounter at the Yarra camp was no longer indicative of relations in the grasslands beyond. While the lower Yarra's swamps and wastelands were not yet the refuges for Aborigines they would soon become, less than twelve months after the arrival of the *Enterprize* the famous camp was already one of the safer, if not saner, places on the Port Phillip frontier.

PART IV

DECISION TIME

THE COLONIES RESPOND

THE REMARKABLY RAPID SPREAD of Britons and their animals during Melbourne's first year was a direct consequence of the response taken by the governments of Van Diemen's Land and New South Wales to the squatter invasion. Today the legend endures that government was a passive onlooker, unable to influence events, but this fails to recognise that *inaction* by political leaders can be just as effective and deliberate a policy choice as *action*. The governors of both Van Diemen's Land and New South Wales were careful not to formally sanction trespass on crown land. However, the fact that both only stated existing policy and law, without attempting to uphold it, amounted to an informal sanction, without which the speculative investment flowing to the Port Phillip venture would soon have dried up.

During the critical first months of the project, in the spring of 1835, this policy was Lieutenant Governor Arthur's alone. The physical distance between Hobart Town and Sydney, and the relative autonomy of their political and commercial establishments, is revealed by the fact that it took three months for Governor Bourke even to hear that Port Phillip had been settled. Arthur was in no hurry to notify Sydney, and Bourke does not seem to have had information from any other source. Arthur himself stayed well informed, maintaining close contact with Swanston and Simpson in particular, and even meeting privately with Batman shortly after his return from Port Phillip. (Batman informed Wedge in a letter of 18 June that he was soon to have an interview with the 'little man.'[1])

Arthur did not inform the British government of the Port Phillip project until 4 July 1835, more than a month after Batman's return. More significant still is that even when he did so, he used a request for policy direction as an excuse not to implement the existing policy in the interim, even though, as the voyage took from three to six months, answers to policy queries usually took about twelve months to arrive.

Arthur's decision not to implement British government policy on the unauthorised settlement of crown land represented decisive support for the Port Phillip settlement. If Arthur were genuinely neutral or passive on the issue, the appropriate action would have been to try to prevent settlement proceeding until advice from the Colonial Office was received.

Furthermore, when Arthur finally wrote to the Secretary of State for the Colonies in July, asking to 'be made acquainted at the earliest period, with the views which His Majesty's Government entertains upon this important subject,' he did not withhold his own enthusiasm for settlement. Arthur argued that 'The settlement of this district would unquestionably be highly advantageous to Van Diemen's Land. Its extensive plains and rich pastures are capable of supporting large herds of cattle and sheep, and as the distance between the two coasts might be traversed by a steam boat in about 24 hours, it might very rapidly be covered with flocks and herds from this colony.' And although he did not see 'any valid grounds' for recognition of the Association's purchase of land from the Aborigines – because the land had already been 'taken possession of by David Collins in 1803 and on a number of occasions subsequently'[2] – he once more requested that Port Phillip be placed 'temporarily' under Van Diemen's Land's jurisdiction.

Arthur took even longer to write to Governor Bourke with news of the Port Phillip project, only forwarding relevant reports on 7 and

12 August. Bourke recognised that the delay was due to Arthur's hope that Port Phillip would be incorporated into Van Diemen's Land, and by return mail the Governor of New South Wales asserted his jurisdictional authority, citing existing British government land policy and the exclusive crown claim to the land. The letter from Bourke's Colonial Secretary to Arthur, dated 1 September 1835, advised that in putting Arthur's correspondence before the New South Wales Executive Council, the Governor also:

> laid before it a dispatch received from the Right Honourable the Earl of Aberdeen dated 25th December 1834, stating the opinion of His Majesty's Government upon the proposition to extend the location of settlers beyond the present authorized limits, and directing the Government to discountenance any plan which may be hereafter proposed for settling the territory beyond those limits. As the result of the deliberations of the Council, I do myself the honour by the command of Sir Richard Bourke to transmit to you the accompanying copies of a proclamation he has issued, notifying that any bargain or contract made with the aboriginal natives of New Holland for the possession of any lands within the limits of the Government of New South Wales will be held to be null and void as against the rights of the Crown, and that all persons found in possession of any such lands will be considered as intruders and dealt with accordingly, with a request that you will … cause copies to be furnished to Mr Batman and the other parties associated with him, with a communication to the effect that though this Government is fully satisfied of the great respectability of the parties, and highly approves of the regard expressed for the welfare of the aboriginal natives, it has nevertheless been deemed necessary to announce in the most formal and public manner the right of the Crown of England to the territory in question, and the absolute nullity of any grant for its possession made by any other party.[3]

The proclamation in question, dated 26 August 1835, was enough to send shivers down any Van Diemonian property speculator's spine:

> I the Governor, in virtue and in exercise of the power and authority in me vested, do hereby proclaim and notify to all His Majesty's subjects and others whom it may concern, that every such treaty, bargain, and contract with the aboriginal natives ... for the possession, title, or claim to any lands lying and being within the limits of the Government of the Colony of New South Wales, as the same are laid down and defined by His Majesty's Commission; that is to say, extending from the Northern Cape or extremity of the coast called Cape York, in the latitude of 10 degrees 37 minutes south, to the southern extremity of the said Territory of New South Wales, or Wilson's Promontory, in the latitude of 39 degrees 12 minutes south, and embracing all the country inland to the westward, as far as the 129th degree of east longitude, reckoning from the meridian of Greenwich ... is void and of no effect against the rights of the Crown; and that all persons who shall be found in possession of any such lands as aforesaid, without the licence of authority of His Majesty's Government, for such purpose, first had and obtained, will be considered as trespassers, and liable to be dealt with in like manner as intruders upon the vacant lands of the Crown within the said Colony.[4]

Such a clear statement of existing policy immediately slowed the flow of capital to the Port Phillip venture. Four of the Association members reportedly sold their shares or part of them,[5] and Batman delayed his planned departure to Port Phillip, presumably to deal with the fall-out, before deciding to test the political waters and defy the proclamation. He informed Arthur that 'I propose immediately to proceed with my family to Port Phillip, to take, with Mr Wedge, the direction of the affairs of the Association, and the arrangements with the native tribes,' and asked the Lieutenant Governor 'to fully inform His Excellency General Bourke of the proposed plans of the Association, their capacity to carry them into execution, and the principles under which they wish to establish a colony at Port Phillip.' Batman also signalled a significant strategic shift: the Association was now calling for immediate government intervention, on the basis that other new settlers, 'in defiance of our occupation of the land from the natives,' would 'materially check, if not destroy, the principles of colonisation, unless controlled by a competent authority.'[6] In effect the Port Phillip Association acknowledged that there was no local political support for its claim to exclusive possession and was now prepared to give up its monopoly land claim in return for government sanction of the settlement.

It is highly likely that this momentous strategic shift was made in consultation with Arthur, or at least in recognition of the Lieutenant Governor's views, as Arthur shortly after provided a very public display of support for Batman's violation of Bourke's proclamation. The *Hobart Town Courier* records Arthur visiting Launceston and George Town in October to see at first hand the progress being made for Batman's imminent departure to Port Phillip, complimenting the work being done and publicly advising that the Lieutenant Governor would be joining the call for the appointment of a resident government authority.[7]

Despite the short-term uncertainty, it soon became clear that Bourke had no intention of carrying through the implied eviction notice anyway. While the proclamation was sent as far as the Swan River, for some reason (never explained) it didn't make it to Port Phillip. Bourke then took six weeks to inform London of events, and when he did so, he advised that he too would await instructions before taking any further action. He informed the British Secretary of State, Lord Glenelg, that:

I have considered it incumbent of me immediately to protest against any consequences derogatory to the rights of the British crown that might be imagined to flow from the alleged treaty. I have accordingly issued, with the advice of the Executive Council of this Colony, a Proclamation of which I transmit a copy. It is not my present intention, and I shall probably not see cause to take any other step in this matter until I have had the honour to receive Your Lordship's commands on the subject. In the meantime, there is little doubt that Mr Batman and his Party will continue to convey cattle to Port Phillip and to invest capital in building and other improvements at that place.[8]

Bourke acknowledged the 'weighty objections' to Batman's actions, 'not only in the irregular mode he has had recourse to for obtaining Land, but on account of the absence of any provision for the control and government of the inhabitants of the intended settlement,' but nevertheless backed the squatters' call for the 'interference and protection of Government.'

Bourke's October 1835 dispatch made it clear that he was as enthusiastic about colonising southern Australia as Arthur, and that he saw the trespass as an opportunity to overturn the existing policy of concentrated settlement. Bourke did admit, 'as every reasonable person must, that a certain degree of concentration is necessary for the advancement of wealth and civilization, and that it enables Government to become at once efficient and economical,' but he could not 'avoid perceiving the peculiarities which, in this Colony, render it impolitic and even impossible to restrain dispersion within limits that would be expedient elsewhere.' He then stated his famous dictum, which has become a cornerstone of Australian history:

The wool of New South Wales forms at present, and is likely long to continue, its chief wealth. It is only by a free range over the wide expanse of native herbage, which the Colony affords, that the production of this staple article can be upheld at its present rate of increase in quantity, or standard of value in quality ... The colonists must otherwise restrain the increase, or endeavour to raise artificial food for their stock. Whilst nature presents all around an unlimited supply of the most wholesome nutrient, either course would seem a perverse rejection of the bounty of Providence, and the latter would certainly require more labour than can at present be obtained in the Colony, or immigration profitably supply. Independently of these powerful reasons for allowing dispersion, it is not to be disguised that the Government is unable to prevent it. No adequate measures could be resorted to for the general and permanent removal of intruders from waste lands, without incurring probably a greater expense than would be sufficient to extend a large share of the control and protection of the Government over the country they desire to occupy ... I do not, however, mean to admit the claim of every wanderer in search of pasture to the protection of civil or military force. The question, I would beg leave to submit, is simply this: How may this Government turn to the best advantage a state of things, which it cannot wholly interdict?

The Governor concluded that such 'considerations induce me to believe that it will be more desirable to impose reasonable conditions on Mr Batman and his associates than to insist on their abandoning their undertaking,' and proposed that 'a township be marked out ... in some eligible spot on the coast, to which Mr Batman's party has proceeded.'[9]

Remarkably, given the political context of the time, Bourke's oft-cited dispatch is as significant for what it neglected as for what it asserted. There was no reference to the impact of Port Phillip colonisation on the Aborigines. While government intervention would later be justified in part by the protection that it supposedly afforded them, this was not a factor in Bourke's critical early support for the project.

Even when Arthur belatedly raised the protection argument in his letter to Bourke of 14 November 1835, it had less to do with protection for the Aborigines than for the invaders. He forwarded Batman's letter seeking a government authority to be appointed and reiterated Wedge's view (which was one Arthur had himself once put in relation to Van Diemen's Land) that:

> little dependence ... can be placed upon them [the Aborigines] unless impressed with that appearance of strength and determination among the white settlers which the latter will not be able to present if they are not united among themselves and if their intercourse with the Blacks be not marked by uniformity of purpose as well as by a mild and conciliatory spirit.

It was to achieve the necessary 'strength and determination,' that Arthur recommended that the 'District be placed under some form of Government.' The alternative was likely an 'exterminating war' between settlers and Aborigines.[10]

It was by now clear that with their petty jurisdictional dispute settled, Bourke and Arthur were of one mind on Port Phillip colonisation (and they would in fact maintain a friendly correspondence for many years). In a May 1836 letter to Bourke, Arthur expressed his commitment to the colonial ideal, which was ultimately far more important to both men than the legality of the enterprise: 'Great Britain and Ireland are over-peopled, surely every effort should be made to occupy the whole tract of country in question comprehending many millions of acres of the finest land.'[11]

Such was the Governors' shared faith in the underlying virtues of this private colonisation project that even major problems understood to be caused by the blatant disregard for the law were used to press the case for British government sanction. Bourke backed

Arthur and Batman's proposal to establish a government presence at Port Phillip in his dispatch to Glenelg on 21 December 1835, specifically noting that Batman had now admitted 'the impossibility of maintaining peace and order in the proposed establishment without the assistance of civil or military force.'[12]

Now that both colonial governments supported the Port Phillip settlement, an ever-increasing pool of potential investors was prepared to stake money and reputation on what remained, it is important to remember, an act of trespass. On a tour of Van Diemen's Land in late 1835, the Reverend John Dunmore Lang reported that he 'found almost every respectable person I met with preparing, either individually, or in the person of some near relation or confidential agent, to occupy the Australian El Dorado,'[13] and Gellibrand wrote in early 1836 that 'the people of Van Diemen's Land are all mad for emigration and several Companies are forming for the export of sheep.'[14]

Thomas Brenan of Launceston complained to Bourke in February 1836 that the illegal occupation of land was unfair to men like him who sought permission through the proper channels. He noted that the very day 'previous to the receipt of your communication [denying official permission to settle], a vessel had sailed for that place, with several passengers, amongst whom were men of considerable capital, and taking with them stock of every description.' Brenan presented a realistic appraisal of how government policy was understood by investors in Van Diemen's Land:

I have reason to believe that the ideas which these individuals have formed on the subject in question are these; they argue that having selected a quantity of land, and taken possession of the same, they may consider it fairly as their own, resting assured that His Excellency ... will not interfere with them, until he has received instructions from His Majesty on the subject, who they seem to think will never instruct His Excellency to disturb the first possessors (no matter how possession was obtained) but should such an event as a matter of necessity occur, a highly advantageous preference will be given to them; this is the foundation upon which they build their hopes.[15]

Brenan must have been a man of cautious character, as by April even the Chief Justice of Van Diemen's Land, Sir John Pedder, had reportedly placed sheep and shepherds on the grasslands of Port Phillip,[16] and it was almost universally appreciated that Bourke's rejection of applications for land was little more than a gesture until London ordered otherwise.

Governor Bourke's determination to do all he could to support the colonisation while he awaited further instructions from the British government meant that he seized on the opportunity provided by the sealer attack on the Aborigines at Westernport in March 1836. On 18 May, the *New South Wales Government Gazette* formally proclaimed that the Aborigines of Port Phillip were under the Governor's protection:

Whereas it has been represented to me that a flagrant Outrage has been committed upon the Aboriginal Natives of Western Port by a Party of White Men, and that other Outrages of a similar Nature have been Committed by Stockmen and others upon the Natives in the Neighbourhood of Port Phillip; Now, therefore I, The Governor ... do hereby Proclaim ... that the whole of the Country on the Southern Coast of New Holland extending westward from Wilson's Promontory to the One Hundred and Twenty-ninth Degree of East Longitude ... being within the limits of New South Wales, all Persons residing or being within the same, are subject to the Laws in force in the said Colony, and the promptest measures will be taken by me to cause all Persons who may be guilty of any Outrage against the Aboriginal Natives, or any breach of the said Laws to be brought to Trial before the Supreme Court of New South Wales, and Punished accordingly.[17]

It was this incident which enabled Bourke to send Police Magistrate George Stewart down to the Yarra, both to investigate the killings and to provide a report of the settlement. Stewart's short sojourn of eight days from May 25 marks the first government presence in the Port Phillip district, and his sympathetic report of 10 June ends the period in which the New South Wales government viewed the settlers, in even the most token sense, as trespassers. The visit also clarified the New South Wales government's agenda to the squatters, and in a petition to Bourke, conveyed through Stewart, they adopted the same logic used by their political leaders: without a government presence, there would be conflict with Aborigines, the district would be a haven for runaway convicts, there would be smuggling and loss of revenue, and ongoing difficulty in enforcing law and order.[18]

Stewart's report confirmed that the problems caused by colonisation now formed the principal argument for sanctioning the settlement. As Bourke probably expected from the police magistrate of the frontier Goulburn district, his investigator excused the settlers from any responsibility for the conflict with the Aborigines, even as he distributed Bourke's proclamation of protection.[19] Stewart believed relations were generally peaceful, although the Port Phillip Aborigines 'like all savages ... will steal when they can find any opportunity.' He noted that since there were already eleven vessels 'now employed in bringing stock from Van Diemen's Land,' a 'branch of the Customs' should be established – which would amount to a formal government presence – as he was sure that the residents would 'feel much gratified if this Government would extend to them its protection.'[20]

While Bourke remained unwilling to station officers permanently at Port Phillip until he heard back from London, he did introduce legislation that signalled his determination to achieve a change in settlement policy. In July 1836, the New South Wales government passed a law which ensured that the question of trespass on crown land could now be determined according to the class of the occupier.

The 'Act to Restrain the Unauthorised Occupation of Crown lands' of 29 July[21] noted that 'it shall not be lawful for any person to occupy any Crown Lands in New South Wales ... without having first obtained a licence for such purpose.'[22] Those with a licence would no longer be trespassers – in effect they would no longer be squatters, although this term remained in use – while those without licences could now be evicted without setting a precedent that threatened the legitimacy of all. Although Bourke acknowledged to Glenelg that 'There is a natural disposition on the part of the wealthy stock holders to exaggerate the offences of the poorer class of intruders upon Crown Land, and an equal unwillingness to submit themselves to such restraints as are essential to the due and impartial regulation of this species of occupancy,'[23] there is no doubt that the new measures were primarily targeted at the poor. The Colonial Secretary, Alexander McLeay, was explicit about this, reassuring members of the landowning elite, many of whom were also squatters, that licences would only be provided to those persons 'upon whom reliance can be placed' and denied to 'those of an opposite character.'[24] This was not just a matter of reserving the land for the rich but of achieving social and economic order on the frontier. Poor squatters were believed to 'harbour the settlers' runaway servants ... steal the cattle and sheep ... receive stolen goods ... sell spirits on the sly ... entice shepherds from the care of their sheep; and ... shelter and feed bushrangers, and afford them information.'[25]

Thomas McCombie provided a succinct summary of the perceived problem and the government's solution in his 1858 *History of the Colony of Victoria*: 'A very objectionable class ... began to settle ... on the Crown lands at this period; this was composed of runaway prisoners of the Crown and expiree convicts, who erected huts and became "sly grog" sellers, cattle stealers, and receivers of stolen property. In order to suppress this system and to legalise the occupation of Crown lands by respectable persons, for grazing purposes, the Squatting Act was framed …'[26]

The regulations accompanying the new law confirmed that poor squatters were the only ones likely to face eviction. Applicants to government 'to depasture the vacant Crown Lands beyond the limits of location' needed to be 'accompanied by a certificate of character from the nearest Justice of the Peace, or Commissioner of Crown Lands.' This was not readily obtainable for any but the most select group of former convicts. Further, it was now prescribed that 'every such licence will be chargeable with a fee of ten pounds,' a significant sum only to the poor. Finally, 'any person who shall be convicted of any breach of law' was now liable 'to have his licence cancelled' – a major hurdle for highly policed emancipists, who went before the magistrates for a large array of minor offences, especially drunkenness, in vast and disproportionate numbers. If any doubt remained as to the objective of the legislation, the Proclamation concluded that 'these regulations consequent upon it are now promulgated, as the fittest mode of putting an end to *the mischief arising from* the unauthorized occupation'[27] – that is, the unauthorised occupation itself was now no longer under question. It is true that the considerable autonomy given to the Commissioners of Crown Lands to grant licences and administer law and order meant that many squatters would later complain about the Commissioners' arbitrary power, but in the 1830s there was no question that the new regulations were primarily targeted at former convicts seeking independence and freedom in remote lands. While a licence was not land title – which rested in the crown until the land was surveyed and sold – or even a lease over a particular piece of territory, in practice, as will be explored later, licensed 'squatters' claimed exclusive possession and evicted others, white and black, from 'their' land.

This Act provided the potential legal foundation for the settlement of Port Phillip. However, until there was a change in the British government's policy of concentrated settlement, 'uncertainty' remained the project's 'essential characteristic,' as the *Launceston Advertiser* put it in March 1836. While the 'land is good' and the 'natives have not yet been troublesome ... one obstacle to success remains to be stated – the active interference of government. Will it take place or not?'[28] The colonial governments had provided essential policy and legislative assistance, but the long-term future of the camp on the Yarra and the vast pastoral project it supported was a matter that ultimately only the British government could decide.

THE EMPIRE DECIDES

As SOON AS HE WAS ADVISED OF the private invasion of the southern coast of New Holland, the Secretary of State for the Colonies, Lord Glenelg, made it clear that the Port Phillip trespassers would *not* be sanctioned by the British government. Glenelg informed Lieutenant Governor Arthur in January 1836 that:

> I am very much averse to the principle of encouraging the settlement in the un-located districts of Australia of private individuals either singly or associated. All schemes ... have of late years been discouraged by H. M. Government as leading to fresh Establishments, involving expense, exposing both natives and the new settlers to many dangers and calamities. And there is so much prudence and of justice and I think I might add of humanity in this policy, I do not feel disposed to depart from it in the present instance ...[29]

Yet despite the long-established principle expressed in this dispatch, by early April Glenelg had reversed his position. Little more than two months after rejecting the Port Phillip project, the same Secretary of State now advised Governor Bourke that he looked forward to Port Phillip becoming a centre of trade that would:

expedite the general occupation by the people of this Kingdom or their descendents of those vast territories, in which
our national wealth and industry have already, in the last half
century, converted an unproductive waste into two great and
flourishing provinces. In producing and multiplying such
results as these, it has, I believe, always occurred, and is perhaps inevitable that the sanguine ardour of private speculation
should quicken and anticipate the more cautious movements of
the Government.[30]

How did the 'dangers and calamities' of January become an
exemplar of the 'sanguine ardour of private speculation' by April?
And why did the British government, at the height of evangelical
political concern for native peoples, decide to approve the private
conquest of Aboriginal land, even though as recently as December
1835 the South Australian Commissioners had only broken their
deadlock with the government by offering to 'give precise and posi-
tive instructions' to prospective settlers 'not to colonize any district
which the Aborigines may be found occupying or enjoying or possessing any right of property in the Soil'?[31] Moreover, the Colonial
Office had recently rejected a private scheme to colonise New Zealand and was still immersed in its South African intervention, in
which the seizure of Xhosa land was to be reversed.

In considering the dramatic policy change, it is first necessary
to remember that Glenelg's two dispatches were addressed to different men. In January 1836 Lieutenant Governor George Arthur,
normally highly skilled in dealing with the Colonial Office, was
experiencing the loss of trust and influence which would soon con-
tribute to his recall. Arthur's biographer, A.G.L. Shaw, has observed
that 'During the English winter of 1835–36 criticism of Arthur was
constant,' and at least in the short term it had a significant effect on
his reputation in London.[32] The Colonial Office also had serious
concerns about unauthorised expenditure and there had been

understandable disquiet when the British government was belatedly advised during 1835 that the Tasmanian Aborigines did not want to be on Flinders Island and how few of them were still alive.[33] The news that the Aborigines were dying out in their imposed exile was guaranteed to disturb even the most pragmatic evangelical soul, and probably played a role in the firm rebuff given to Arthur's proposals concerning the colonisation of Port Phillip. One of the Association's lobbyists, Joseph Ball, experienced the result of Arthur's loss of influence: 'I found after dancing attendance for months I could get nothing from the Colonial Office and the circumstance of Colonel Arthur's recall has been much against any interest there.'[34]

The recent focus on South African affairs had, by contrast, turned Governor Bourke into something of an evangelical hero. Bourke's policy in the Cape in the late 1820s had provided what was increasingly portrayed as a template for humanitarian colonisation, and it lent credibility and influence to his views on pastoralism (the Cape was also sheep country) and native peoples. The fact that Bourke was a close friend of the former Colonial Secretary and current Chancellor of the Exchequer, Thomas Spring Rice (a fellow Irish protestant landowner), further aided relations with the Whig administration. The April dispatch was not just a case of the British government giving the New South Wales government the go-ahead to colonise Port Phillip, but of *Glenelg* giving permission for *Bourke* to do so.

The change in the government's position might also have reflected a changing of the guard in the bureaucracy. It is significant that although both dispatches were signed by Glenelg, they were written not only *to* different men, but *by* different men. During this time the evangelical James Stephen, a long-time legal adviser to the Colonial Office and in recent years its deputy head, became the permanent head of the department, replacing R.W. Hay, who had been influential in the defence of the policy of concentrated settlement. Hay had drafted the first dispatch rejecting the Port Phillip project and in his accompanying memo to the Colonial Secretary had accurately foreseen its long-term implications, arguing that 'if every one were allowed to follow his own inclination by selecting a fit place of residence on the coast of New Holland all hope of restricting the limits of our settlements in that quarter must be at once abandoned.'[35]

On what basis did Stephen reject Hay's analysis? The essence of the argument put by the new head of the Colonial Office was that the private invasion of settlers and their sheep could not be stopped because it *should not* be. In landmark logic, which remains largely accepted in Australia 175 years later, the dispatch drafted by Stephen in April 1836 argued that New South Wales was 'not only marked out by nature for a pastoral country' but that:

> It is wholly vain to expect that any positive laws, especially those of a very young and thinly peopled country, will be energetic enough to repress the spirit of adventure and speculation in which the unauthorised settlements at Port Phillip and Twofold Bay have originated. The motives which are urging mankind, especially in these days of general peace and increasing population, to break through the restraints which would forbid their settling themselves and their families in such situations, are too strong to be encountered with effect by ordinary means. To engage in such a struggle would be wholly irrational. All that remains for the Government in such circumstances is to assume the guidance and direction of such enterprises, which, though it cannot prevent or retard, it may yet conduct to happy results ...[36]

The dispatch thus expressed both the fatalism – there was nothing the government *could* do – and the faith in the forces driving colonisation – there was little the government *should* do – which were to drive the conquest of the Australian continent for the rest of the nineteenth century and beyond.

James Stephen understood the likely consequences of British settlement for the Aborigines, and as these became increasingly evident, he came to emphasise the powerlessness of government to confront human 'will.' In October 1836, in a long letter to the South Australian Colonization Commissioners, who were concerned about the effect of the easy availability of land at Port Phillip on land sales in their province, he wrote that:

> in New South Wales the 'Squatters' (to employ the significant local term) ... instead of being condemned and opposed, are countenanced and supported by the society to which they belong ... the local authorities have experienced the impossibility of making an effectual resistance to the general will. The case of Port Phillip is but an example and illustration of this prevailing triumph of popular feelings over positive law ... If it be answered that the Governor should have been directed to coerce this lawless invasion of the lands of the Crown by force, it might be replied that there is not in the Australian colonies any power, civil or military, available for such a service ... it is undeniable that, immediately on receiving intelligence of the proceedings at Port Phillip, the Government adopted the only means which it was in their power to adopt or which in sound reason they could adopt with a view to arrest the further progress of the impending danger.[37]

In a November 1838 minute to the Parliamentary Under-Secretary Sir George Grey, a fellow evangelical, Stephen acknowledged that 'the colonists of New South Wales and the natives are in collision with each other at a great many different points' and that 'the causes and the consequence of this state of things are alike clear and irremediable.' Yet he did not 'suppose that it is possible to discover any method by which the impending catastrophe, namely, the extermination of the black race, can long be averted.' At this point, Stephen's fatalism seems more characteristic of a late nineteenth-century social Darwinist than a mid-century evangelical (although he would admit that 'of course, nothing that can be done ought to be omitted'[38]).

The dramatic reversal in policy probably also reflected the need to resolve the legal uncertainty arising from Batman's treaty with the Aborigines. The January dispatch explicitly put off considering the treaty, but the Port Phillip Association having obtained advice that seemed to challenge the legal foundation of all previous British settlement, the matter could be delayed no longer. In the April dispatch to Bourke, Glenelg famously observed that to recognise the treaty's validity 'would subvert the foundation of which all proprietary rights in New South Wales at present rest, and defeat a large part of the most important Regulations of the Local Government.'[39] In other words, if native title and Aboriginal sovereignty were now to be recognised, the foundation on which 'crown' land had been leased and sold since 1788, and local laws promulgated, would be brought into question.

The rejection of the treaty was not in itself surprising. For more than two hundred years British government policy had been that only the Crown had the right to purchase land from native people (although there had been inconsistency on this). Evangelicals, including Thomas Fowell Buxton and the Select Committee on Aborigines, were also usually against private treaties on the basis that they allowed unscrupulous individuals to exploit people who could have little real understanding of the nature of the transaction (such sentiments were also expressed in Glenelg's dispatch to Bourke). It was seen to be the role of government, and of those it delegated to act on its behalf, to purchase, reserve or annex land and ensure compensation was provided. On these grounds, Henry Reynolds has argued in *The Law of the Land* that the British government was not denying the right of Port Phillip Aborigines to sell their land, but asserting that only the Crown, or those to whom the Crown had conceded this right, could purchase it.[40]

Bain Attwood suggests in *Possession*, however, that it would be more accurate to say that the Colonial Office 'couched its repudiation of the Association's treaty' in the terms Reynolds describes, but that the British government was effectively putting 'the matter of Aboriginal title aside altogether.'[41] Attwood argues that the judgment expressed in the 1836 dispatch amounted to a rejection of Aboriginal sovereignty per se and a new assertion of the perfect territorial sovereignty of the British Crown over the vast (and largely unoccupied) area covered by the Governor's Commission. The complex legal questions reviewed by Attwood, Reynolds and the legal historian Lisa Ford[42] deserve more specialised attention than is possible here, but it is important to emphasise that the question was not whether the British territorial claim extended to Port Phillip, but whether perfect sovereignty (that is, full legal control over people and land) reached beyond the surveyed and settled districts. Attwood's convincing argument is that the British government's response to the treaty affirmed that perfect sovereignty extended to all of New South Wales, including regions that were not in any practical sense 'governed.'

If Attwood is correct, the legal position adopted in response to Batman's treaty is integral to the approval given to the colonisation of Port Phillip. With crown land around the Yarra now having the same legal status as crown land around Sydney Harbour, settling Port Phillip became an internal matter for the governor of New South Wales to regulate, and could be framed as an extension of existing settlement rather than an expansion of empire such as the annexation of Xhosa territory or the proposal to colonise New Zealand.

It is equally true, however, that this legal view could have been used to *restrict* settlement. Indeed, with their legal powers clarified, the capacity of the New South Wales governor and the British government to control settlement in frontier districts had seemingly been *enhanced*. Ultimately the decision to sanction the settlement of Port Phillip was not a question of law but of conviction.

Although the rights of the Aborigines were taken seriously in London, they continued to be seen largely through the prism of class, with the lower order of settlers, of which Australia had more than its share, perceived as the greatest threat to the fulfilment of the imperial mission to convert and civilise native peoples and colonise empty lands. In lobbying for support, the Port Phillip Association played to these sentiments and concerns with some success, and while there could be no question of upholding a treaty with the Aborigines or a monopoly land claim, this rhetoric played a significant role in muting the criticism which might have been expected to follow a major unauthorised territorial expansion. Even the leading parliamentary campaigner for native peoples, Thomas Fowell Buxton, was regarded by the Association as a potential ally and only shied away from public support for its cause because of his prior commitment to the *crown* land claim. The lobbyist Joseph Ball wrote, 'I found after trying in every way and devoting much time to it, I could not succeed in inducing Mr Buxton to take up the business. His opinion is very favourable as to the success of the association but he says he cannot on principle be connected with it, as they recognise the right of the Government to alienate the right to the soil.'[43]

Glenelg was also sympathetic to the Port Phillip Association and alluded to its members' respectability and benevolent approach to the Aborigines in much of his correspondence. He was even prepared to give the Association 'a priority in the purchase, on moderate and easy terms, of any lands which they may have already occupied, or on which they may have actually effected any improvements.' Bourke, believing this would undermine the integrity of the land-sales system, later persuaded him that a £7000 government lump sum was a more appropriate form of compensation.[44]

Even more significant than the Association's campaign to shape evangelical views of Port Phillip was the influence of the House of Commons Select Committee on Aborigines (British Settlements), which began sitting a few weeks before the *Enterprize* docked on the banks of the Yarra and reached its conclusion in 1837 as Melbourne was already becoming an important centre of imperial commerce.[45]

On first impressions, it would seem improbable that the colonisation of Port Phillip might be facilitated by a committee justly famous for its concern for indigenous peoples. Its final report argued that 'the native inhabitants of any land have an incontrovertible right to their own soil: a plain and sacred right' and condemned Europeans who 'have entered their borders uninvited, and, when there, have not only acted as if they were undoubted lords of the soil, but have punished the natives as aggressors if they have evinced a disposition to live in their own country.'[46] How then could the Select Committee have come to legitimate rather than criticise and repudiate the private seizure of Aboriginal land?

One reason is that the final report of the committee was, by necessity, a political compromise. Buxton himself noted in 'comments' published in 1837 by the Aborigines Protection Society that 'in some respects the Report is defective. Facts of deep importance ... are more than once passed over altogether or only incidentally alluded to.'[47] Furthermore, the committee uncritically accepted the assumptions underpinning the population debate, including the 'the national necessity of finding some outlet for the superabundant population of Great Britain and Ireland ... and to find a soil to which our surplus population may retreat.'[48] Nevertheless, to explain the paradox of the committee's de facto approval of Port Phillip, one must return to the conflict with the Aborigines of Van Diemen's Land, now becoming infamous in evangelical circles, and the interpretation of this provided by the committee's two Van Diemen's Land informants, the soon-to-be Bishop of Australia, W.G. Broughton, and George Arthur.

Despite having being the senior Church of England cleric in the Australian colonies since 1829, Broughton had very little experience of Aborigines outside Sydney, although he had temporarily chaired one of the great whitewashes of Australian history, the Van Diemen's Land Government Inquiry of 1830, established to consider 'the origin of the hostility displayed by the black natives of this island.' This inquiry had infamously concluded that 'acts of violence on the part of the natives are generally to be regarded, not as retaliating for any wrongs which they conceived themselves collectively or individually to have endured, but as proceeding from a wanton and savage spirit inherent in them.' Furthermore, the inquiry was sure that 'manifold insults and injuries' committed *in the past* by 'dissolute and abandoned characters' (that is, the convicts) had led to the 'universal and permanent excitement' of hostility and resulted in Aborigines indiscriminately attacking 'a different and totally innocent class.' In short, it was the character of savages, white and black, rather than the seizure of Aboriginal land, which was the cause of the fighting.[49] In his evidence to the Select Committee on Aborigines, Broughton now repeated this analysis. Even though it was often factually incorrect (as in his testimony that only fifty Tasmanian Aborigines had been happily removed to Flinders Island), the story he told went unchallenged, and it is not surprising that the committee's final report concluded that the cause of the fighting in Van Diemen's Land was not the conquest of Aboriginal country but 'the deadly antipathy which was excited between the Aborigines and the bushrangers.'

The wild white-man narrative was also reflected in the committee's general analysis of the situation in the Australian colonies. While the theft of land was acknowledged, it was largely presented as an unfortunate fact of history, in contrast to the commendable present-day impulse to bring law and missionaries to the frontier: 'Whatever may have been the injustice of this encroachment [on Australian Aborigines' land], there is no reason to suppose that either justice or humanity would now be consulted by receding from it.' Rather, in a convict colony there were advantages to respectable conquest: 'If the whole of New Holland be part of the British Empire, then every inhabitant of that vast island is under the defence of British law,' and even a small percentage from the sale of the land could fund missionaries to 'instruct' and protectors to 'defend' the former owners of the soil. The committee therefore viewed the conquest of Port Phillip as part of a larger imperative to bring civilisation, Christianity and law to the frontier, thereby saving the Aborigines from those who represented the principal threat to the Empire's divine mission: former convicts living beyond the authority of government and outside the social order.

The committee's notion that an unauthorised land grab could be made legal and just would soon be reflected in the British government's decision to establish an Aboriginal protectorate at Port Phillip. Given the dearth of detail available to the Select Committee concerning land settlement in Australia generally and in Port Phillip in particular, it is odd that the only concrete policy outcome of its work concerned this locality. The explanation for this revolves around the committee's other principal informant on Van Diemen's Land, George Arthur.

When Arthur left Hobart to return home in October 1836, it may have seemed as though his role in the Port Phillip story was over. Yet the irony of his recall was that it not only restored but enormously increased his influence over the ambitious colonisation project. On his return to London in early 1837, Arthur became almost a full-time lobbyist both for his own reputation (on which his future career depended) and for government action on the Aborigines – and it is no reflection on the sincerity of his convictions to point out that the two were closely linked. Arthur was in Britain when the Select Committee's final report was being written – largely by a small group of evangelical women connected to Buxton, including Anna Gurney[50] – and played a very important role in framing its analysis.

Arthur had returned to England not only with a clear historical narrative of what had gone wrong in Van Diemen's Land, but also a practical plan to apply these lessons in Port Phillip. Arthur's work ensured that the 'lesson' of Van Diemen's Land, which Henry Reynolds suggests 'haunted' Glenelg and his colleagues,[51] directly contributed to the decision to give approval to the conquest of Port Phillip and the official founding of Melbourne.

Arthur's plan was based on the proposals Robinson had presented in frantic correspondence conducted in the three days before Arthur's departure from Hobart: 'the plan which I have taken the liberty to submit was much on my mind before I left Van Diemen's Land; and I discussed it at great length with Mr Robinson.'[52]

The history of Van Diemen's Land Arthur had been telling for the past five years, which emphasised the critical importance of reaching an understanding (he called it a 'treaty') on first contact, had now been modified in two crucial respects. First, Arthur now believed that using force was almost always wrong, confessing to his former boss, Lord Glenelg, that:

> I fell into some very wrong notions in the early part of my Government, from which very injurious consequences followed ... No provocation, no demonstration of hostility, no recollection of injuries they may have inflicted can constitute a justification for any act of violence towards them [the Aborigines] – nothing indeed, short of self-defence in the last extremity ... Conciliatory measures ... known to every member of the community, and most especially to the distant stock keepers and other persons employed at remote stations – ought, therefore, to be adopted from the very first, and notwithstanding any, and even often repeated, acts of violence on the part of the savages, pursued with calm and determined perseverance.[53]

Although these sentiments were replicated in the committee's report (and were hardly original in evangelical discourse), they would have no impact in Port Phillip or anywhere else in New South Wales, where the frontier necessity of teaching a lesson to Aborigines who killed stock, let alone people, continued to be accepted by Bourke and his successors.

Arthur's other new idea, an Aboriginal protectorate across southern Australia, was of more practical import. The concept of protectors, modelled on Robinson's early work in Van Diemen's Land, was not new, and had been promoted by Arthur since 1834, but this was a much more ambitious and comprehensive proposal intended to guide settlement across the region. On 22 July 1837 Arthur wrote to Glenelg:

> If Your Lordship should be pleased to direct the acceptance of Mr Robinson's services, I submit that his head station should be at Port Phillip; from whence he should traverse the surrounding country himself, and be in communication with two assistant protectors who should occupy the country extending to the eastward and northward; and with two other assistant protectors, who should occupy the country to the westward and northward, which will embrace the fine territory lately explored by the Surveyor General of New South Wales, and even so far as Gulf St Vincent – and the scheme might still further be extended so as to include King Georges Sound and Swan River.

The scheme would even generate a good profit:

> From what has happened within the last four years in Van Diemen's Land, Your Lordship has the proof of the extraordinary effect of personal security upon the value of land; for no sooner was that country relived from the dreadful outrages of the Aborigines, and from the lawless conduct of the convicts,

than land, almost suddenly, rose in value from 50 to 100 per cent at least!

The relocated Aborigines at Flinders Island were integral to Arthur's project, as they would be 'most useful auxiliaries in conciliating the natives of Australia.'[54]

Glenelg seized on the idea with enthusiasm, and only five days after Arthur's letter was written James Stephen advised his staff to 'Prepare the draft of a dispatch to Sir John Franklin [the new Lieutenant Governor of Van Diemen's Land] instructing him to offer this place [of Protector of Aborigines at Port Phillip] to Mr Robinson ... It is almost superfluous to acknowledge this letter, as Sir George Arthur is in such habitual intercourse with Lord Glenelg that he will probably dispense with that ceremony.'[55]

Robinson would be in charge of four white assistants, but although Stephen believed that it might be 'practicable and expedient to break up the aboriginal establishment at Flinders Island, and to remove the natives together with Mr Robinson to Port Phillip,' this aspect of the plan was left up to the New South Wales government to decide (who in 1838 vetoed the relocation, with the exception of some of Robinson's closest assistants – a concession which Robinson would stretch to the limit).[56]

Arthur's view of the role of the protector was that he would 'watch over the rights and interests of the natives' and defend them 'as far as he can ... from any encroachment on their property and from acts of cruelty, oppression and injustice.' A protector would travel with Aborigines and 'make them feel that he is their friend.' This would involve learning Aboriginal languages and administering 'religious instruction to them and their children in the dialects most likely to arrest their attention.'[57] The contradiction of protecting the Aborigines from encroachments onto their land within a land policy based on allowing settlers to self-select unlimited quantities of prime grasslands was not addressed. Indeed, at the heart of the proposal, and of evangelical faith, was the assumption that harm to Aborigines was *not* intrinsic to the colonisation of their land.

While this evangelical belief now seems so unrealistic that it is hard to take seriously, most Britons in the early nineteenth century still assumed that land could be shared. For centuries in Britain the question of the ownership of land had been quite distinct from the right to use it. Land was always owned by someone, but complex local custom with a legal foundation in common law determined grazing, fuel, fishing, hunting, transport and multiple other commoner rights, which often required specific parliamentary legislation to extinguish. The attack on common rights was long and relentless, and by the 1830s had largely succeeded in evicting hundreds of thousands of ordinary people from their own country, a process which had more similarities with that being simultaneously played out in the empire than is usually recognised. But resistance had been strong, and it was still widely assumed that ownership (let alone a lease or licence) did not automatically imply an exclusive right of access or use.

The historian J.M. Neeson has pointed out that we now 'know relatively little about common right ... and even that is disputed among historians,' and one of the reasons for this is 'a failure of the imagination ... imagining something that has disappeared is difficult; after all loss *is* loss.'[58] We need to be careful, therefore, not to project our own difficulty in imagining how the grasslands of Australia could realistically have been shared onto the policy-makers of the 1830s. It is likely that for them the goal of co-existence was not just convenient evangelical fantasy but quite consistent with a view of the world rooted in centuries of practical experience. In a private letter to Spring Rice, Bourke hoped that the Chancellor of the Exchequer would 'remember enough of the ways of *sheep*, and especially of *Kerry sheep*, to believe that ... the doctrine of concentration is ill applied to them.'[59] In Ireland sheep traditionally roamed with little constraint in the common pastures of the hill country. When in April 1839 Governor Gipps informed Glenelg that a pastoral licence 'gives only a general right to depasture cattle or sheep on the Crown lands, in the same way as a right of Common is enjoyed in England,' he explicitly drew on this rich Anglo-Irish cultural heritage.[60] The problem, of course, was that by this time it was already perfectly evident that the licence-holders themselves saw their entitlements in terms of the modern right to exclusive possession, and the government took no serious action to challenge this.

Thus it was that the British government gave its blessing in both a political and religious sense to Port Phillip colonisation, and on 1 September 1836, almost exactly a year after the first permanent tents had been pitched on the Yarra's banks, Governor Bourke received the welcome news that he could authorise the legal settlement of the district. Aided by the fact that planning was already underway to send Captain William Lonsdale to investigate the recent killing of Aborigines by Henry Batman's party, Bourke was able to establish a government presence at Port Phillip within a few weeks of receipt of the dispatch from London.

The establishment of a centre of government on the Yarra River implied more than just the movement of troops and officials to the new territory. The rejection of the monopoly land claim of the Port Phillip Association, the removal of any remaining legal risk, the provision of military protection and the confirmation that there were to be no limits of location, meant that the last barrier to a full-blown squatter land rush had been removed. While James Stephen continued to argue that the new policy was the only way to control settlement, there was no plan in place to achieve this. Instead, with some of the richest grasslands in the world now able to be legally occupied by the first 'respectable' men to put sheep upon them, the movement of capital, stock and men intensified to an extent never before seen in Australian history. The Hobart-based periodical *Bents News* reported on 24 September 1836 what happened when news of the British government's decision reached town:

within twenty-four hours of the above intelligence coming to Hobart Town numerous persons of every grade were contriving how to get to Port Phillip ... certain it is that the Colony is now beyond a doubt to become one of the very greatest importance in the hemisphere, and that at any early period, as its progression is greater and more rapid than any other known in any part of the world ... the only feeling existing among men of capital here appears to be that of jealousy who shall have the first and best hold of land and stock at Port Phillip.

With the remaining risk to capital removed, the annexation of the hunting grounds of Port Phillip degenerated into a frenzied land rush. The Select Committee's concern that Aborigines 'found upon their own property' had been 'treated as thieves and robbers' and 'driven back into the interior as if they were dogs or kangaroos' was being replicated at Port Phillip even before the committee's final report was written.[61] By the end of 1836 it was already clear that the new Protectors of the Aborigines were going to have a very difficult job indeed.

PART V

THE AFTERMATH

14.

EXPLOSIVE GROWTH

THE GOVERNMENT HAD JUSTIFIED its decision to sanction the squatter invasion of Port Phillip by the need to exert control over the land grab. Yet rarely can regulation have been applied with such a light hand. The official placed in charge of the Port Phillip district, Police Magistrate William Lonsdale, was instructed by Governor Bourke not to 'prevent free persons either with or without stock from passing into the District, nor ... disturb the occupation of those already there.' Bourke made it clear that Lonsdale had the legal authority to expel those he deemed to be trespassers, but also expressed a hope that 'the necessity for so disagreeable a proceeding may be wholly avoided.'[1] He even decided to delay issuing squatting licences in case it caused Lonsdale any difficulties, explaining in late 1836 that 'to authorize the Police Magistrate at Port Phillip to grant licences would only embarrass him by requiring an unpleasant exercise of his discretion.' And although Bourke encouraged Lonsdale to discourage 'occupation before sales can be regularly effected,' there is no evidence that any such 'discouragement' ever occurred, and the subject was not mentioned again.[2]

Such laissez-faire policies brought forth a predictable response from property speculators in the south. In his final missive as Lieutenant Governor of Van Diemen's Land, a satisfied George Arthur wrote to Bourke that 'the rage for Port Phillip seems quite unabated.' A number of competing associations had now been formed and, according to Arthur, it was not only the Port Phillip Association that claimed as its object 'the civilization of the natives.' But with his departure imminent, Arthur was refreshingly frank about the settlers' motive: 'it is better for all parties to be sincere and plainly state that the occupation of a good run for sheep has been the primary consideration, if not the only one.'[3]

Bourke's visit to Port Phillip in early March 1837 symbolised the depth of his government's commitment to extending the domain of sheep and settler. It was Bourke who named the settlement after the Whig prime minister Lord Melbourne (whose family name happened to be *Lamb*).[4] He also approved the surveyor Robert Hoddle's 'rectangle in the bush' town plan.[5] Military-camp style, it defined a grid of streets ninety-nine feet wide and lanes thirty-three feet wide. In later life Hoddle would take credit for the former but blame Bourke for the latter, although perhaps neither deserves much praise given that, as an 1849 pamphleteer observed, 'the only skill exhibited in the plan of Melbourne is that involved in the use of square and compass'![6] Bourke's final vice-regal act was to confer the street names that mostly survive to this day – the most notable loss being Stephen Street, which became Exhibition Street – informing his son that 'I have had the satisfaction of affixing Whig names in the bush.'[7]

Bourke retrospectively endorsed the actions of those whom he had once proclaimed trespassers, and publicly pledged his support for further extensions to the squatters' domain. In his address to the inhabitants of Melbourne on 4 March 1837, he praised the settlers' 'lucrative pastoral objects' and assured them that 'the fostering care of His Majesty's Government will … be never wavering to promote and protect to the utmost those useful pursuits.' Bourke also addressed 120 Aborigines, whom he 'exhorted … to good conduct and attention to the Missionary.' The Kulin were given blankets and four favoured men, who had been recommended for 'honorary distinctions' by Lonsdale, were awarded brass plates. Any doubts the Governor might have harboured about the prospects of

Melbourne were removed by his delight in finding that during the first week of his visit, five ships, with 2700 sheep on board, reached the port.[8]

In May 1837 Henry Batman was appointed acting Commissioner of Crown Lands, the official charged with overseeing the squatters. Given Batman's role in the 1836 massacre, the appointment further signalled the government's squatter-friendly approach. His permanent replacement, the 21-year-old Peter Snodgrass, took full advantage of Bourke's support for the status quo and did little more than license the numerous runs of the principal squatters before resigning to join their ranks. So inseparable was government policy from private practice that there was considered nothing wrong with officials engaging in land speculation or becoming squatters themselves, and in the early years of settlement most supplemented their wage, sometimes many times over, by doing so. 'Charles Latrobe, William Lonsdale, Foster Fyans, James Blair, Acheson French and Benjamin Baxter do not exhaust the list of senior public servants who were engaged in land speculation and squatting.'[9] Indeed, it is difficult to identify a police magistrate or commissioner of crown lands who did not dabble in land. Some of these men also became bankers, still the most profitable component of the Port Phillip project.[10]

An even more significant factor in the co-option of officialdom was the influence of their peers. In a small community that still saw itself as under threat from both a distant bureaucracy and local Aborigines, 'fitting in' depended on upholding the squatter cause. A letter written by Snodgrass's replacement, H.F. Gisborne, on his arrival in Melbourne in September 1839, describes how the embryonic establishment worked:

> I have come here as Commissioner of Crown Lands, with a salary of £500 a year and some other allowances, bringing with me overland two horse teams, five troopers, besides a great

> mob of attaches in the shape of servants &c ... The folk here
> have been extremely polite. I found myself invited to parties
> and made an honorary member of this [Melbourne] club before
> I had time to get off my horse ... I suppose we shall soon have
> to fire some blank cartridge at the blacks [his position included
> responsibility for the newly formed border police]. They are
> very troublesome towards the westward, but I think that half
> my army, amounts in all to a baker's dozen, will be able to keep
> 'em quiet.[11]

It was day one and yet Gisborne already seemed to have forgotten, or had never been made aware, that the Commissioner of Crown Lands was also meant to *protect* the Aborigines. Indeed, one of the many paradoxes of a government presence was that the earlier incentive to maintain peace – to avoid open conflict until the government decided the squatters' fate – was much reduced now that official sanction had been given to the seizure of land.

Beginning in 1837, but really taking hold during 1838, the conquest of the Port Phillip district was dramatically accelerated by the opening of a second front in the aftermath of Surveyor-General Thomas Mitchell's journey through what he named 'Australia Felix' ('Fortunate Australia') from June to October 1836. Mitchell left behind him a road clearly marked by wagon wheels ('the Major's Line') that became the highway to the south. Mitchell believed the grasslands he traversed were 'specially prepared by the Creator for the industrious hands of Englishmen'[12] and Bourke encouraged settlers to send men and stock overland by having Mitchell's report published in the *Government Gazette* (taking care to censor the sections relating to 'a very unfortunate conflict with the aboriginal natives in which,' he informed London, 'I fear a considerable number of these unhappy savages were slaughtered'[13]). The New South Wales establishment was not slow in taking up the Governor's invitation and sent what must have seemed to the Aborigines like whole tribes to the south. For example, in 1837 Alexander Mollison moved thirty men (plus an overseer and three Aborigines), five thousand sheep, 634 cattle, twenty-eight working bullocks and twenty-two horses south from the Murrumbidgee.[14] Such was the number of squatters who had already crossed the Murray that Mollison had some difficulty finding a run 'sufficiently extensive, and secure from intrusion, to form even a moderately good run for our stock.'[15] By 1838 the 'Major's Line' was reported to be 'crowded with sheep and cattle' traveling from Yass.[16]

The easily traversed and difficult to defend topography, a supportive government and the opening of the second front now led to an occupation of Aboriginal land that Richard Broome believes was 'as fast as any expansion in the history of European colonisation.'[17] From 1837 to 1842 the European population of Port Phillip swelled from about one thousand to twenty thousand, but even more dramatic was the increase in stock and enlargement of territory. Official estimates of sheep numbers rose from 26,000 in June 1836 to 310,000 in September 1838 and 700,000 in 1840.[18] This number doubled again by 1842,[19] by which time half of the Port Phillip District (almost all of the best grasslands) was occupied and the region was producing as much wool as the rest of New South Wales combined.[20] During this frenetic invasion, the frontier extended at a rate of around one hundred miles a year to the west and north, with the consequence that the Aborigines were largely dispossessed of a territory bigger than England in just five years.[21] In late 1839 Gisborne reported that he was able to traverse the 267 miles from Melbourne to Portland Bay via Corio, the Barwon River, Lake Colac, Lake Corangamite and the Grampian Hills, while making 'a station every night except the night before we arrived at Portland Bay, and even then it would have been possible to have reached one of Mr Henty's sheep stations, had I been aware of its locality.'[22]

J.H. Patterson recalled the speed of the conquest:

In November 1836, I had shipped six cargoes of sheep from V.D. Land for Port Phillip, and landed myself in December … I took up the Greenhill Station about 25 miles north, and posted an out-station at what is now called Bacchus Marsh … Soon after my occupation, say early in 1837, Messrs James Clarke, Bacchus, Whyte Brothers, and … Messrs Powlett and Green, took up the country beyond me to the west … and in an exceedingly short space of time that whole country was stocked with sheep from V.D. Land, as the arrivals at Geelong, with sheep, pressed up the Morrabool till they came in contact with the pioneers from Williamstown. In 1838, the Whyte brothers traveled west, with their stock, in search of another run, and took up a country about the Wannon, but met with great difficulties from the determined ferocity of the aborigines, which ended in conflict and great loss of life to the latter.[23]

There was literally no limit to how many runs each licensed squatter could claim, provided he stocked each with shepherds and sheep. The Commissioners of Crown Land granted a general licence to graze animals on crown land, not a lease over any particular territory. Ironically, given the denial of indigenous property rights, the only legal claim a squatter had to a particular piece of land depended on common-law rights associated with possession. But what constituted possession? In the absence of any policy guidelines on the matter, commissioners assumed that it fell to whoever was the first to place stock upon the land in question. This led to the farcical situation of newly arrived Europeans vigorously disputing each other's claims to the hunting grounds of a 40,000-year-old culture on the basis of who was there first. H.W. Haygarth recalled that 'Adversaries searched for an old-timer who could interlard his testimony with remarks upon "the first sight of the district."'[24] But even when this was agreed, it was not clear how to substantiate occupancy. The custom, one newly arrived squatter, Niel Black, explained in 1840, was to 'plant stations at every 3 or 4 miles distance where water can be had [and] a hut keeper is required at each station.'[25] However, as John Weaver explains, squatters often occupied much larger areas than such 'rules' suggested:

> Grazing needs were estimated at one sheep to three acres, although in some circumstances, the ratio might be one to one or one to six. Ideally, a flock of a thousand sheep was tended by three men, but on open plains a single shepherd could tend a flock of 1500 to 2000 sheep on a run. Three flocks often made up the stock for a station. Accordingly, a station could have runs occupying roughly 25 square miles. Additionally, squatters reserved land for lambing, old ewes, and diseased sheep. That might bring the area to 30 square miles.

Furthermore, squatters frequently had several stations on a single licence and 'used the land between the stations, so that a home station under one licence might control sixty to a hundred square miles.'[26] If one secured control of a water source, this could lead to the effective monopolisation of still larger areas, as sheep could only survive a day's drive from a major source of water (which generally meant about six miles). Thus, although runs would usually only extend a short distance from a river, creek or lake, a much greater area of country was effectively secured. In 1846 C.P. Hodgson observed that 'by obtaining a station high up the creek, interlopers are excluded, and he [the squatter] knows no one can come above him.'[27]

Squatters moved scarce men and sheep around their many runs to try to maximise the area they 'possessed.' Niel Black noted that with 'a view to keep the country only one shepherd with one flock consisting of about 600 is sent to each station'[28] – although at the height of Aboriginal resistance between 1840 and 1843, such a low labour ratio could not be sustained. George Russell, the manager of the Scottish–Van Diemonian concern the Clyde Company, managed to secure seventy thousand acres in 1839 with fewer than eight thousand sheep. Needless to say, his animals had a highly nomadic grazing regime, and on at least one occasion Russell resorted to borrowing sheep from a neighbour to prove possession.[29] A squatter's relationship to the Commissioner of the Crown Lands became critical because it was he who decided whether the removal of stock was 'temporary' and thus whether land was occupied or not.[30]

Throughout the frenetic period of expansion from 1837 to 1842, the New South Wales government's formal policy continued to be that a licence-holder's right to use crown lands for grazing afforded him no exclusive or pre-emptive rights. However, this bore so little relation to reality that local officials made no effort to uphold the Governor's line. Squatters and public servants alike assumed that first possession of a grassland conferred an exclusive right which could then be bought and sold: 'Strictly speaking, vendors sold their licence, but they and buyers assumed much more.'[31]

The frontier reality was that government regulation achieved little more than the exclusion of the poor, who were deemed ineligible for a licence; the distribution of the grasslands was largely left for the elite to work out among themselves. This fostered a culture of assertive demonstrations of local power. In a very practical sense, might was right. Young men increasingly represented their powerful families on the ground in Port Phillip, backed up by seasoned overseers and managers. Disputes about boundaries were common and Commissioners of Crown Land spent much of their time adjudicating these.[32] The level of competition among the select group of licence-holders, especially in the early years, should not, however, be exaggerated. Once a region's grassland had been carved up, it was in every squatter's interest to band together against the external threats posed by new claimants, more conscientious officials (especially the Aboriginal Protectors) and, of course, the traditional owners. This often involved neighbours drawing up detailed agreements and boundary maps, the validity of which was largely accepted by the government after 1845. Established squatters had an incentive to work together not only to secure the land they already possessed, but also to seize the 'empty' country beyond. It was very difficult for newcomers to jump over the territory of a body of men who monopolised the supply of animals, labour and goods, and controlled the water sources, stock routes and information required to move into more remote country. The system fostered the continual expansion of already large holdings, although in the race to seize 'empty' land as quickly as possible, it also encouraged, as would soon become evident, dangerously high levels of debt.

Bourke's successor, Governor George Gipps, did attempt to assert some control in 1844 by requiring a separate licence for each station, setting a maximum station size of twenty square miles, and ensuring that one licence should not cover more than four thousand sheep and five hundred cattle. However, the New South Wales establishment was so enmeshed in squatting by this time – Gipps warned the Secretary of State, Lord Stanley, that 'almost anybody who has any property at all, is a Squatter'[33] – that even these modest reforms were successfully resisted. Pressure from the squatter-dominated Legislative Council and lobbying in London led to an Act being passed at Westminster in 1846 which, against Gipps' advice, allowed for leases up to fourteen years, compensation for improvements, and granted squatters some pre-emptive rights.[34]

As important as this prominent, bitter and lengthy land-policy debate undoubtedly was, when the larger question of the fate of the Aborigines is remembered, the dispute between Gipps, who considered that the sheep runs were 'the rightful patrimony of all the people of the United Kingdom,' and the squatters, who argued that 'these wilds belong to us, and not to the British Government' because they are 'our rightful and first inheritance,' seems macabre.[35]

In the frenzied grab for land, motivated bush-wise labour remained at a premium, and the familiar trade-off, in which a large measure of freedom and independence was afforded conscientious shepherds who protected stock and property, again came into play. Until the mid-1840s the majority of these men were former convicts from Van Diemen's Land, especially in the Van Diemonian stronghold of the western districts.

Squatters defended the utility of their convict workers in the face of widespread anti-convict hyperbole. John Hepburn observed that 'I have had many ... old prisoners in my service, and have in general found them very good servants.' He did, however, question the value of convicts sent direct from England – 1700 of these so-called exiles arrived between 1844 and 1847 – as 'English training avails little in this country.'[36] Hepburn's assessment points to the rarely acknowledged skills and productivity of the emancipist workforce. By 1846 fewer than six thousand permanent workers were tending three million sheep and a third of a million cattle. These men were shepherds, shearers, bullock drivers, builders, carpenters, splitters, sawyers, fencers, hunters and mercenaries, often all in one.[37] The squatters did not let moral judgments distort their verdict on the capacities of emancipist bushmen. Archibald Cunninghame might complain that Van Diemen's Land was a 'polluted and polluting stream,' but he did not hold back in recruiting Van Diemonian labour.[38]

Such was the demand for skilled workers from the penal colony that labour shortages soon occurred. In July 1838 Phillip Russell wrote to his brother in Port Phillip that 'I find great difficulty in getting men – at least such as I would like to send to you. I intend dispatching two tomorrow Morning: they do not seem first rate hands; they are to get £20 each, and I hope you will find them useful. I will endeavour to get three more that can shear.' Shortly after he advised that 'I have used every endeavour to get sheep shearers, without success; all the sheep shearers in this district are Ticket of leave men [who, still under sentence, were not allowed to leave the colony]. I have hired three men who I hope will be useful as shepherds.'[39]

The situation of the overlanders was somewhat different, because in the early years most brought their assigned convicts with them – but this was not necessarily the advantage it seemed, given the challenges involved in motivating largely unsupervised men to protect property and stock. Some convicts took advantage of the proximity of sealing and whaling gangs and the new colony of South Australia to abscond. Police Magistrate Foster Fyans noted in 1840 that the convicts assigned 'to squatters and others in this district are absconding to a great number, and if not speedily checked, in my opinion not one of them will remain.'[40]

The problem proved to be a short-term one. In late 1837 Bourke received instructions from London that, given projected changes in the penal system, he was to 'abstain to the utmost practicable extent from the assignment of convicts to the settlers in the Port Phillip District.' Instead he was ordered to 'take measures as soon as possible for directing immigration to this settlement,' and in a short period of time a large number of migrants began to arrive in Melbourne straight from the United Kingdom (which then included Ireland).[41]

Passage to Australia was prohibitively expensive for ordinary working people, and so in the 1830s and 1840s it was widely accepted that government subsidies were indispensable if some of the 'surplus' poor and destitute were to be relocated to the Australian colonies. It was also accepted that colonial development depended on an abundant supply of labour, both to provide a workforce and supply a market. Inspired in part by the work of theorists of colonisation such as Edward Gibbon Wakefield, from 1831 revenue from the sale of colonial lands was used to support the emigration of the poor. Between 1836 and 1839, public officials selected the migrants, but when this arrangement was complemented with a 'bounty system,' in which 'mobilization, selection and conveyance were all performed by private enterprise,' the number of assisted migrants exploded: from 1622 in 1838 to 20,103 in 1841. In all, almost exactly forty thousand bounty migrants came to New South Wales (two-thirds of all arrivals) from 1838 to 1842, and while it is not clear what proportion of these reached Port Phillip, they were sufficient to change the face of the district, not least because many were women.[42]

Not surprisingly, divisions soon opened in Melbourne between the 'old' settlers and the new. Garryowen recalled that:

Originally, the population was bi-sected into branches known as the 'ex-convict' and 'immigration' sections. The Expiree contingent was, as a rule, the older – and at one time it would be something rare to find a resident over forty years of age who had not previously expiated some breach of the criminal law in chains, gangs or prisons. At first what for convenience sake were termed the 'bond' and 'free' did not take kindly to each other. The Expirees regarded the others with a feeling of pitying contempt, a species of simpletons who should have stayed at home. They called them 'Johnny Raws' and 'New Chums.' On the other side, the immigrants snapped their fingers at those whom they inelegantly denominated 'The Old Lags.' Time, which softens everything, soon mitigated these asperities. There was one line of demarcation between the two castes which took several years to remove, *viz.*, in their style of apparel. The English, Irish, and Scottish appeared clad in heterogeneous garb, the men's upper and nether garments of every known cut, fashion and material – cloth, frieze and corduroy – and the headgear either a felt hat or bell-topper, then stylishly known as the 'Caroline.' Their coats were mostly not over-long swallow-tailed, and the would-be swellfish portion went for glaring brass buttons. With the Expirees there was more uniformity of costume, for their dress was a cabbage-tree hat, a cloth jacket, 'loud' necktie and moleskin or drill trousers.'[43]

Despite the rapid increase in 'New Chums,' and the move towards a more healthy gender balance, Melbourne did not altogether cease to be a Van Diemonian town. After transportation ended to New South Wales in 1840, the number of convicts coming to Van Diemen's Land increased rapidly just as the island's long economic stagnation really set in. The result was a very large surplus labour supply, which for the employers of Port Phillip meant cheap labour. Societies such as the Portland Emigration Society and the Port Phillip Emigration Society were formed to bring over workers who had their passage paid and work guaranteed. Early in January 1845 one such syndicate advertised in Hobart's *Colonial Times* seeking men 'who will engage at reasonable wages' to work 'in the district of Geelong,' promising that those who signed up would sail within the week, passage paid. Many others arrived under their own steam. In 1846 the newly elected Mayor of Melbourne, James Palmer, estimated 'there was a continuous stream of immigration proceeding from Van Diemen's Land of the worst and profligate part of that community to about one hundred and fifty persons per month.'[44]

The concern about immigration from the south, which within a few years would lead to the government trying to turn ships back, check people's identity papers and illegally attempt to deport ex-convicts, reflected a self-importance that was the fruit of economic success. Those who survived the 1842–43 recession prospered mightily by buying up failed runs and businesses on the cheap. As the landed and business establishment solidified, so did Port Phillip's view of itself as a place built by *free* men and *free* enterprise. Nevertheless, one might have expected Mayor Palmer to have more pressing concerns, for by the 1840s the once bountiful and healthy Yarra camp had degenerated into a cesspool of disease and distress.

The most fundamental advantage of Australian life for the majority of early settlers was the gift of free and clean water provided by the creeks and rivers abutting first settlement sites. Only when these waterways became heavily polluted did old-world disease patterns reappear, and the health of the poor become little better than that of their brethren in London or Birmingham. Because of particularly rapid growth, this environmental transformation happened faster in Melbourne than in other Australian urban centres. By the early 1840s 'household and slaughter-house refuse ... deposited promiscuously in the streets' (amplified by the new industry of boiling down dead animals for tallow) had made the Yarra a dangerous drain. Georgiana McCrae noted in 1842 that 'Infantile cholera and dysentery are just now decimating the children,' and 'colonial' or typhoid fever proved equally destructive.[45] Thomas McCombie suggested that 'at one period the deaths in Melbourne ... were from 15 to 20 a week'[46] and on this matter he can be said to be expert, having chaired a landmark 1848 Melbourne Corporation (Council) inquiry which found that 'the diseases which prevail at particular seasons in Melbourne may be attributed to the crowding, the want of water, the absence of sewerage, the non-removal of decayed animal and vegetable refuse and the poisonous liquid and gaseous matter generated within the city.'[47] Such progressive sentiment, however, did little for the reputation of the swamps, which were blamed for all manner of ills. McCombie wanted the 'dense wood that lies between the town and the bay' cleared to let the sea breeze in so as to counter the 'dangerous exhalation' emanating from the marshes.[48]

The elite's distaste for the swamps and woods meant that they provided an increasingly important refuge for the landless and poor. The new estate marked out for cashed-up settlers in Brighton was already a world apart from the 'brick makers' camp' which Garryowen recalled was located 'south of the river on the flat running from Government House reserve round by Emerald Hill'[49] and the camps of the Aborigines who lived 'along by the new Botanic Gardens and round towards Studley Park and the Yarra Bend ... with two or three nooks in the Merri Creek.'[50]

Despite the disease, squalor and social divisions, there is no doubt that, as Edward Curr put it, Melbourne was a 'bustling, stirring sort of place from the very pip.'[51] By the end of 1839 there were seventy-seven warehouses, shops and offices where almost anything could be bought, sold or consumed in this (to use Lady Jane Franklin's idiom) 'money-making place'.[52]

The fact that Melbourne had not been established as either a military camp or a penal establishment brought an unusual freedom, which was as much expressed in the town's vernacular architecture as in its people. Curr noted in 1839 that there was none of the 'continuous rows of uniform or similar buildings such as one expects to find in streets ... as everyone built as he liked, in the most independent way, and to suit the requirements of the moment. Here and there houses were of brick ... others were of weatherboards, wattle-and-daub, or slabs.'[53] During the building boom the town took on a more English air, but Charles Griffiths, who arrived in 1840, observed that while 'the general appearance of the town is more that of an English country town than of anything else to which I can compare it ... The weather-boarded houses and numerous stores [give] it ... a character peculiar to itself.' It was the distinctive human society Griffiths most remarked on: 'the long teams of bullocks, with their wild-looking drivers, occasionally a straggling tribe of natives, followed by a host of mangy dogs, remind you that you are not in the British Isles.'[54]

Such was the rate of growth in Melbourne that the historian James Bellich is probably right that the mainstay of the boom was not the sale of wool but 'supplying the local market in the service of growth itself.'[55] The speculative nature of this growth was most visibly expressed in the explosion in property prices. Melbourne's first town lots were sold at auction on 1 June 1837, and with loans freely available from the three resident banks, during 1839 they increased in value 1000 per cent. In September of that year, C.H. Ebden sold for £10,250 a town block in Collins St that had cost him £54 little more than two years before. At this time Melbourne became renowned for its 'champagne' lunches, at which beverages were freely supplied to those attending the latest auction; in 1842 Gipps quipped that 'the whole country for miles, almost for hundreds of miles, round Melbourne, is strewed to this day with champagne bottles'.[56]

The government received only a paltry return on this speculation. Some 234 acres of central Melbourne earned the Sydney government about £62,000 – a miniscule proportion of its value in 1840. However, the sale of rural land, which commenced in 1838, proved far more lucrative. The coffers of the New South Wales Treasury were soon overflowing, as the government became Port Phillip speculator-in chief. From the commencement of rural land sales at Port Phillip in 1838 until 30 June 1840, more than 159,000 acres were sold for £219,000, a figure considerably exceeding the annual budget of Van Diemen's Land.[57] However, this proved to be but a modest beginning, after a sum exceeding this total was realised in the first six months of 1840 alone. Gipps reported that during this half-year period, £233,219-2s-8d was realised by the sale of 125,554 acres, at an average price 'which far exceeds, as I apprehend, the average of any other colony under the Crown.' At this time the average price of rural land around Port Phillip was £1-15s-5d per acre compared to an average in the rest of the New South Wales of 13s-3d per acre. A single Port Phillip land sale on 10 and 11 June, Gipps gleefully informed the new Secretary of State for the Colonies, Lord John Russell, realised £104,000.[58] Given these prodigious returns, it is perhaps not surprising that with Britain in the middle of the most severe recession of the nineteenth century, which lasted from 1837 to 1842, the pace of squatter settlement remained largely unquestioned and once-powerful voices of conscience struggled to be heard. In effect the colonisation of Port Phillip had become what its Van Diemonian backers had originally intended: a gigantic land speculation, albeit on a vastly larger scale than anyone could have possibly imagined in 1835.

The dramatic end to growth that came with the crash of 1842–43 was the inevitable cyclical bust that follows such a debt-driven boom, but it was reinforced by dwindling land supply. By 1842 the only large area of unclaimed grassland was in the dry and highly variable Mallee country of the north-west, and so the demand for new livestock to secure new runs evaporated. Sheep that had fetched as much as three pounds before the crash now sold for as little as one shilling, although at least there was finally an abundance of fresh meat for shepherds and labourers alike. Sheep prices did slowly recover, primarily driven by demand for animals for tallow, but it took some years for the pastoral industry to be put on a sustainable basis, and many squatters, bankers and other speculators went broke in the process. Of the 481 people who held pastoral licences in 1840, fewer than half remained by 1845.[59] Having bought out their over-mortgaged neighbours, these men were wealthier than ever. It was this group, reinforced by those who had bought up failed holdings from outside, who became the venerated patriarchs of the landed families that were to wield so much political and economic power in Victoria for generations to come.

15.

CONQUEST CONFIRMED

As EARLY AS 1839 THE MISSIONARY Joseph Orton observed that Aborigines were 'almost in a state of starvation and can only obtain food day by day, by begging.' The practice of hunting had been almost 'abandoned on account of their game being driven away by the encroachment of settlers, and the roots on which they used partially to feed have been destroyed by the sheep.' In a letter to the Wesleyan Missionary Society in London Orton condemned the 'Squatters Act,' 'under which settlers may establish themselves in any part of the extensive territory of New South Wales, and no reserve whatever of land is made for the provision of the natives, neither in securing to them sufficient portions of their own native land as hunting ground, nor otherwise providing for their necessities.' Orton considered that 'nothing less than the "hue and cry" of persevering Christian philanthropists will (I am apprehensive) move the Imperial Parliament to the consideration and adoption of measures on a comprehensive and liberal scale likely to be efficient in their operation ...'[60]

Unfortunately, Orton's hope of imperial action, emboldened by his recent reading of the House of Commons Select Committee Report on Aborigines, was already out of date, with Lord Glenelg having being forced to resign in early 1839 over his handling of the rebellion in Canada, and evangelical political power on the wane.[61] The small group of activists focused on the condition of native peoples had finally been made aware, as an 1840 Quaker report put it, that 'regulated emigration' was a greater danger to Aborigines than 'the old evils of squatters, runaway convicts and deserters,' but the British government was no longer listening.[62]

The land rush simply swept all before it. The tentative agreements concerning access that the Kulin had negotiated with the Port Phillip Association and other early settlers in 1835–36 soon became as irrelevant as evangelical discourse. Although in remote regions there could still be practical advantages in what Alexander Mollison called 'sitting down' with local Aborigines,[63] the political and practical necessity underpinning deal-making largely disappeared once the government gave its blessing to squatter settlement. Licence-holders' unconditional permission to settle whatever Aboriginal country they chose meant the balance of power rapidly shifted on the frontier. Having paid their ten-pound licence to use 'crown' land, newly arrived squatters understandably believed that they had the right to assert their claim vigorously until such time as the government accepted its responsibility to provide them with the protection they were almost certain to need.

The New South Wales government, as unwilling to face the reality created by its open-lands policy as it was to surrender its humanitarian rhetoric, proved reluctant to commit to active policing of the frontier. As a result, in June 1837, forty-four squatters appealed directly to Bourke for police protection against the Aborigines. This led to the appointment of Foster Fyans as police magistrate for the western district, but in May 1838 Lonsdale reported that the situation continued to deteriorate: 'The excitement among the settlers has been general and with much reason as the depredations of the blacks have been numerous, and their attacks can seldom be guarded against … Mr James Smith's, Mr George Smith's and Mr Simpson's stations have been attacked besides those I have already reported.'[64] In the following month squatters called on Governor Gipps to take stronger action against the Aborigines, employing

almost the exact language, logic and 'lessons from history' many
had used in petitions to the Van Diemen's Land government less
than a decade before:

> certain tribes on the road to and in the neighbourhood of Port
> Phillip have lately assumed a hostile attitude towards the set-
> tlers and have committed many murders and other outrages
> upon them ... they are assembled in large numbers armed and
> attacking such persons as are most unprotected and within
> their reach so that many have been obliged to abandon their
> stations leaving in some cases their flocks and herds at the
> mercy of the hostile tribes ... the intercourse by land between
> this part of the territory and Port Phillip, if it has not already
> ceased, has become one of imminent danger to life and prop-
> erty ... the natives, unrestrained by moral principles and plac-
> ing little or no value on human life, have been stimulated by
> their natural cupidity and ferocity in perpetrating the outrages
> ... these untutored savages ... attribute forbearance on our
> part solely to impotence or fear, and are thus rendered only
> more bold and sanguinary. This opinion, founded on past
> experience, will receive ample confirmation on reference to the
> history of this Colony and the acts of the former Governments
> ... coercion was ultimately found unavoidably necessary,
> which, if earlier adopted, would have saved much bloodshed on
> both sides. It is only when they have become experimentally
> acquainted with our power and determination to punish their
> aggressions that they have become orderly, peaceable, and been
> brought within the reach of civilization ...[65]

Gipps advised the petitioners that troop reinforcements, including the highly effective mounted police, would soon be forthcom-
ing, and that 'a discretionary power has been given to the Police
Magistrate at Melbourne to cause parties of infantry to advance, if

necessary, into the interior.' It was his 'intention to establish posts at convenient distances along the road, from Yass to Port Phillip, in order to keep open the [lines of] communication, and that a permanent addition to the Mounted Police will be made for this purpose.'[66] Gipps further assured the squatters that while 'a deep feeling of their duties' to the Aborigines existed among both the New South Wales and British governments (the Select Committee Report and evangelical influence over policy were being widely blamed for a lack of government resolve), 'there is nothing in the Governor's instructions to prevent his protecting to the utmost of his power the lives and property of settlers in every part of this territory.'[67]

Such were the reports of conflict Gipps was receiving 'from both the north and south' that in March 1838 he told London that he considered it 'desirable to defer the publication' of regulations ensuring Aborigines' equal legal status, despite such equality being central to evangelical discourse.[68] Gipps was particularly concerned to avoid giving 'offence … to the officers and men of the Mounted Police.'[69]

The war over Port Phillip's grasslands peaked between 1840 and 1843 as the land rush reached a crescendo. During this period, new squatters were left in no doubt about what was required to secure their land claim. Niel Black noted in December 1839 that he had been told that to take up a run it was necessary 'to slaughter natives right and left,' although he believed the numbers killed were exaggerated because 'many persons bounce [brag] about their treatment of the natives.' Nevertheless, Black thought 'that two thirds of them does not care a single straw about taking the life of a native provided they are not taken up by the Protector.'[70]

The infamous squatter henchman Frederick Taylor, the subject of an investigation for the killing of Aborigines as early as 1836,[71] became renowned for his ability to secure a new run. A neighbour, Charles Gray, noted that only a week after Taylor arrived in his district in 1839 there were obvious signs of slaughter. The missionary Orton viewed the official deposition in which it was reported that men had 'formed themselves into an extended line with Taylor being at the centre' and while the Aborigines were sleeping 'fired upon them and killed the whole party save one consisting of thirty-five men women and children.'[72] The aptly named Whyte brothers were equally notorious for their resolve to teach Aborigines an early and unambiguous lesson. The squatter John G. Robertson recalled that:

> The first day I went over the Wando Vale Station to look at the ground I found old Maggie (that Sir Thomas Mitchell gave the tomahawk to) fishing for muscles with her toes, in a waterhole up to her middle, near where the Major crossed that stream ... nearly all her male relatives were killed three days before I arrived on the Wando by [the] Whyte brothers. Three days after the Whytes arrived, the natives of this creek, with some others, made up a plan to rob the new comers ... They watched an opportunity, and cut off 50 sheep from [the] Whyte Brothers' flocks, which were soon missed ... they had taken shelter in an open plain with long clump of tea-tree, which the Whyte Brothers' party, seven in number, surrounded, and shot them all but one. Fifty one men were killed, and the bones of the men and sheep lay mingled together bleaching in the sun at the Fighting Hills ... the females were mostly chased by men up the Glenelg, and the children followed them. This I learnt since from themselves ...[73]

William Moodie was given a still more shocking version of the same incident by an Aboriginal man: 'Blackfellow all runem along scrub in creek, lubra look up scrub, white fellow shoot her down. Two hundred fine fat lubra shot.'[74]

George Augustus Robinson was a voluminous chronicler of frontier violence. In early 1840, when the Chief Protector belatedly ventured from Melbourne and reached Hutton's station, ninety miles from Melbourne on the Goulburn River, with its 'tens of thousands [of acres] on every side' of good sheep country, he recorded that:

> Mr Hutton avowed his [policy towards the Aborigines] to be
> terror; to keep the natives in subjection by fear, and to punish
> them wholesale, that is, by tribes or communities. If a member
> of a tribe offend, destroy the whole. He believed they must be
> exterminated. This, in his opinion, was the best ... Mr Hutton
> said that these blacks will never be any good until they are
> scared as the Murrumbidgee blacks were: three parts killed.[75]

The killing and dispersal of Aborigines was not only the practice of brutes but also of comparatively sympathetic settlers who deplored crude slaughter. Alexander Mollison believed that he largely avoided trouble with Aborigines because they knew 'we were prepared to punish them for any aggression.'[76] Annie Baxter expressed in words and actions her sympathy for the Aborigines and yet participated in some of the thirteen armed raids which she mentions in her journal.[77] From the Wedge family holding, Charles Wedge wrote to his uncle – who had been pursuing the Port Phillip Association cause and promoting its humanitarian intent in London – that he had lost stock to the Aborigines, adding, 'You may depend I do not allow these things to be done with impunity.'[78] Samuel Winter, with whom many Aborigines found refuge, nevertheless had a large swivel gun mounted at the home station.[79] The government official C.J. Tyers made reference to Wedge and Winter in his journal in February 1840, noting first that at Wedge's station in the Portland Bay district:

> the natives have been very troublesome ... lately, endeavour-
> ing to burn them [the squatters] out and steal the sheep. They
> succeeded in burning the country for some miles around the
> station and one of the huts of the out-station with everything

in it, but were prevented from getting any of the sheep by the timely arrival of some of the men. Mr Codd also told me that five native blacks had been shot at Mr Winter's station while making an attack on the shepherds and carrying off some sheep.[80]

Rolf Boldrewood, a squatter who had initially defied settler warnings 'to keep the blacks at a distance' on the basis that 'it was their country after all,' also accepted the necessity for 'concerted action' once 'war broke out.' Boldrewood openly acknowledged that the local people were largely wiped out before the issue was settled 'for good and all, [and] we pioneers were enabled to devote ourselves to our legitimate business.'[81] Even the aforementioned John G. Robertson, who was fiercely critical of the killing of Aborigines, admitted that 'I have on four different occasions, when they committed murders, gone out with others in search of them, and *I now thank God* I never fell in with them, or there is no doubt I should be like many others, and feel that sting which must always be felt by the most regardless of the deed done to those poor creatures.'[82] The few squatters who disowned the use of violence, most notably the Aboriginal advocate James Dawson, had invariably taken up runs that had already been secured.[83] The reality created by the conquest of Aboriginal land was that despite some variation in local principle and practice, almost 'every station,' as C.B. Hall recalled, 'has some tragic tale connected with this subject.'[84]

The dispossession of the Aborigines was more rapid and more complete than might be suggested by the large size of the runs and the low density of the European population. This was because of the exclusive control asserted over productive country and reliable water supplies. Port Phillip's pastures were not of uniform quality, and the 'young and sweet'[85] grass of the best sheep-lands was the same country on which native herbivores and the Aborigines relied. The competition for water was equally intense. Although settlers were now much less likely to be guided to springs and waterholes, Aboriginal campsites, often marked by substantial huts, were a sure sign that water was nearby. Tyers 'found' the 'best water we had tasted since leaving Mr Fisher's station' by moving to where Aborigines were camped. He fired a gun to alert the Aborigines that he was coming and was surprised when the people ran off despite him holding up what was surely now a superseded symbol: the 'green bough in token of friendship'.[86]

Aborigines were dependent on these water sources not just for drinking water, but for food. In the winter months the fish, eel and birds of the rivers and marshes provided their major source of nutrition. The infrastructure supporting this food supply – huts, traps and extensive channels – could not easily be replaced after it was destroyed by squatters or fire. Niel Black admitted that he demolished permanent Aboriginal structures on his runs as a clear sign 'that we did not want them near us.'[87] Game was also quickly driven off runs by men and dogs, and waterholes and plant foods (especially the yam daisy) were damaged by over-grazing. The fact that 1840–41 was particularly dry made the situation worse. From 1840 most of the Aborigines of Port Phillip were hungry and malnourished, which weakened their capacity to resist disease and flee the armed parties pursuing them.

The shortage of food and the extent of the land occupation meant that by 1840 it is probable that even Aborigines who sought to avoid Europeans and were not actively engaged in the resistance had no option but to kill stock. In responding to such 'crimes' government officials invariably accepted the norms of frontier culture, a mindset not helped by the fact that even Aboriginal Protectors were reliant on squatter hospitality. While Robinson was at Hutton's station two Aborigines were shot, but even the Protector didn't dispute the legality or legitimacy of this, as there had been an attack on Hutton's sheep, and instead merely argued against further reprisals, considering two deaths to be 'sufficient … for the wrongs committed.'

Unfortunately a Mr Russel of the Mounted Police thought differently: he 'said the natives ought to be taught a wholesome lesson; that it was quite out of the question people were to be disturbed by such wretches.'[88]

Nor was the indiscriminate killing of Aborigines as a punishment for the killing of sheep or cattle only a frontier norm; it was also sanctioned by the authorities and courts in Melbourne. While Charles La Trobe, the 'superintendent' in charge of the Port Phillip district from 1839, expressed some concern about the many reports of frontier violence, the government was keen for squatters to accept primary responsibility for the defence of their runs. In September 1840 Fyans suggested to La Trobe that he should insist that 'the gentlemen in the country ... protect their property, and ... deal with such useless savages on the spot.'[89] And in late 1841 the recently arrived resident judge of the Supreme Court, John Walpole Willis, upheld the legality of squatters forcefully asserting exclusive rights of possession over their runs on the basis that Aborigines had 'no right to trespass.'[90] In the trial of a squatter, George Bolden, who had actually confessed to a Protector that he had killed an Aborigine, Willis reportedly instructed the jury that:

> I have no hesitation to say that, if a person has a run, for which he pays a licence, and a man or any person comes to that run the owner or lessee has a right to use every lawful means to recover any property that may be attempted to be carried away. I care not whether they are white or black – I may turn them off my property. I will go further: if Government takes upon themselves to assume the ownership of the soil, the lessee have aright to look to them for a sufficient guarantee of their property, and they have a clear and distinct right to turn any person off their property that may come on to it for the purpose of aggression or not.[91]

For all the humanitarian rhetoric that could still issue from the pen of La Trobe and Gipps, only one European was convicted for shooting an Aborigine in the Port Phillip district between 1835 and 1850. This was John Stokell, an overseer on George Armytage's station in the Wimmera, using a gun borrowed from Robert Officer, Jr (all three of these men were originally from Van Diemen's Land). The fact that the dead body had been sighted (although identification was disputed) and that there was a white witness willing to testify overcame the two standard reasons for avoiding prosecution. Stokell was convicted of grievous bodily harm in 1848 and served two months in prison.[92]

Although squatters undertook most clearances themselves, police units were also a formidable presence, more than compensating for the withdrawal of the British military from the Australian frontier after 1838. By 1842 there were border police, mounted police and native police actively committed to defending the squatters' exclusive claims. In 1842 the total Port Phillip expenditure on mounted police was £5540, which, along with the £4273 spent on border police, amounted to more than 11 per cent of government expenditure in the district.[93]

The key to both private and public military success was that in open grassland country, the principal British weapons, the horse and the gun, could operate to maximum efficiency. Whereas the dense scrub and forest-covered hills and gullies which fringed the grassland valleys of Van Diemen's Land had dragged fighting out for years because of the difficulty of hunting down guerilla warriors in such terrain, in the vast open pasturelands of Port Phillip there were few refuges from mounted settlers or police. Moreover, people could not find safety by moving to more remote territory because of the obvious reason that this was the defended homeland of another people.

Even when they survived the initial occupation of their land, Aborigines attempting to stay in their own country could be continually harassed. Community life became impossible and this destroyed health and spirit. As Jan Critchett concludes in her comprehensive study of the western district frontier, for the Aborigines and the local squatters the frontier was 'a very local phenomenon,' where 'the enemy was not on the other side of neutral ground' but located in 'the very land each settler lived upon.'[94]

The speed and totality of the invasion meant that Aboriginal resistance was unable to slow the overwhelming white advance, although the infamous Faithfull massacre of April 1838, in which a party of convicts and other employees driving a large group of sheep and cattle south were attacked near present-day Benalla, with seven whites killed, does seem to have temporarily slowed the pace on the northern front. Fifteen years after this incident, George Faithfull remained proud of the part he played in the protracted campaign:

> The country was left to us for some years in consequence of the hostility of the blacks … I and my men were kept for years in a perpetual state of alarm. We dared not move to supply our huts with wood or water without a gun, and many of my men absconded from my service … from sheer terror of the blacks. This may appear too absurd for belief; nevertheless, it is a fact. At last it so happened that I was the means of putting an end to this warfare … I ordered my men to take deliberate aim, and to fire only with certainty of destruction … I fired my double-barrel right and left … the war thus began continued from about ten o'clock in the morning until four in the afternoon … and I trust and believe that many of the bravest of the savage warriors bit the dust. It was remarkable that the children, and many of the women likewise, had so little fear that they boldly ran forward, even under our horses' legs, picked up the spears, and carried them back to the warrior men … The fight I have described gave them a notion of what sort of stuff the white man was made, and my name was a terror to them ever after.[95]

The sheer scale of the pastoral operations made operations like those of the Faithfull brothers vulnerable to attack. Their overseer James Crossley reported that at the time of the first ambush he was proceeding with eighteen men, two drays, 3472 sheep and 395 head of cattle.[96] Yet it also makes the fierce reprisal raids that often followed the killing of even a single sheep difficult to explain on economic or security grounds alone. Robert Kenny has suggested that the Aboriginal attacks on sheep, which could include driving them into the bush or even into temporary stock yards as well as spearing, might have been partly meant to 'evoke a power against the settlers,' who were seen to be 'mystically linked to the sheep.'[97] And perhaps the vigorous white defence of their flocks also had a symbolic meaning. After all, pastoral patriarchs of the Promised Land – with whom the Australian squatters were occasionally compared – had, according to scripture (which provided a wellspring for the settler imagination even for those who never read the Bible), sometimes cleansed conquered country by killing every living thing. Certainly, the nonrational dimensions of the conflict should not be underestimated as the brutal emotions released by war can never be easily contained. If the Aborigines were chiefly killed in what was seen as a necessary 'war' to secure lives and property, they could also be killed for no 'reason' at all.

Although the capacities of the battle-scarred Van Diemonian workers who led the initial invasion are still persistently underestimated, there remains a large degree of consensus about the level of violence. Geoffrey Blainey has referred to the sealers and whalers in his recent *History of Victoria* (2006) as 'the advance troops of an invasion which suddenly was to shake and then shatter the old Aboriginal way of life.' Blainey asserts that the 'Aboriginals were the victims of massacres,' that 'the protectors could rarely offer strong protection, and the law and the courts did not protect the Aboriginals,' and that 'at least 400 must have been killed by firearms.'[98] His casualty count is broadly similar to that given by Henry Gyles

Turner, who personally knew men like Fawkner and Wedge and estimated in his *A History of the Colony of Victoria* (1904) that 'the total number of the Aborigines who fell in conflict with the whites within the Port Phillip district might be stated approximately at 350.'[99] Richard Broome's estimate is that about one thousand were directly killed, and some have proposed a significantly higher figure than this. What there is no dispute about is the fact that a large number of Aboriginal people were slaughtered. This truth was also accepted in the nineteenth century, and indeed a body of early Victorian historiography was devoted to countering what seems to have been a strong *white* oral memory of more extensive violence. Turner suggests that numbers killed 'were not so numerous *as generally supposed*' and 'At no time did it rise to a condition of warfare.'[100] In 1903, Rolf Boldrewood did not dispute that violence had been widespread (a subject covered in his novels as well as his memoir) but rather sought to justify the killings by restating old prejudices concerning Aboriginal character: 'under an apparently peaceable, even grateful, demeanour, lurks an untrustworthy treacherous disposition, ready at all times to assert itself in acts of violence.'[101]

What of the Aboriginal Protectors? How could it be that the officials charged by the imperial government with the duty of protecting the rights and lives of the Aborigines achieved little more than documenting the extent of their abuse?

George Faithfull argued that the work of the Protectors only made matters worse, as 'People formed themselves into bands of alliance and allegiance to each other, and then it was the destruction of the natives really did take place.'[102] McCombie also believed that the Protectors were in part to blame for the violence because of their 'antagonistic position' to settlers.[103] While this argument is both self-serving and far-fetched, it is likely that clearances were sometimes hastened to prevent future interference. Even when the presence of the Protectors discouraged massacres, the incentive for huts, fish traps and whole villages to be quickly obliterated remained, both to encourage the Aborigines to move on and to disguise the extent of their occupation. The main limitation on the Protectorate, however, was that the five under-funded and over-worked officials worked within a land policy that nullified their work, and there was no political will to change this. Their sometimes valiant efforts were simply overwhelmed by the speed and magnitude of the conquest. In recent decades, the work of the 'much-maligned Protectors'[104] has been more generously appraised by historians who rightly emphasise the impossible context in which they worked. The real question is whether they could have done more to change this context.

All four of George Augustus Robinson's assistants were appointed in England (three were Wesleyan schoolmasters) and did not reach Melbourne until 21 March 1839, a few months after the Chief Protector himself had arrived from Flinders Island. After dividing the Port Phillip district among his subordinates, Robinson ordered them 'to take the field forthwith.'[105] The letters and journals of these men during the next decade provide a comprehensive catalogue of the violence, degradation and abuse of those in their charge. There is no doubt that they were privately appalled about the situation of the Aborigines, but should more have been expressed in *official* reports? In particular there seems a disturbing gulf between the concern detailed in Robinson's now published journal (a critical resource for historians that was of course unavailable to his contemporaries) and the reports that would be read in Sydney and London. The Chief Protector arguably failed in his duty to ensure that the British government was succinctly and hastily advised of the full reality of the Port Phillip frontier, the true impact of its land policy, and what was needed to achieve change. Although Robinson would become the most widely travelled government official in Port Phillip, spending approximately three years of his eleven years' service moving around the country,[106] he didn't visit the most violent part of the Port Phillip district, the western district, until March 1841.

His official report of this trip came to 264 pages with six appendices but, although the fighting was intense and the dispossession was then reaching its climax, Robinson chose to focus on matters of anthropological interest – languages, clan names, cultural practices, accounts of meetings and so on – that were irrelevant to the immediate crisis. Gipps was overwhelmed by the report's detail and asked for 'somebody to read this report and make notes on its contents.' The clerk who did this commented 'there is not much information to be obtained by its perusal' although 'the case of cannibalism is I believe something new.'[107] Robinson presented no strong case for immediate government action, made no specific policy recommendations and passed no judgment on the squatting licence system, even though his journal makes it clear that he was passionately concerned and knowledgeable about such matters and that he had met with scores of Aborigines who had told him they had been forcefully evicted from their land.

The point of such advocacy was not that government officials did not already know the human consequences of their land policy; rather, if the Chief Protector were to set out the situation unambiguously, it might become a political problem requiring a political response. The possible cost of Robinson's caution is made clear by the British government's response when the Chief Protector belatedly set out the horrific reality of the Port Phillip frontier and the fallacy of co-existence in his 1845 and 1846 annual reports. Henry Reynolds has observed that it was in consequence of Robinson's advocacy that in February 1848 the Secretary of State, Earl Grey, informed Governor Fitzroy that pastoral leases were 'not intended to deprive the natives of their former right to hunt' or to 'wander over them in search of subsistence ... except over land actually cultivated or fenced in for that purpose.'[108] The sad truth was that, at least in the grasslands of Port Phillip, there were by then so few Aborigines left alive that, even had this instruction been acted upon, it was already too late to make a difference.

Robinson's misplaced prudence had probably arisen from a concern not to undermine the small local political backing his work received. From 1840 the Chief Protector reported directly to La Trobe, and Robinson struggled even to have his travel expenses authorised by the equivocal but ultimately unsupportive Superintendent. Assistant Protector Dredge agreed with Robinson that 'the measure of protection to the natives is extremely unpopular here, and that this government ... will do everything it can to neutralize its efficiency.'[109]

If colonial officials were never enamoured of the London-imposed Protectorate, their response to the Methodist missionaries who established themselves at Buntingdale on the Barwon River about thirty miles from Geelong shows that the neglect of the Aborigines was rooted in much more than disdain for outside interference. The New South Wales government proved reluctant to set aside even a single run for the Wesleyan mission. Gipps advised Magistrate Lonsdale that 'the quantity of the land which it may be in His Excellency's power to secure to this mission will be dependent on the locality in which it may be selected. If fixed on valuable land or such as in demand by settlers it will be quite out of the Governor's power to give the quantity of two square miles as asked for.'[110] In the following year, the Surveyor-General of New South Wales, S.A. Perry, objected to reserving mission land for five years, pointing out, apparently without irony, 'the irregularity of any body of men anticipating the arrangements of the Government and thereby placing obstacles to the general improvement of the country.' Perry informed Gipps that he had 'received information from an authentic source that there is a very valuable tract of country in that direction, and I am aware that a vast number of persons already civilised, and whose example would go far to promote the objects contemplated, anxiously look forward to establishing themselves with their families in the district in question.'[111] Perry was assured that the land to be reserved for the Wesleyan mission had been reduced to 640 acres.[112] This was all too much even for Foster Fyans, an official not otherwise known for his advocacy of the Aboriginal cause, who pointed out that were the missionaries to become squatters, 'they could keep the [larger area of] ground for a few pounds yearly.'[113]

The government-run reserves that were eventually established as part of the Protectorate were even more vulnerable to neglect. Squatter land hunger meant they were being continually carved up and their residents pushed out into more marginal country. Little effort was made to provide food and blankets (or even religious instruction) at these reserves. In 1847, at the western district protectorate of Mt Rouse, there were virtually no Aborigines present, largely because there was nothing to be had there.[114]

The lack of a local commitment to the Protectorate or even to traditional missionary work after 1839 is a deeply troubling dimension of the early history of Port Phillip, and a more accurate measure of the political priority given to Aborigines than the rhetoric expressed in imperial dispatches, the occasional proclamation or much-publicised prosecution. There is no reason to question the accuracy of Robinson's assessment: 'It is painful to witness these scenes. The stock keeper and shepherd has tobacco and bread to give but I have nothing. If I were to purchase I should be surcharged. It is a common mockery. I am called to protect and the means of protection is withheld.'[115]

As Robinson regularly pointed out, this paucity and neglect was occurring at a time when New South Wales government coffers were overflowing with hundreds of thousands of pounds in revenue from the sale of Aboriginal lands. Robinson knew that the neglect of the Aborigines was not primarily a product of ignorance, misunderstanding or perennial budget complaints, but accurately reflected the priority given to the conquest and settlement of their homelands.

16.

MELBOURNE'S CROSS-CULTURAL ENCOUNTER

DESPITE THE RAPID COLLAPSE IN THE population of the indigenous Boon wurrung and Woi wurrung,[116] the speed with which Aborigines were dispossessed across Port Phillip in the late 1830s and early 1840s gave rise to an unexpected development: the Aboriginal population of Melbourne actually *increased* due to the arrival of hundreds of refugees. Furthermore, as these people fled their homelands to the town, they became more visible to European observers.

Between 1836 and 1838, the concentration of Aborigines in Melbourne was a public policy choice. The Port Phillip Association had made the town a distribution centre for food and supplies, and this practice was continued by Governor Bourke, who instructed Lonsdale to 'endeavour to establish them [the Aborigines] in a village, and to induce them to offer their labour in return for food and clothing.'[117] In 1837 the government appointed a missionary, George Langhorne, who sought to develop this village on the southern banks of the Yarra around the present-day Botanic Gardens.

The native village concept was inspired both by the famous Kat River settlement of the Cape Colony and, more surprisingly, by the Owenite community at Lanark in Scotland. Langhorne believed that the principle of a 'community of goods' on which Lanark was based was similar to Aboriginal notions of property.[118] Robert

Owen, the working-class leader who believed that society could be transformed by experimental communities in which possessions were held in common, and social and economic activity was organised on a co-operative basis, thus became the inspiration for a cultural experiment which Bourke hoped (according to Langhorne) would eventually see 'the two races of whites and blacks (the lower class of whites) ... amalgamated.'[119] While the number of Aborigines who permanently lived on the mission was never high, the fact that so many came into Melbourne for their own reasons meant that considerable numbers had some contact with the missionary. For example, at the end of March 1837 Langhorne reported that 'It being the time for the annual meeting of families from different tribes for the purpose of arranging their quarrels and other matters, a considerable number of blacks, between two and three hundred men, women and children, have been during the past month congregated in Melbourne.'[120]

Despite the official welcome given to Aborigines at this time, during 1837 the town's environs became securely British and the Aborigines more vulnerable than they had been during Melbourne's first year. Less than a year after it commenced operation, three Aboriginal residents of the Melbourne mission were shot and killed after seeking nourishment in a neighbouring potato field; several others, including one known as Tullamarine, were subsequently arrested over the incident, although they famously escaped by burning down their jail.[121] During 1838 the mission was even attacked by the police. Langhorne informed Sydney that 'the conduct of some of the police on this occasion was brutal in the extreme' and reported that he had expressed to Lonsdale his regret that the police magistrate 'should have considered it advisable to take a step, the consequence of which was converting the Mission into a scene of bloodshed and confusion.' Langhorne accused Lonsdale of lying about the claim that the police 'had fired in the air,' pointing out that 'from the direction the shot took they must have

fired directly upon the flying blacks.'[122] However, with the recall of
his patron, Governor Bourke, Langhorne's political influence had
already evaporated and not only were the missionary's allegations
ignored, but the new Governor ordered that in order 'to preserve
the subordination which ought to exist in every department of
Government,' Langhorne was to 'regard the Police Magistrate of
Melbourne as your immediate superior, and to obey all orders that
may be conveyed to you by or through the Police Magistrate, and to
send your reports to the Government also through that officer.'[123]

After George Augustus Robinson arrived as Chief Protector of
the Aborigines in early 1839, he sought to improve cross-cultural
relations by arranging for the Aborigines to put on an exhibition for
the Melbourne establishment. He recorded the event in his journal:

> 11 am went to the entertainment given by to the native tribes
> ... between 4 and 500. Refreshment was also provided: choice
> wines and viands for the respectable white inhabitants. Six
> tents were provided for the white visitants. All the respectable
> inhabitants were present on this occasion all in best attire ...
> I served out the dinner to the Natives ... After dinner the
> Natives engaged in different amusements: racing for toma-
> hawks which I gave them; climbing a greasy pole for hand-
> kerchiefs; throwing the spear. In the evening corrobery and a
> grand display of fireworks ... the entertainment went off with
> exclamation.[124]

Given the escalating crisis in Kulin country and beyond, the
Aborigines no doubt had serious business to discuss during this
customary autumnal gathering. Perhaps their engagement with the
white elite was even a deliberate ploy. But the reality is that their
participation in Robinson's festival was primarily motivated by
hunger: Robinson was unsuccessfully trying to get food for 'famish-
ing' Port Phillip natives at this time. Shortly after the grand event,

Robinson records that 'A large party of women and children attended this afternoon and were most unfortunate in their application for bread or food of any description. Said they were plenty hungry. Whilst taking some refreshment ... they were surrounding the table and craved every morsel I put to my mouth. It is a crying sin to allow these poor creatures to perish for want.'[125]

The suffering in the town camps at this time was soon exacerbated by outbreaks of disease. In May 1839, Robinson reported that:

Sievwright called and reported that the natives were encamped on the opposite side of the river near to his tent, and that five deaths had happened among them and that several other deaths might be expected. They were all afflicted with dysentery and their state truly deplorable. One little girl of tender years, supposed about eight years, was grievously afflicted with venereal.[126]

When Robinson visited this camp himself, he found the Aborigines:

in a deplorable state of disease and wretchedness. Six deaths had taken place within a few days, one this morning. I visited each abode of misery and famine and was intensely excited at the scenes of misery I beheld, particularly when I contrasted it with the appearance possessed by the Europeans derived from their lands and the sale of their lands. Land has been sold in Melbourne for £1200 per acre, 90 and 100 per cent is also the acreage return for flock masters yet the original occupiers of the soil are perishing with disease, want, and the extreme of wretchedness. This is a disgrace to humanity.[127]

Dr P. Cussens, the settlement's medical officer, also attended the camp and noted both the widespread disease and that the 'people lacked food and were without blankets in over-night May temperatures of 10° [Farenheit].'[128]

With Charles La Trobe's appointment as superintendent of the Port Phillip District, government policy towards Aborigines in Melbourne would change dramatically. Robinson noted in his journal that in December 1839 the superintendent told him that 'force must be made use' to effect the eviction of the Aborigines from Melbourne, as 'Captain Lonsdale used force and they all respect Captain Lonsdale.' La Trobe, who had supposedly been appointed partly because of his evangelical credentials, believed that Robinson's charity had made the Aborigines 'the masters.' Robinson's reply illuminated how little any sense of reciprocal obligations or memory of the treaty (John Batman had died earlier that year) now remained: the Aborigines, Robinson explained, 'had received nothing,' and when La Trobe cited a recent blanket distribution, the Chief Protector responded that these blankets had been 'given exclusively to the sick and aged and there were but 25 in all.'[129] On the day when the government mission was moved to Narre Warren (the base for the new native police), and the Aborigines were evicted from their old mission site, William Thomas, the assistant protector responsible for the Melbourne region, wrote in his diary: 'From sunrise to sunset spent in arguing, reasoning, and persuading the natives – They declare that they will not remove. They had camped on private property ... I tell them again that they make *willums* on White Man's ground, and cut down trees and cut off bark, make White Man sulky – they say no White Man's ground Black Man's.'[130]

Although government assistance to Aborigines in Melbourne had now ceased (although Thomas would re-establish a small protectorate and school at Merri Creek in late 1842[131]), and there was neither land nor rations reserved for them, the Aborigines continued to come into the town. Edward Curr was one of many observers who noted that a 'feature of Melbourne was the blacks, who constantly wandered about in large numbers.'[132] In April 1840 over 400

Kulin camped just north of Melbourne for five months and refused to obey La Trobe's orders to leave. On 11 October 1840, taking advantage of Thomas's absence, the camp was forcibly broken up with a young Woi wurrung clan head, Winberry, killed. The people were herded through the town and thirty-three were imprisoned for five weeks without charge. Ultimately ten Aborigines were convicted of stealing sheep and sentenced to transportation for ten years (all but one escaped). Yet even after this display of terror, visits to Melbourne did not cease. In January 1844 there were said to be 675 Aborigines resident[133], and as late as June 1846 La Trobe ordered Thomas to burn the camps of the Boon wurrung and Woi Wurrung to force them to move on.[134]

There can be little doubt that the people's unbridled determination to come into Melbourne reflected their level of desperation. Despite its dangers, the town was safer than most of their homelands, and through work, begging and prostitution food could often be had. In the winter of 1844 Thomas lamented: 'I do not think that of the five tribes who visit Melbourne that there is in the whole five districts enough to feed one tribe.'[135] The survival of waste- and marsh-lands near the town centre, too prone to flooding to build on or farm, provided camping sites for scattered groups of dispossessed people. For a time urban visibility disguised the severity of the overall population decline, but the reality of Melbourne after 1838 is that Aboriginal people, including those who had played a central role in the founding of the town, such as the Sydney Aborigines, Batman's Tasmanian companions and Kulin elders like Derrimut and Billibellary, were vulnerable, largely powerless and often sick from the ravages of disease, malnutrition and alcohol.[136] The brief period when the village on the Yarra was a genuinely multicultural camp lasted for less than three years. From 1839 Melbourne was British at its core, with large numbers of homeless Aborigines surviving wherever and however they could on the geographic, social and economic margins of the town. By the time

Victoria separated from New South Wales in 1851, with most Aborigines dead, and catastrophic population decline stemming the flow of survivors into the semi-sanctuary afforded by Melbourne's swamps, the city's well-publicised cross-cultural encounter had effectively come to an end.

Derrimut survived until 1864, long enough to receive posthumous recognition, when the nostalgic city patriarch and proud member of the Legislative Council, John Fawkner, successfully organised a subscription for a memorial stone. Derrimut's last documented words were ones of despair: 'You have all this place, no good have children, no good have lubra, me tumble down and die very soon now.'[137] Aborigines gradually rebuilt their community from the temporary sanctuary of Coranderrk, established near Healesville in 1863, and other small reserves scattered across the bloodstained plains of Port Phillip, although their struggle to survive total conquest had only just begun.[138]

PART VI

UNDERSTANDING CONQUEST

17.

FRONTIER TRUTHS

NOT THIRTY YEARS AFTER the founding of Melbourne, only about two hundred people remained from all five of the clans that made up the once populous Kulin nation, and the population decline across Victoria as a whole was at least 80 per cent.[1] It is now almost universally accepted that the suffering of the Aborigines and the rate of their demise were proportionate to the speed of the land grab. Given this, why is the unrestricted opening of the grasslands to white settlement still not understood to have been a disastrous mistake? How can it be that 175 years after this defining decision in Australian history was taken, it is yet to be condemned? There are at least four factors which have prevented this apparently self-evident conclusion from being reached.

Adaptation and resistance
On 4 July 1837 Alexander Mollison noted in his journal that after crossing the Murray River he met with a local Aborigine, 'Jimmy,' who 'has been daily pressing me to make my station on his ground.' Jimmy had presumably seen for himself some of the potential benefits, especially in food and supplies, which came with an ongoing white presence. Yet on that very same day Mollison also records meeting three men who had 'just been much frightened by a tribe of blacks' and he 'gave them some powder' to deal with the potential threat.[2]

Such disparate responses to European settlement point to the complexity of the frontier, something which has in recent decades been the subject of much research. Underpinning this new historical work is a concern to see Aborigines as more than mere victims of conquest and to understand how they both resisted and adapted to the British presence. But if this well-intentioned research has led to a much greater understanding of the complexity of the frontier, it has also tended to give a distorted sense of the experience of the overwhelming majority of Aborigines in the immediate aftermath of conquest.

While exceptions can always be found, genuine cultural encounter, real exchange and effective adaptation require temporal and geographical space. The unprecedented speed of the land grab and the open topography of the grasslands ensured few such spaces existed in Port Phillip's squatter lands before 1850. Adding nuance to the frontier story is a worthwhile enterprise, but it cannot alter the fact that Port Phillip had become such a terrible place for Aborigines that within fifteen years of the founding of Melbourne almost all of them were dead. This does not diminish (but rather magnifies) the extraordinary achievement of those who somehow survived the onslaught.

It is also important to remember that the historical record is inevitably biased towards cross-cultural meetings – after all, there can be no record of a *non*-meeting – and it is likely that most Aboriginal people sought 'to stay clear of the newcomers' for as long as they could.[3] When Land Commissioner Gisborne travelled through the western district in late 1839, he noted that in the whole overland journey from Geelong to Portland Bay, 'I do not recollect having seen a single native, and I have understood that they very rarely visit the stations.'[4] Around the same time, Joseph Orton also observed that the Aborigines 'seclude themselves as much as possible from Europeans so that it is extremely difficult to fall in with them.'[5] Hugh Murray from Colac similarly recalled: 'We had very little intercourse with them [the Aborigines] for the first 18 months.'[6] Henry Dwyer from Victoria Valley wrote that: 'The niggers have always been shy of coming to or showing on this country.'[7] William Adeney, who came to Port Phillip in January 1843, explained why few Aborigines were seen: 'the dread which many of the stockkeepers inspire in those poor wandering tribes is extreme. They will often run at the sight of one of these men.'[8]

Undoubtedly there were, even in these terrible times, examples of real meeting and genuine exchange. Nevertheless, it is not until after 1850, when the squatters experienced a serious labour shortage with the discovery of gold, and so many Aborigines had died that they no longer posed even a potential threat to land or property, that Port Phillip's grasslands can cease to be portrayed as primarily pastures of death.

Disease

Although there is relatively little argument about widespread violence on the Port Phillip frontier, for nearly 170 years there has been dissent about the conclusions which can be drawn from this. The debate largely revolves around the question of deaths from disease. The principal dispute does not concern whether or not most Aborigines died from violence or disease, but whether disease *qualifies* or *compounds* the culpability of the invaders. While there is no question that the majority of Aborigines died from some form of disease, some see this as an integral part of conquest, others as a force operating independently of human agency. Recently the latter conception, common in squatter memoirs, has again become resurgent.

Evangelicals saw *both* violence and disease as evidence of injustice. As the House of Commons Select Committee concluded, the Aborigines' 'territory has been usurped; their property seized; their numbers diminished; their character debased; the spread of civilisation impeded. European vices and diseases have been introduced amongst them, and they have been familiarised with the use of the most potent instruments for the subtle or the violent destruction of human life, viz. brandy and gunpowder.'⁹ George Augustus Robinson drew the same connections, reflecting in April 1839, 'What are the evils accruing to the Aborigines by occupancy of their lands by the whites? Disease of fatal character, hunger and distress, murder and rapine.'¹⁰ Even Foster Fyans, the battle-hardened Police Magistrate of Geelong, could see the direct relationship between government neglect and disease: 'I trust that His Excellency may feel pleased to grant us another supply of female clothing, as a vast number of these poor people are in a deplorable state of misery from disease and want, and must be lost during the approaching winter, excepting something is done to relieve their situation.'¹¹ The squatter Samuel Winter blamed the high death rate in the winter of 1843 on the lack of 'large well constructed winter huts,' which had been destroyed in an effort to force Aborigines from their land.¹²

The single biggest killer was probably (as in the European population) tuberculosis, which 'thrived in deprived bodies.'¹³ Large numbers of Aborigines also died from influenza and venereal disease, although VD's relative prevalence could be exaggerated to 'deflect settlement's consequences onto the natives' [and lower-class white men's] moral incapacity.'¹⁴ Whatever the diagnosis, it is indisputable that Aboriginal deaths from disease after 1835 were the direct result of the rapid and comprehensive conquest of their homelands. But what of deaths from disease that occurred *before* settlement?

Did smallpox, perhaps introduced to the continent by Macassan traders from Indonesia, decimate the Aborigines of south-eastern Australia before 1835? Were the pasturelands already largely emptied before the British arrived? It is now widely believed that two epidemics, the first around 1789 and the second around 1830, greatly reduced the Aboriginal population of eastern Australia.¹⁵ However, population density was too small, and travel times too slow, for this vast region to be considered as a single interactive population in epidemiological terms,[16] and the smallpox thesis remains highly speculative in relation to Port Phillip. There is some evidence for the first epidemic, principally observations of pock-marks, the scarring left on smallpox survivors, but there is little doubt that the second either never reached or did not penetrate far into the Port Phillip district.[17]

As discussed, by 1830–31 the coastal areas of Port Phillip were regularly visited by Europeans involved in the sealing, whaling and wattle-bark industries, yet no European records any sign of a smallpox epidemic at the time. Moreover, this was only four to five years before Melbourne was founded. If smallpox had deci-mated the population only a few years before, such a transforma-tive event would almost certainly have become known to early settlers. William Buckley, who had lived with the Aboriginal people for over thirty years, was explicit on the matter: 'I never observed any European contagious disease prevalent, in the least degree' (although he did recall that many Aborigines died from a 'dreadful swelling of the feet,' which some historians argue could have been a symptom of smallpox).[18] Indeed, almost no whites, even the most pro-Aboriginal, record pockmarks at this time, although it would have been politically helpful for the illegal tres-passers at Port Phillip to present themselves as saviours of an already ravaged race.[19] Furthermore, the many accounts of a diverse and healthy population, including the elderly and infants (those most vulnerable to disease), do not suggest a population recovering from an epidemic.

One day after his first landing at Port Phillip, John Batman met with an old woman, 'quite a cripple,' and a group made up of 'only women and children; twenty of the former, and twenty-four of the latter.' Batman noted that 'the children were good-looking and of a healthy appearance,' and during the next couple of years there are numerous similar observations.[20] Nor is it necessarily significant that the squatters *later* recalled prevalent pockmarks. The fact that the same men failed to mention such poignant signs in journals or letters written at the time of the invasion is far more historically significant and serves to highlight the unreliability of the later claim. It is obvious enough why the self-proclaimed founding fathers of Victoria might belatedly emphasise the role played by smallpox once almost all the original owners of their land were dead. It is important to keep in mind how self-serving memoir (and even memory) can be.

It is sometimes argued that 'nothing could have saved the First Australians from the microbes European explorers, sealers and settlers inadvertently carried with them,' or that 'Aborigines with no prior immunity often succumbed to "pulmonary" disease simply by standing downwind of a European.'[21] But the destruction wrought by introduced diseases can never be explained by biology alone.[22] Such statements need to be given a precise geographical and social context, or else it becomes difficult to explain why so many more Aborigines survived in some regions than others, why there were few deaths in Melbourne's first year but so many after this, or indeed how any indigenous people survived European settlement at all.

In the end historians are confined to the evidence available, and this means that the only definitive conclusion which can be drawn is that very high rates of mortality among Port Phillip Aborigines occurred *after* Aborigines were dispossessed, lost their traditional food supply (including their main sources of protein) and were concentrated together in places where sanitary conditions, water quality, housing and diet were more akin to those of a Manchester slum than a traditional camp.

The high death toll from disease at Port Phillip does not mean government or settlers *intended* to kill Aborigines with disease (even if some found it convenient that the population was annihilated so rapidly). But nor does it mean that the invaders were not culpable. The link between disease and conquest was well under-

stood, and those who called for better provision for the Aborigines
– land reserves, decent food supplies, blankets, proper support and
protection – explicitly did so on the basis that without this assistance the Aborigines would soon all be dead largely from disease.
Despite these pleas, few measures were taken.[23] The point is not the
one made by former prime minister Paul Keating, in his Redfern
Park Speech of 1992, that 'we brought the disease,' but rather that
Europeans created the conditions in which diseases flourished and
did almost nothing to ameliorate these.

Scapegoats

In the 1830s, evangelicals argued that it was lower-order Europeans,
not the seizure of land, who were largely responsible for the suffering
of the Aborigines. It is a view that has proved remarkably resilient.
Former convict shepherds have predominantly borne the blame for
the violence at Port Phillip, with their well-publicised character flaws
deflecting attention from how they came to be in the frontline in the
first place. Although there is no doubt that these men did most of the
killing and that some were brutal and wantonly cruel, they no more
set the context for their deeds than do frontline soldiers in war.

The scapegoating of convicts is in part a legacy of the vitriolic
anti-transportation campaign of the late 1840s and early 1850s,
when convicts were frequently depicted, in Melbourne at least, as
even more 'savage' than the Aborigines. At a public meeting in the
Queens Theatre on 1 March 1847, one speaker asked, 'Will you agree
to receive such men as a Jeffrey, who violated the mother and then
dashed out the infant's brains while the unconscious innocent was
smiling on its brutal murderer? Or will you agree to receive such
men as the cannibal Pearce, who, according to his own dying con-
fession, devoured the flesh and muscles of seven of his fellow creatures?'[24] Such was the level of anti-convict hysteria that in 1852 the
Victorian Parliament passed laws designed to stop emancipist immigration from Van Diemen's Land – an estimated nineteen thousand

people crossed the strait that year[25] – by legislating that former convicts possessing only a conditional pardon (that is, the large majority) were to be treated as felons at large and sentenced to hard labour for three years. London intervened, but unrepentant Victorian Members of Parliament continued to pass discriminatory legislation until 1856. These efforts had no impact on boat arrivals – the lure of gold ensured that by the mid-1850s there were more Van Diemonian emancipists living in Port Phillip than on their home island– but they were successful in pushing Victoria's convict heritage underground. In such an atmosphere, blaming former convicts for the violence against the Aborigines, with a special emphasis on their sexual depredations, was not only expedient but commonsensical.

Henry Gyles Turner gave a standard account in his *History of the Colony of Victoria,* claiming that workers on the stations were 'debased and reckless characters ... In the sullen monotony of their animal life they risked anything for the companionship of the native women, and being practically outside the region of law, they took by bribery, by force, by murder if necessary, that which they coveted.' He concluded that the most important reason for the eventual reduction in fighting was that:

> under the stimulus of immigration the colony was being rapidly populated, and by a far superior type of man to the prison waifs and hardened ruffians who had in the earlier years been to the aborigines the representative of civilization ... the old, bad element gradually died out, or reverted to its old condition under lock and key, and the new element treated the natives, as a rule, with firmness and justice, respected the laws which aimed at their protection, and gave them no cause for personal revenge as the answer to brutal license.[26]

It was doubly convenient that the passing of the Aborigines could be blamed on savage Europeans who had also vanished into history. Illiterate men like James Gumm, who ended up a hermit in the Plenty Ranges, were unlikely to proclaim their own past in a virulently anti-convict society.[27] Persecuted in law and legend, the denigrated founding fathers seemed to fade into the landscape, forgotten when they were not despised. Ultimately no one wanted 'Marvellous Melbourne' to have been founded by this lot – and with the help of the mass immigration of the gold-rush years, it didn't need to be.

While few have been prepared to acknowledge, let alone defend, the convicts, the squatter-friendly slant of traditional history has long been disputed in Victoria. With the emergence of class-based politics in the second half of the nineteenth century, an anti-squatter sentiment developed, accompanying a campaign to redistribute large landholdings and achieve democratic reform. This sometimes saw the squatters blamed for all manner of ills, including the near-demise of the Aborigines, with as little rigour and as much prejudice as others blamed the emancipist workforce.

The effect of this often-bitter ideological divide has been to divert attention from the larger picture. The truth is that while there were the usual scattering of callous brutes and compassionate saints among both the squatters and their workers, individual actions were much less significant in deciding the fate of the Aborigines than was the policy decision to open Aboriginal lands to unrestricted white settlement. It was the government policy to encourage squatters to take possession of whatever land they chose, and not settler character, that largely explains why almost all the original inhabitants of Port Phillip's vast grasslands were dead so soon after 1835.

The mystery of existence
There is a final reason why the policy to open Aboriginal lands to unrestricted private conquest has escaped analysis: the recognition that not just Melbourne but the Australian nation was constructed on the foundation of open access to indigenous land and resources.

How can this fact of history now be condemned, given that we might not exist had the choice not been made? Yet while it is true that the origins of contemporary Melbourne and modern Australia lie in an approach to settlement decided 175 years ago, this need not prevent scrutiny of the decision that was taken. No part of the past can be quarantined from the present. Every city and every nation (and for that matter, every individual) is the product of past choices, good and bad, but if this mystery of existence is allowed to act as a barrier to critical study, history comes to an end. The moral consequences of the political commitment to open Australia's 'crown' lands to unrestricted private settlement cannot be evaded by arguing that there would have been no European Australia without it.

At any rate, historical choices, including the one under scrutiny, invariably have more complex implications than a choice between existence and non-existence. The primary decision that had to be made after the founding of Melbourne in 1835 was not *whether* there would be European settlement of the grasslands, but *how, when* and *to what extent* settlement would occur.

18.

WHAT IF?

ONLY FIVE YEARS AFTER the uncontrolled conquest of Port Phillip began, the terrible consequences were obvious even to distant government officials. Governor Gipps was concerned about the suffering of the Aborigines but consoled himself with refining the thesis that there was nothing the government could do, even suggesting to the Colonial Office that:

> As well might it be attempted to confine the Arabs of the Desert within a circle, traced upon their sands, as to confine the Graziers or Woolgrowers of New South Wales within any bounds that can possible be assigned to them ... [for] as certainly as the Arabs would be starved, so also would the flocks and herds of New South Wales if they were so confined, and the prosperity of the Country be at an end.[28]

This was the Governor's best argument for not restraining a squatter invasion that already stretched from Wilson's Promontory to Hervey Bay, but it is surely not a convincing one. Although Gipps's dispatch is still routinely presented as evidence of an overdue recognition of Australian 'reality,' it – like similar oft-cited dispatches from Governor Bourke – amounts to little more than determinist hyperbole. The woolgrowers were not nomads, but farmers. Flocks didn't need more land, *more* flocks needed more land (if no improvements were made to it), and no sheep would face 'starvation' as a result of a change in land policy – outside of environmental constraints that neither squatter nor government could change.

Nor, most critically, would 'the prosperity of the country' have been brought to an end if the resource rush had been reined in. The 'limits of location' were not, as many historians assume, an 'absurd' imposition.[29] In fact, there is a strong case to be made that removing them constrained economic growth in the long term by encouraging speculative rather than productive investment. The government's land policy ensured that the most profitable short-term action for the individual squatter was to monopolise enormous areas of 'free' grasslands and spend the minimum possible amount of his own capital in exploiting them. Whether the greater good was served by this means of disposing of the most valuable natural resource of the continent is highly doubtful, even without reference to the situation of the Aborigines. It was widely recognised in the nineteenth century that a larger number of improved and more concentrated holdings would have produced greater economic and social benefits. The fact that by 1849, some 1019 squatters occupied nearly 17.7 million hectares in eastern Australia[30] did not reflect a rational public-policy choice or Australian 'reality,' but the power of a vested interest.

Given the way the grasslands were possessed, it is not surprising that the conquest of Australia has never been celebrated in the way that the American move west has been. Although the inevitability of continental expansion has generally been taken for granted, the sentiment associated with this often seems closer to manifest resignation than manifest destiny. The response to the fate of the Aborigines reflects this mood. Well into the twentieth century, most Europeans believed the Aborigines were doomed to disappear following white settlement, but once the initial conflict had passed, they generally expressed regret about this. Today, while the survival of the Aborigines is no longer in question, the assumption underlying this perspective persists. The Aborigines might not have died out, but white people still *had* to colonise their lands. Indeed, the inevitability of a rapid and comprehensive continental conquest, for good or ill, arguably remains the central (and generally unacknowledged) assumption underpinning the telling of Australian history.

Whether based on belief in providence, Marxist or free-market economics, political 'reality,' the 'forces of history' or – the ultimate fall-back – 'human nature,' for 175 years policy-makers, historians and social commentators have shared the view of Governor Gipps that the rapid seizure of land and eviction of the Aborigines from their country could not have been prevented by government action. Judgments have varied on whether the pattern of settlement was on balance a good thing – this attitude is most evident in traditional progress narratives – or bad – as in much Aboriginal and environmental history – but in both cases policy-makers are assumed to have had no other choice.

Despite its radical nature, and even more radical consequences, the state-sanctioned private conquest of the Australian continent after 1835 is now taken for granted, so much so that the original policy *choice* seems to have been virtually forgotten. Analysis invariably starts from the position that, in the words of the eminent historian A.G.L. Shaw, 'the government could not control, even had it wished to, the squatters.'[31] Even those historians who deplore the environmental and human consequences of the land grab accept that the government legitimised 'that which it could not prevent.'[32] Or, as Henry Reynolds puts it: 'it is hard to see how it could have been otherwise. The result was predetermined.'[33] Even a scholar as critically immersed in the frontier as Reynolds assumes that officials in both Sydney and London 'lacked the power or the means to bring the squatters and their flocks and herds back within the settled districts' and that 'it was *obvious* that the future of New South

Wales was dependent on the wool industry and that the flocks needed a "free range over the wide expanse of herbage", as Governor Bourke phrased it.'[34] Historians have been remarkably constant on this matter across time and political persuasion, and indeed have barely diverged from the position put by Bourke in October 1835, when he advised London that 'no adequate measures could be resorted to for the general and permanent removal of intruders from waste lands.'[35]

Despite the end in the 1980s of what Stuart Macintyre calls 'the age of confident determinism,' when 'grand theories' linked past and future[36], we are still constrained by the idea that there were forces at work in the conquest of Australia so powerful that they overwhelmed political choice. So it is important for reasons of historical accuracy, moral honesty and future freedom to remember that Governors Arthur and Bourke, the Colonial Office in London and not least the Port Phillip Association knew that a policy choice *was* made. The case put by those who sought a change in land policy – that there was no alternative to sanctioning the squatters – was an argument in favour of a preferred position, not a statement of self-evident truth.

Contrary to what is often assumed, it was not standard imperial policy or practice to sponsor the unrestricted seizure of indigenous land by individual settlers. While British colonial expansion is a sorry history of policies, regulations, treaties and agreements violated, bypassed and ignored, there are no direct parallels with the unfettered freedom to appropriate Aboriginal land granted in Australia after 1835. Even the other white settler colonies of New Zealand, South Africa and North America, which all experienced their own land grabs and squatter incursions, paid occasional regard to boundaries, borders and limits. The land rush for Australia's productive grasslands was part of a global phenomenon manifested across the empire and particularly in what is sometimes called the 'Anglo-world,' but it was also a distinctively *local* phenomenon.[37]

There were, in fact, many possible responses to both the planned and actual dispersal of sheep and men, and had different choices been made in Hobart, Sydney or London, a different form of land settlement would have been achieved.

What has been missed by historians is that while the movement of *people* could not be easily controlled, the movement of *capital* could. The invasion by sealers, whalers and wattle-bark collectors along the coast of Port Phillip was difficult to control precisely because capital investment was diffuse and limited. The squatters' movement of flocks and shepherds was another matter altogether. In this case, the significant necessary investment was made by a small group of landowners, officials, bankers and merchants whose interests relied in large measure on their relations with the government. Highly sought-after convict labour, government office and, above all, land leases and title were in the power of the government to regulate and bestow.

Above all else, the squatters sought long-term leases and, ultimately, freehold title over their runs. Securing land was the whole point of their project, and it remained so even after annual licences were granted over what remained crown land. It is because of this fundamental motive that Governor Bourke's proposition that 'no adequate measures could be resorted to for the general and permanent removal of intruders from waste lands' and James Stephen's assertion that the Governor could not have prevented the 'lawless invasion of the lands of the Crown' because there was 'not in the Australian colonies any power, civil or military, available for such a service' are absurd. The power to control the squatting invasion rested not with troops, but with title.

What if it had been made clear to investors that those who occupied land without government sanction would be barred from leasing or purchasing crown land in the future?[38] *What if* the owners of sheep placed illegally on crown land were also automatically denied the right to receive convict labour or be considered for government office? *What if* the Protectors of Aborigines had been given the power to renew or cancel squatting licences according to whether the squatter upheld the Aborigines' right to access the resources of their country? *What if* London hadn't waited until the late 1840s to insist on clauses in pastoral leases that specified that Aborigines were not to be deprived 'of their former right to hunt over these Districts, or to wander over them in search of subsistence, in the manner to which they have been heretofore accustomed'?[39]

The truth revealed by these genuine policy options is that the conquest of almost all of Victoria's vast grasslands in less than a decade, and almost all of eastern Australia in a single generation, didn't occur in spite of policy or political action, but because of it. Politics was not overwhelmed by the market, but instead drove the resource rush. While some level of violence and suffering could not have been avoided, with sufficient political will the colonisation of Port Phillip could have been properly regulated, the Aborigines could have been better protected, and the land settlement process dramatically slowed to allow time for cultural adaptation and change. Policy-makers could not have prescribed peace, but they could have bought time. The speed and totality of the resource rush on the grasslands of Australia after the founding of Melbourne could – and should – have been avoided. In 1835 the future of the British and Aboriginal residents of the grasslands of Port Phillip was, in fact, no more predetermined than is our own.

This book has sought to resurrect the prime place of government decision-making in the conquest of Australia. In the 175 years following the founding of Melbourne and the overturning of the policy of concentrated settlement, we have come to assume that economic forces set the parameters of government power. It has become difficult to remember that, as the Aborigines Protection Society put it in 1837, the uncontrolled, comprehensive and ruthlessly fast conquest of the Australian continent was not 'an appointment of Heaven.'[40]

Given the depth and urgency of the current environmental crisis, this conclusion might be one of more than historical interest.[41] Perhaps the most pressing public-policy issue of our time is the necessity to rein in the continent-wide resource rush that began with the seizure of the grasslands in 1835. Could there be a connection between the ingrained assumption that the squatter conquest of Australia could not have been slowed down and properly regulated, and the national difficulty in imagining that governments might do the same to coalminers today? If Guy Pearse is right that it is 'our inability to *imagine* something different [which] is digging us deeper into danger as the immensity of the climate crisis hits home,' then it is not Aborigines alone who live with the dangerous legacy of the political decisions made after the founding of Melbourne in 1835.[42]

EPILOGUE

Stand at the crossroads and look,
ask for the ancient paths,
ask where the good way is, and walk in it,
and you will find rest for your souls

— *Jeremiah* 6:16

SINCE 1835 IT HAS BEEN IMPORTANT TO tell the story of the
founding of Melbourne with care. For the squatters, facing eviction
or prosecution, it was vital that imperial rulers understood that the
new settlement was convict-free and committed to the care and civilisation of the Aborigines. For the local governors, who sought to
exploit the act of trespass so as to overturn existing land policy, the
forces of colonisation had to be portrayed as too powerful for the
government to control. For the British government, cognisant of the
interwoven value of wool, land and God, squatter trespass needed to
be imbued with the inevitability and blessing of Providence. For the
landed elite in the proud young colony of Victoria from the 1850s, it
was best that many aspects of Melbourne's foundation, including its
legal status, be passed over altogether.

Money, respect and reputation were at stake in how Melbourne's
creation story was told, which the discovery of gold in the 1850s and
the end of the pastoral phase of the city's birth only confirmed. It was
surely fitting that a marvellous imperial metropolis of the liberal

free-market age had been founded through private initiative and free-settler enterprise, and that an impotent government had been reduced to playing catch-up.

What is more surprising is that such myths are still with us. The former Van Diemonian convicts who made up the overwhelming majority of the founding fathers of Melbourne remain forgotten or denigrated. The policy of concentrated settlement is still presented as out of touch with Australian 'reality.' Governments continue to be seen as powerless to regulate effectively the invasion of the continent. Enterprise remains imbued with a quasi-divine energy beyond the means of flesh-and-blood people to control. The land rush is still presented as a natural wonder in which human agency never stood a chance. Principle continues to be described as an irrelevant irritant in the 'real world' of the frontier. Even the horror of what happened to the Aborigines is often shied away from as we search for indigenous opportunities for growth amid the rubble of one of the fastest and most comprehensive conquests in the history of the British Empire.

Part of the reason that the founding fables have endured is that there is truth and legitimate sentiment to be found in them. The speed with which Melbourne grew and Victoria was settled *is*, when seen from the victor's perspective, 'one of the romances of modern colonisation.'[43] If anything, perhaps in part out of sensitivity to Aboriginal people, historians now tend to downplay what an extraordinary settlement story the founding of Melbourne represents. When R.V. Billis and A.S. Kenyon published *Pastures New* in 1930, they believed that 'there can be no room for doubt that the pastoral occupation of Port Phillip … was the most remarkable colonisation feat in the annals of the British Empire.' The only question for these historians was whether this had 'no parallel since the wonderful achievements of the ancients,' or if, for 'effective land settlement results, even ancient history furnishes no similar example.'[44] They had a point. During the past thirty years the gold rushes have to a large degree supplanted pastoralism in Australian history-writing. Yet at the commencement of the gold rushes, Victoria was already home to nearly 100,000 people, Melbourne was the continent's second-largest urban centre, and squatters had seized control of a tract of land stretching from the South Australian border to southern Queensland. It was the opening up of the grasslands, not the discovery of gold, that began the 'rush that never ended.'[45]

By the time Anthony Trollope visited Melbourne, then a city of 206,000 'souls,' in the early 1870s, the city had already largely turned its back on the Yarra, drained the swamps, filled in the lakes and flattened the hills, so that Trollope knew 'of no great town in the neighbourhood of which there is less to see in the way of landscape beauty.'[46]

There were also, however, the new parklands, and while the young trees planted in these were largely exiles and immigrants, they were already becoming an important part of home. Like so many other people, I have long enjoyed Melbourne's now magnificent collection of deciduous trees, but it was only in undertaking the preparatory pilgrimage for this book that I became aware of their even older indigenous companions: the ancient river red gums. Given the extent to which Melbourne's landscape has been remade, it is surely something of a miracle that such stupendous living connections with the Yarra world of 1835 have survived. There are two especially beautiful specimens in the Botanic Gardens around the lower lagoon, once part of the reserve in which the Kulin took early refuge before being expelled into less valuable swamps. The open grassland beneath one of these trees also became a meeting ground of early Britons, and it was even given a name, the 'Separation Tree,' in honour of the spontaneous party that occurred there in 1850 on the news that Victoria was to become a separate colony from New South Wales. A number of other pre-settlement river red gums survive along the Yarra and one even stands guard at the entrance to the sacred turf of the Melbourne Cricket Ground.

These trees have become a living symbol to me. I return to them often in my imagination because their roots, endurance, graceful hospitality, silent majesty and very survival seem to testify that perhaps rational choice and decent public policy do not provide our only source of hope to survive the challenges of the *next* 175 years. As the imperial elms and their human guardians shrivel in the heat (and may we both be saved), the river red gums stand as a reminder that perhaps the Colonial Office gentlemen were right in one respect at least: there is some force greater than us.

Acknowledgments

One day I would like to write a book with my publisher, Chris Feik. Only his name on the cover will ensure he receives the recognition he deserves. His contribution to *1835*, as to my previous book, *Van Diemen's Land*, has been immense. Nor can I imagine a more appropriate patron for a book on the founding of Melbourne than Morry Schwartz. In founding Black Inc., Morry has created a Melbourne institution in the noblest traditions of this spirited city. John Fawkner once edited and printed the *Patriot* from a room in his pub in Flinders Lane. I can well imagine, if freedom demanded it, Morry and the Black Inc. team doing the same. I thank all the talented collective for their vital work in creating this book: Sophy Williams, Caitlin Yates, Thomas Deverall, Elisabeth Young, Nina Kenwood, Nikola Lusk, Elke Power, Duncan Blachford, Phoebe Wynne, Kate Goldsworthy and the brilliant wordsmith Denise O'Dea.

Writing this book was more of a solitary venture than was perhaps wise, but I have drawn guidance and strength from the advice and work of many people, including John Hirst, Inga Clendinnen, Robert Manne, Pete Hay, Hamish Maxwell-Stewart, Bain Attwood, Peter Ryan, Grant Finlay, David Treanor, Penny Edman, Don Pitcher, Margaret Boyce, Catherine Campbell and Remo Di Benedetto. The staff of the School of Geography and Environmental Studies at the University of Tasmania, especially Elaine Stratford, Paulene Harrowby, Tracy Payne, Patricia McKay, Aidan Davidson, Stewart Williams, Darren Turner, Jim Russell and Andrew Harwood, have provided indispensable support for their usually invisible honorary associate, without which I could not have sustained the privileged but marginal occupation of self-employed writer. I am also grateful to the invariably friendly and helpful library staff of the university. The owners and staff of Hobart's wonderful bookshops, especially Fullers, Hobart Bookshop and Dymocks, always made me feel as though I might become a real writer yet, and passionate distributors Debbie McGowan and Andrew Hopwood do an amazing job of getting books out there. I also owe much to my family, especially my parents, Peter and Lorinne Boyce, and my blessed own (and very beautiful) Emma, Clare and William.

I also want to acknowledge my friends from years of studying and working as a social worker in Melbourne, who have helped me maintain my personal connections with the city and who, through their decades of work in the front line, have kept me in touch with the reality of big town life, especially Julie Boffa and Ken McNamara, and my rarely seen but never forgotten friends from the Footscray Office of the then CSV, Sunshine Hostel and Brotherhood of St Laurence.

And from the State Library of Victoria I don't want to forget Tim Hogan, who despite it being going-home time still climbed the stairs for the pesky Tasmanian who wanted to find the separation tree!

Notes

Preface

1 Even though by the early 1830s squatters were breaking out of imperially imposed borders on every side, the recent influential theorising of Edward Gibbon Wakefield had seemed to strengthen the case for occupying 'empty' land in a systematic, regulated way. In 1829 Wakefield published two influential tracts, *A Sketch of a Proposal for Colonizing Australasia* and *A Letter from Sydney* (both were in fact, perhaps not inappropriately given his subject, written while Wakefield was an inmate of London's Newgate Gaol). The new colony of South Australia had been established on Wakefieldian principles by an Act of the British Parliament just a year before the squatter invasion of Port Phillip commenced.

2 Richard Broome, *Aboriginal Victorians: A History Since 1800* (Sydney: Allen and Unwin, 2005): 54. It was only the environmental barriers around the British outposts in Perth and Darwin, and the remoteness of the northern half of the continent, that delayed the squatting invasion extending to Australia's north, west and centre until the second half of the nineteenth century.

PART I.

Chapter 1

1 Tim Flannery (ed.), *The Birth of Melbourne* (Melbourne: Text Publishing, 2002): 1.

2 Rhys Jones, 'Fire-Stick Farming', *Australian Natural History* 16, 1969: 224–8. More recent research which challenges the claim that the Aborigines' use of fire had much long-term impact on the environment cannot explain the rapid change in pasturelands no longer subject to Aboriginal burns.

3 Flannery (ed.), *The Birth of Melbourne*: 7–8.

4 Gary Presland, *The Place for a Village: How Nature Has Shaped the City of Melbourne* (Melbourne: Museum Victoria, 2008): 84–5.

5   *Ibid.*: 84–8.
6   *Ibid.*: 91–2.
7   This change in the grasslands began with intensive grazing, and was completed by the introduction of improved pastures. In the early 1850s, one landholder reflected that after just a few years of farming 'many of our herbaceous plants began to disappear from the pasture land; the silk-grass began to show itself in the edge of the bush track, and in patches here and there on the hill. The patches have grown larger every year: herbaceous plants and grasses give way for the silk-grass and the little annuals, beneath which are annual peas, and die in our deep clay soil with few hot days in spring, and nothing returns to take their place until later in the winter following. The consequence is that the long deep-rooted grasses that held our strong clay hill together have died out; the ground is now exposed to the sun, and it has cracked in all directions, and the clay hills are slipping in all directions; also the sides of precipitous creeks – long slips, taking trees and all with them.' Thomas Francis Bride (ed.), *Letters from Victorian Pioneers* (Melbourne: Trustees of the Public Library, 1898): 168–9.
8   Presland, *The Place for a Village*: 138.
9   *Historical Records of Victoria (HRV)* 1: 65.
10 Presland, *The Place for a Village*: 168–72.
11 Geoffrey Blainey, *A History of Victoria* (Melbourne: Cambridge University Press, 2006; first published as *Our Side of the Country*, 1984): 12–13.
12 Batman Journal, 1 June 1835, in C.P. Billot, *John Batman: The Story of John Batman and the Founding of Melbourne* (Melbourne: Hyland House, 1979): 90–1.
13 Presland, *The Place for a Village*: 183–5.
14 *Ibid.*: 218–9.
15 The Aboriginal population at the time of the founding of Melbourne is not known and estimates vary widely. Richard Broome estimates the pre-contact population at about 60,000, but believes this was halved by a small-pox epidemic around 1790 and halved again in an 1830 epidemic, leading to a population of about 15,000 in 1835. Broome, *Aboriginal Victorians*: 9. In his most recent book, Gary Presland also gives a figure of 15,000 for the Port Phillip District as a whole at the time of first settlement. *First People: The Eastern Kulin of Melbourne, Port Phillip and Central Victoria* (Melbourne: Museum Victoria, 2010): 90. However, the population in 1835 might have been higher than this estimate, especially given the dearth of evidence for the 1830 epidemic (a question that I discuss in chapter 17 of this book). Indeed, the many recorded observations of healthy children and pregnant women suggest that the population might even have been recovering in the early 1830s.

16 Presland, *First People*: 12–16 (Presland refers to these five language groups as the Eastern Kulin). Historically there have been many different spellings used for the different groups of Aborigines who visited the Melbourne region. In 1996, Ian D. Clark, in conjunction with the Victorian Aboriginal Corporation for Languages, sought to make modern spelling reflect pre-colonisation pronunciation. Clark's recommendations are employed in this book except for quotes, when the original is retained. Ian D. Clark, 'Aboriginal Language Areas in Victoria: A Report for the Victorian Aboriginal Corporation for Languages' (Melbourne: Victorian Aboriginal Corporation for Languages, 1996).

CHAPTER 2

17 This chapter draws on my previous book: James Boyce, *Van Diemen's Land* (Melbourne: Black Inc., 2008).

18 J.M. Tuckey, *General Observations of Port Phillip*, 26 October 1803, Mitchell Library (ML) Brabourne Papers CY 1747.

19 *Sydney Gazette*, 5 April 1817, cited in Stephen Murray-Smith, 'Beyond the Pale: The Islander Community of Bass Strait in the 19th Century,' *THRA Papers and Proceedings* 20/4 (1973): 170.

20 Ruth Gooch, *Seal Rocks and Victoria's Primitive Beginnings* (Hastings, Vic: Warrangine Word, 2008): 1–3.

21 *Historical Records of Australia (HRA)* 3/5: 827.

22 Will Lawson, *Blue Gum Clippers and Whale Ships of Tasmania*, facsimile edition (Melbourne: D&C Book Distributors, 1986): 23.

23 The sites where bay whaling occurred have been detailed in Michael Nash, *The Bay Whalers: Tasmania's Shore-Based Whaling Industry* (Canberra: Navarine Publishing, 2003).

24 *Ibid.*: 93.

25 Gooch, *Seal Rocks and Victoria's Primitive Beginnings*: 8–11.

26 Keryn James, 'Wife or Slave: Australian Sealing Slavery', in Anne Chittleborough, Gillian Dooley and Rick Hosking Rick (eds), *Alas, for the Pelicans! Flinders, Baudin and Beyond: Essays and Poems* (Sydney: Wakefield Press, 2002): 175–6.

27 Lynnette Peel (ed.), *The Henty Journals: A Record of Farming, Whaling and Shipping at Portland Bay, 1834–1839* (Melbourne: The Miegunyah Press, 1996): 46.

28 *Ibid.*: 371.

29 N.J.B. Plomley, *Friendly Mission: The Tasmanian Journals of George Augustus Robinson* (Launceston: Queen Victoria Museum and Quintus Publishing, 2008): 249.

30 Wedge to Colonial Secretary, Van Diemen's Land, 8 October 1836, *HRV*

2A: 52.

31 Wedge to Montagu, 15 March 1836, *HRV 1*: 34–5.

32 George Stewart to Colonial Secretary, 10 June 1836, *HRV 1*: 39–43.

33 Peel (ed.), *The Henty Journals*: 125.

34 On 30 December 1830 Robinson recorded meeting Edward Tomlin, a 'half-caste young man', the son of 'Bullrub'. On 28 December 1832, he met 'the sealers Kelly and Tomlins' at the Lovely Banks Inn on his way to Launceston. Plomley, *Friendly Mission*: 336, 743.

35 It is uncertain whether or to what extent the Aboriginal population of this district was reduced by smallpox in the early 1830s. Whereas it is almost certain that the epidemic evident in some regions of south-eastern Australia at this time did not extend to Port Phillip Bay, it may have reached Portland Bay.

36 Peel (ed.), *The Henty Journals*: 39.

37 *Ibid.*: 89, 93–4, 105, 123, 163, 169, 176, 214, 252–3, 258.

38 Gary Presland (ed.), *Journals of G.A. Robinson May to August 1841*, Report of the Victorian Archeological Survey, 1980: 2–3.

39 *HRV 2A*: 176–90.

40 *Ibid.*

41 See Inga Clendinnen, *Dancing with Strangers* (Melbourne: Text Publishing, 2003).

CHAPTER 3

42 James Bellich, *Replenishing the Earth: The Settler Revolution and the Rise of the Anglo-World, 1783–1939* (Oxford: Oxford University Press, 2009): 267.

43 R. Torrens, *Colonization of South Australia* (London: Longman, Rees, Orme, Brown, Green and Longman, 1835; facsimile edition, Public Library of South Australia, 1962): 222–3.

44 Charles Darwin, *The Voyage of the Beagle* (London: J.M. Dent, 1961): 430.

45 Arthur to Glenelg, 21 October 1835, Archives Office of Tasmania (AOT) CO 280/68.

46 Arthur to Rice, 14 May 1835, AOT CO 280/57.

47 Arthur to Rice, 14 May 1835, AOT CO 280/57.

48 Arthur to Stanley, 14 May 1834, AOT CO 280/47.

49 Gordon Forth, 'The Hentys, Whales and Sheep,' *Royal Historical Society of Victoria Journal* 55/4), December 1984: 1–9. Arthur to Hay, 18 April 1834, AOT CO 280/47.

50 *HRV 2A*: 6–7.

51 Arthur to Goderich, 7 January 1832, AOT CO280/33.

52 Arthur to Hay, 24 September 1832, AOT CO280/35, my emphasis.

53 Arthur to Goderich, 10 January 1828, *HRA* 3/7: 26–9.

54 *HRV* 2A: 6–7, 12. Arthur to Rice, 10 March 1835, AOT CO280/56. A nascent version of this proposal was first put in a dispatch of September 1832.

55 Only a select group of Aborigines, including Truganini, were allowed to accompany Robinson from Flinders Island. It is noteworthy that Robinson took with him all the surviving Aborigines with whom he had negotiated the original agreement. Two of the men became the first people hanged at Port Phillip after they resumed armed resistance.

56 Letter to Secretary of State of the Colonies from certain settlers of Launceston, August 1834, AOT CO280/59.

57 Alfred Stephen to Colonial Secretary Burnett, 3 November 1834, State Library of Victoria (SLV) M5082 Box 52/2 (3).

CHAPTER 4

58 Arthur didn't provide the New South Wales government with any information on the Hentys' move across Bass Strait until October 1836. Arthur to Bourke, 6 October 1836, *HRV* 1: 60–1.

59 Richard Waterhouse, *The Vision Splendid: A Social and Cultural History of Rural Australia* (Fremantle, WA: Curtin University Books, 2005): 19–20.

60 *Ibid.*: 19–21.

61 Alan Atkinson, *The Europeans in Australia: A History, Vol. Two: Democracy* (Melbourne: Oxford University Press, 2004): 92.

62 *Ibid.*: 94.

63 Elizabeth Elbourne, *Blood Ground: Colonialism, Missions and the Contest for Christianity in the Cape Colony and Britain, 1799–1853* (Montreal: McGill-Queens Press, 2002): 255.

64 Richard Elphick and Hermann Giliomee, *The Shaping of South African Society, 1652–1840* (Middletown, CT: Wesleyan University Press, 1989): 494–5, 497–8.

65 C.M.H. Clark (ed.), *Select Documents in Australian History 1788–1850* (Sydney: Angus and Robertson, 1950): 226–7.

66 Rex Harcourt, *Southern Invasion Northern Conquest: Story of the Founding of Melbourne* (Melbourne: Golden Point Press, 2001): 180–1.

CHAPTER 5

67 J.F.C. Harrison, *The Early Victorians, 1832–1851* (London: Weidenfeld and Nicolson, 1971): 151.

68 Geoffrey Finlayson, *England in the Eighteen Thirties: Decade of Reform* (London: Edward Arnold, 1978): 19–21.

69 Alan Lester, 'British Settler Discourse and the Circuits of Empire', *History Workshop Journal* 54 (2002): 24–48, 24.

70   To take one example, perhaps the best known of the politically influential evangelicals of this era, James Stephen, drew on a broad theological and intellectual tradition as seen in his regular essays in the *Edinburgh Review*. Stephen was also engulfed in a post-retirement controversy related to his doubts about eternal damnation.

71   Derek Whitelock, *Adelaide, 1836–1976: A History of Difference* (St Lucia: University of Queensland Press, 1977): 3.

72   Robert Kenny, *The Lamb Enters the Dreaming: Nathanael Pepper and the Ruptured World* (Melbourne: Scribe, 2007): 72–3.

73   Elizabeth Elbourne, 'Indigenous Peoples and Imperial Networks in the Early Nineteenth Century: The Politics of Knowledge,' in Phillip Buckner and R. Douglas Francis (eds), *Rediscovering the British World* (Calgary: University of Calgary Press, 2005): 79–80.

74   *Report of the Parliamentary Select Committee on Aboriginal Tribes (British Settlements): Reprinted with Comments by the 'Aborigines Protection Society'* (London: 1837): 104.

75   Elbourne, 'Indigenous Peoples and Imperial Networks in the Early Nineteenth Century': 80.

76   Atkinson, *The Europeans in Australia: A History, Volume Two*: 161–2.

77   Robert D. Grant, *Representations of British Emigration, Colonisation and Settlement: Imagining Empire, 1800–1860* (London: Palgrave Macmillan, 2005): 90–4. Elizabeth Elbourne, 'Between Van Diemen's Land and the Cape Colony,' in Anna Johnston and Mitchell Rolls (eds), *Reading Robinson: Companion Essays to Friendly Mission* (Hobart: Quintus Publishing, 2008): 90–1.

78   A.G.L. Shaw, 'James Stephen,' *Oxford Dictionary of National Biography*, www.oxforddnb.com.

79   Elphick and Giliomee, *The Shaping of South African Society, 1652–1840*: 49–50.

80   Anna Johnston, *Missionary Writing and Empire, 1800–1860* (Cambridge: Cambridge University Press, 2003): 167.

81   'An Act to empower His Majesty to erect South Australia into a British province or Provinces, and to provide for the Colonization and Government thereof', 15 August 1834 in *Clark, Select Documents*: 204–8. It should be noted that there was considerably more debate on the Bill than is recorded in *Hansard*, which was at the time a private venture that did not provide a complete record. The parliamentary progress and intent of the Bill is considered by P.A. Howell, 'The South Australia Act, 1834', in Dean Jaensch (ed.), *The Flinders History of South Australia: Political History* (Adelaide: Wakefield Press, 1986): 26–52.

82   Torrens, *Colonization of South Australia*: ix, 4–9, 175. The proposal drew

on the theories of colonisation proposed by Edward Gibbon Wakefield, which relied on the sale of land to fund immigration.

83 Henry Reynolds, *Dispossession: Black Australians and White Invaders* (Sydney: Allen and Unwin, 1989): 78–9.

84 *Ibid.*: 3–5.

PART II.

CHAPTER 6

1 A legend was put into print by Thomas McCombie in 1858 and a decade later by Batman's biographer, James Bonwick, that Batman senior had come to Australia as a missionary. Even when Bonwick corrected his mistake in the second edition, he still made no mention of William Batman being a convict. Thomas McCombie, *The History of the Colony of Victoria from Its Settlement to the Death of Sir Charles Hotham* (London: Chapman and Hall, 1858): 22; James Bonwick, *John Batman: The Founder of Victoria* (Melbourne: Wren Publishing, 1973; first published 1867): ix.

2 Alastair H. Campbell, *John Batman and the Aborigines* (Malmsbury, Victoria: Kibble Books, 1987): 7–13.

3 Batman to Anstey, 7 September 1829, AOT, CSO1/320/7578, cited in Campbell, *John Batman and the Aborigines*: 31–2.

4 Campbell, *John Batman and the Aborigines*: 64.

5 Thomas Henty to William Humphrey, 17 August 1833, Henty Papers, SLV MSB 450. Henty's geographical reference point was Portland Bay, which he would settle the following year.

6 Bonwick, *John Batman*: 58.

7 Campbell, *John Batman and the Aborigines*: 114–5.

8 *Ibid.*: 62.

9 The group of men who were to become the Port Phillip Association sometimes employed other names for their group even though they broadly retained the same objectives and membership. To avoid unnecessary confusion, I consistently use the name that was eventually to become the accepted one.

10 Billot, *John Batman*: 177–8.

11 Arthur wrote in 1838 that Montagu had invested £3500 of his money 'in a speculation at Port Phillip.' The same year Wedge wrote that Arthur 'is now I believe a member of the association, Captain Montagu, his nephew, jointly with Captain Swanston, having purchased *all* the interests of the late Mr Gellibrand, and it is imagined that Sir George has a share – at all events he has purchased largely of sheep at Port Phillip.' Wedge to Mercer, 2 July 1838, George Mercer Papers, SLV MS 13166.

12 A.G.L. Shaw, *Sir George Arthur, Bart, 1784–1854: Superintendent of British Honduras, Lieutenant-Governor of Van Diemen's Land and of Upper Canada, Governor of the Bombay Presidency* (Melbourne: Melbourne University Press, 1980): 218–9; A.G.L. Shaw, 'Arthur, Sir George Arthur (1784–1854),' *Australian Dictionary of Biography, Volume 1* (Melbourne: Melbourne University Press, 1966): 32–8.

13 Bain Attwood, *Possession: Batman's Treaty and the Matter of History* (Melbourne: Miegunyah Press, 2009): 36–7.

14 This story was told to James Bonwick by George Evans, a member of the first Fawkner expedition, who claimed to have been present when it occurred. Bonwick, *John Batman*: 68.

15 A.G.L. Shaw, *A History of the Port Phillip District: Victoria Before Separation* (Melbourne: Miegunyah Press, 1996): 49.

CHAPTER 7

16 Diane Barwick, 'Mapping the Past: An Atlas of Victorian Clans 1835–1904,' *Aboriginal History* 8.2 (1984): 122.

17 There were nominally two treaties in circulation, one covering the Melbourne region and the other the Geelong region. However, even Batman, the Port Phillip Association and the colonial and imperial governments usually talked of 'the treaty' and treated the two documents as one in their analysis and advocacy, a practice which I continue for reasons of clarity and consistency.

18 Attwood, *Possession*: 33.

19 Richard H. Bartlett, *Native Title in Australia* (Sydney: Butterworths, 2000): 3.

20 Campbell, *John Batman and the Aborigines*: 110–111. See Lisa Ford, 'Before Settler Sovereignty and After Aboriginal Sovereignty: New South Wales in Global Settler Perspective 1788–1836,' in Bain Attwood and Tom Griffiths (eds), *Frontier, Race, Nation: Henry Reynolds and Australian History* (Melbourne: Australian Scholarly Publishing, 2009): 185–209.

21 Alfred Stephen to Colonial Secretary Burnett, 3 November 1834, SLV M5082 Box 52/2 (3).

22 Campbell, *John Batman and the Aborigines*: 174.

23 SLV MS 10258.

24 Batman to Arthur, 25 June 1835, AOT CSO 1/809/2, file 17296.

25 Samuel Crook, *An Account of the Settlement at Sullivan Bay, Port Phillip 1803*, cited in Marjorie Tipping, *Convicts Unbound: The Story of the Calcutta Convicts and Their Settlement in Australia* (Ringwood, Victoria: Viking O'Neill, 1988): 98.

26 Plomley (ed.), *Friendly Mission*: 394. The Aborigines were told that their

removal to Flinders Island would be temporary. For more information on this agreement see Boyce, *Van Diemen's Land*: 261–315.

27 Campbell, *John Batman and the Aborigines*: 30.

28 Billot, *John Batman*: 105–6.

29 AOT CON 31-1-15 (Conduct record). James Gumm arrived on the *Arab* in 1822 with a fourteen-year sentence.

30 Billot, *John Batman*: 90–9.

31 *Ibid.*: 115.

32 J.M. Tuckey, *General Observations of Port Phillip*, 26 October 1803, Mitchell Library (ML) Brabourne Papers CY 1747.

33 Campbell, *John Batman and the Aborigines*: 88–9.

34 *HRV* 2A: 176–90.

35 Kenny, *The Lamb Enters the Dreaming*: 70. Kenny suggests that the Aborigines only knew of the impact of white settlement through 'stories that came down the trade routes' from Port Jackson.

36 Batman Journal, 31 May 1835.

37 Richard Broome, 'Victoria,' in Ann McGrath (ed.), *Contested Ground: Australian Aborigines under the British Crown* (Sydney: Allen and Unwin, 1995): 126.

38 Diane Barwick, *Rebellion at Coranderrk* (Canberra: Aboriginal History Monograph 5, 1998): 23–4.

39 Bride (ed.), *Letters from Victorian Pioneers*: 97–8.

40 Attwood, *Possession*: 56.

41 See for example the Diary of Charles Tyers, 2 and 4 November 1839, *HRV* 6: 348. Rolf Boldrewood claims that when he took up his run the local Aborigines 'sent a herald in advance, who held up a green bough.' Rolf Boldrewood, *Old Melbourne Memories* (New York: Macmillan, 1899): 50.

42 Batman Journal, 7–9 June 1835.

43 *Cornwall Chronicle*, 13 June 1835.

44 William Todd Journal, SLV MS 11243, reproduced in *The Todd Journal* (Geelong: Geelong Historical Society, 1989).

45 *Ibid.*

46 J.H. Wedge, 'Narrative of an Excursion Amongst the Natives of Port Phillip in the South Coast of New Holland August 1835,' AOT.

47 Wedge to Montagu, Bearport, Port Phillip, 15 March 1836, *HRV* 1: 34–5.

48 Jan Kociumbas, 'Genocide and Modernity in Colonial Australia, 1788–1850,' in A. Dirk Moses (ed.), *Genocide and Settler Society: Frontier Violence and Stolen Indigenous Children in Australian History* (Oxford: Berghahn Books, 2005): 93–4.

49 Port Phillip Papers, SLV MS 9142.

50 Wedge to Van Diemen's Land Colonial Secretary, 24 Nov 1836, *HRV* 6: 53–4.
51 *HRV 2A*: 161–7.
52 Colonial Secretary to William Lonsdale, 13 September 1836, *HRV 2A*: 192.
53 Holden to Lonsdale, 25 March 1837, *HRV 2A*: 194.
54 Fyans to Colonial Secretary, 24 May 1838, *HRV 2A*: 198–9.
55 Fyans to Colonial Secretary, 7 March 1839, *HRV 2A*: 199.
56 Governor's minute, 1 April 1839, *HRV 2A*: 199.
57 Wedge to Mercer, 2 July 1838, George Mercer Papers SLV MS 13166.

Chapter 8

58 John J. Shillinglaw, *Historical Records of Port Phillip* (Melbourne: Government Printer, 1879): 29.
59 Campbell, *John Batman and the Aborigines*: 124–5.
60 Margaret Wiedenhofer, *Garryowen's Melbourne: A Selection from the Chronicles of Early Melbourne, 1835 to 1852* (Melbourne: Nelson, 1967): 6.
61 Wedge to Simpson, 9 and 11 August 1835, SLV MS 1436.
62 *Ibid.*
63 Campbell, *John Batman and the Aborigines*: 130–1.
64 Billot, *John Batman*: 162–5.
65 C.P. Billot (ed.), *Melbourne's Missing Chronicle: Being the Journal of Preparations for Departure to and Proceedings at Port Phillip by John Pascoe Fawkner* (Melbourne: Quartet Books, 1982). Fawkner's first plantings included a row of 'pink eye' potatoes which he said had come from New Zealand. This provides some evidence that southern Tasmania's most famous spud might have been bred from those across the Tasman, where the Maoris cultivated a similar variety. There was considerable trade and contact between New Zealand and Van Diemen's Land before British settlement, including but not confined to sealing and whaling. A Maori chief even spent some months in Hobart Town in the early 1820s.
66 Batman to Montagu 30 November 1835, *HRV 1*: 20–1.
67 The spelling of Derrimut's name in Fawkner's journal changes almost by the day.
68 Billot, *Melbourne's Missing Chronicle*: 10–12.
69 C.P. Billot, *The Life and Times of John Pascoe Fawkner* (Melbourne: Hyland House, 1985): 115–16.
70 *Ibid.*: 21.
71 Richard Broome, *Aboriginal Victorians: A History Since 1800* (Sydney: Allen and Unwin, 2005): 12–13.
72 Shirley W. Wiencke, *When the Wattles Bloom Again: The Life and Times of William Barak* (self-published, 1984): 3.

PART III.

CHAPTER 9

1 Letter to the *Argus* from John Fawkner, reproduced in the *Launceston Examiner*, 31 August 1865, reprinted in *Tasmanian Ancestry*, December 1996: 17, 3, 180.

2 Batman to Colonial Secretary of Van Diemen's Land, 30 November 1835, *HRV* 1: 20–1.

3 *HRV* 1: 41.

4 In the original copy of the minutes of the public meeting held during Stewart's visit that was sent to Hobart Town, Bearbrass has a line through it. Thomson to Colonial Secretary of Van Diemen's Land, 2 June 1836, AOT CSO 1 809/2, file 17296.

5 *HRV* 1: 41. The geographic dispersal of the European population was confirmed by the November 1836 census when runs were recorded in a radius extending fifty miles north and west from Melbourne. Census, 9 November 1836, *HRV* 3: 422–7.

6 Fawkner Journal, 29 June and 1 July, in Billot (ed.), *Melbourne's Missing Chronicle*: 90–3. The settlers buried the baby in a new public burial ground in what is now part of Flagstaff Gardens.

7 Martin Sullivan, *Men and Women of Port Phillip* (Sydney: Hale and Iremonger, 1985): 13.

8 See Boyce, *Van Diemen's Land*, especially Parts I and II, for an extensive discussion of the process of environmental adaptation undertaken by the convicts and former convicts of Van Diemen's Land. Note that this immediate environmental *experience* was not a precursor of contemporary environmental *awareness*.

9 For more information on the impact of the dog in Van Diemen's Land see James Boyce, 'Canine Revolution: The Social and Environmental Impact of the Introduction of the Dog to Tasmania,' *Environmental History* 11.1 (January 2006): 102–29.

10 *HRV* 3, 422–7. Campbell, *John Batman and the Aborigines*: 187–9.

11 Gellibrand to Ball, 19 February 1836, SLV MS 10258.

12 Mrs Williams to her father, Mr Reid, 31 October 1836, in P.L. Brown (ed.), *Clyde Company Papers, Vol. II 1836–40* (Oxford: Oxford University Press, 1952): 35–6.

13 Fawkner Journal, 18 April 1836, in Billot (ed.), *Melbourne's Missing Chronicle*: 62–3.

14 Billot (ed.), *Melbourne's Missing Chronicle*: 94.

15 Atkinson, *The Europeans in Australia, Vol. 2*: 145–7; John Fawkner, 'Constitution and Form of Government,' SLV MS 13273.

16 Atkinson, *The Europeans in Australia, Vol. 2*: 71.

17 Batman Journal, 30 May 1835, in Billot, *John Batman*: 88–9.

18 James Grant and Geoffrey Serle, *The Melbourne Scene: 1803–1956* (Melbourne: Melbourne University Press, 1957): 23.

19 Billot (ed.), *Melbourne's Missing Chronicle*: 19–20.

20 Mrs William's Journal, 5 November 1836, in Brown (ed.), *Clyde Company Papers, Vol. II*: 32–3.

21 Ian D. Clark (ed.), *The Journals of George Augustus Robinson, Chief Protector, Port Phillip Aboriginal Protectorate, Volume 1: 1 January 1839–30 September 1840* (Melbourne: Heritage Matters, 1998): 97–8.

22 Billot (ed.), *Melbourne's Missing Chronicle*: 20.

23 Billot, *John Batman*: 90–3; Campbell, *John Batman and the Aborigines*: 87.

24 *The Todd Journal*: 25.

25 This is further suggested by the fact that such was the impact of the dog in Van Diemen's Land, by the mid-1830s the Forester kangaroo had become rare.

26 For example, James Willis blamed 'the enormous appetite of the natives' for the scarcity of wild animals. James Willis Diary, 4 May 1837, *HRV 6*: 191.

27 Letter to the *Argus* from John Fawkner, reproduced in the *Launceston Examiner*, 31 August 1865, reprinted in *Tasmanian Ancestry*, December 1996: 17, 3, 180.

28 Diary of James Willis, *HRV 6*: 182–201.

29 *Ibid.*: 191.

30 There were rare exceptions. Kelp, for instance, was widely eaten in the British Isles and thus provided a food that could be instantly recognised.

31 William Todd Journal, SLV MS 11243.

32 Marilyn Gray and John Knight (eds), *Flora of Melbourne: A Guide to the Indigenous Plants of the Greater Melbourne Area* (Melbourne: Hyland House, 2001): 141.

33 Mollison diary entry, 25 July 1837, in J.O. Randell (ed.), *Alexander Fullerton Mollison: An Overlanding Diary April–December 1837 from Uriara Station on the Murrumbidgee to Port Phillip Victoria* (Melbourne: Mast Gully Press, 1980): 27. In March 1837 Lonsdale reported that some of the convicts in government employ had come down with scurvy because of their reliance on salted provisions, and that because 'I find it impossible to procure vegetables … I have made some of the men gather a wild plant which is a good substitute.' Lonsdale to the Colonial Secretary, NSW, 11 March 1837, *HRV 3*: 246.

34 William Todd Journal, SLV MS 11243.

35 On 23 April 1836 Fawkner 'went out to look for splitting timber did not find much' and on 1 May 'George – Wm and Mackie went out to look for Stringy

bark – were out all day but found none fit to split'; Billot (ed.), *Melbourne's Missing Chronicle*: 64, 68.

36   *HRV 3*: 422–7 .

37   Grant and Serle, *The Melbourne Scene*: 25–6.

38   Charles Griffiths, *The Present State and Prospects of the Port Phillip District of New South Wales* (1845): 2. (Griffiths arrived in Melbourne in 1840.)

39   *HRV 2A*: 176–90.

CHAPTER 10

40   Clendinnen, *Dancing with Strangers*; Grace Karskens, *The Colony: A History of Early Sydney* (Sydney: Allen and Unwin, 2009).

41   Billot (ed.), *Melbourne's Missing Chronicle*: 12. On Monday 16 November 'Steiglitz, Cowie and Stead,' recently landed from Van Diemen's Land, 'took Mackie [Pigeon's brother] for a guide and 8 or 9 days provisions; Billot (ed.), *Melbourne's Missing Chronicle*: 15.

42   *Ibid.*: 23.

43   *Ibid.*: 48.

44   *Ibid.*: 27.

45   *Ibid.*: 70.

46   *HRV 2A*: 178.

47   Presland, *First People*: 37, 40.

48   *Ibid.*: 18.

49   Fawkner to Bourke 7 October 1836, *HRV 3*: 4–7.

50   Lonsdale to Colonial Secretary NSW, 5 February 1837, *HRV 3*: 7–10

51   Billot (ed.), *Melbourne's Missing Chronicle*: 61.

52   Orton to Wesleyan Missionary Society, London, August 1836, *HRV 2A*: 80–9.

53   Billot (ed.), *Melbourne's Missing Chronicle*: 48, 41.

54   Wedge to Mercer, 15 September 1838, George Mercer Papers, SLV MS 13166.

55   Batman to Montagu, 30 November 1835, *HRV 1*: 20–1.

56   Wedge to Montagu, Bearport, Port Phillip, 15 March 1836, *HRV 1*: 34–5.

CHAPTER 11

57   Campbell, *John Batman and the Aborigines*: 151–2; Harcourt, *Southern Invasion Northern Conquest*: 76.

58   Fawkner Journal, 28 March 1836, in Billot (ed.), *Melbourne's Missing Chronicle*: 53.

59   Wedge to Swanston, 23 July 1836, SLV M1447; *HRV 6*: 37–40.

60   Fawkner Journal, 10 July 1836, in Billot (ed.), *Melbourne's Missing Chronicle*: 94.

61 Campbell, *John Batman and the Aborigines*: 171.

62 James Bonwick, *The Wild White Man and the Blacks of Victoria* (Melbourne: Fergusson and Moore, 1863): 1. Buckley himself refused to speak to Bonwick.

63 Jeff Sparrow and Jill Sparrow, *Radical Melbourne* (Melbourne: The Vulgar Press, 2001): 18–19.

64 Wedge to Swanston, 23 July 1836, SLV M1447; *HRV 6*: 37–40.

65 John Montagu to the Colonial Secretary of New South Wales, 18 Aug 1836, *HRV 2A*: 41–2.

66 *HRV 2A*: 45–7.

67 William Lonsdale to the Colonial Secretary, NSW, 7 November 1836, *HRV 2A*: 50.

68 See for example the Police Court hearing into the murder of the Aborigine 'Curacoine,' which involved (among others) the notorious Frederick Taylor. Melbourne Court Register, 25 October 1836, *HRV 2A*: 55–61.

PART IV.

Chapter 12

1   Billot, *John Batman*: 105–6.

2   Arthur to Rice, 4 July 1835 (received 7 December 1835), AOT CO280/58.

3   *HRV 1*: 14–15.

4   *HRV 1*: 12–14.

5   Billot, *John Batman*: 160.

6   *HRV 1*: 19–20.

7   *Hobart Town Courier*, 30 October 1835. Arthur followed through with his public promise to call for a resident authority in a dispatch to Bourke on 14 November and to London in January 1836. Arthur to Hay, 28 January 1836, AOT CO280/64.

8   Bourke to Glenelg, 10 October 1835, *HRV 1*: 15–16.

9   *Ibid.*

10 Arthur to Bourke, 14 November 1835, AOT CO 280/64.

11 Arthur to Bourke, 20 May 1836, *HRV 1*: 26–9.

12 Bourke to Glenelg, 21 December 1835, *HRV 1*: 22–3.

13 William J. Lines, *Taming the Great South Land: A History of the Conquest of Nature in Australia* (Sydney: Allen and Unwin, 1991): 73.

14 J.T. Gellibrand to Joseph Ball, 4 March 1836, George Mercer Papers, SLV MS 13166.

15 Thomas Brenan to Colonial Secretary, 21 February 1836, *HRV 6*: 11–13.

16 The squatter George Armytage recalled that after his initial partner, Charles Franks, was killed by the Aborigines, his sheep were joined with

those of Judge Pedders. Bride (ed.), *Letters from Victorian Pioneers*: 138–41. In becoming a trespasser on crown land, Pedder was following the example of the Chief Justice of New South Wales, who told Governor Bourke in 1834 that he had stock depastured on the Liverpool Plains: 'I have a station there or in plain terms, I am a squatter in the District.' Hazel King, *Richard Bourke* (Melbourne: Oxford University Press, 1971): 180.

17 *New South Wales Government Gazette*, 18 May 1836, *HRV* 6: 38.

18 *HRV* 1: 38.

19 George Stewart to Colonial Secretary, 10 June 1836, *HRV* 1: 39–43.

20 *Ibid.*

21 This Act had 'obvious points of similarity' with the system Bourke had introduced in the Cape Colony. King, *Richard Bourke*: 182.

22 *HRV* 6: 26–8.

23 *HRV* 6: 28–9.

24 *New South Wales LC V&P*, 1836: 490.

25 P.P. King cited in Jan Kociumbas, *The Oxford History of Australia, Vol. 2, 1770–1860: Possessions* (Melbourne: Oxford University Press, 1992): 197.

26 McCombie, *History of the Colony of Victoria from Its Settlement to the Death of Sir Charles Hotham*: 127.

27 *New South Wales Government Gazette*, 5 October 1836, *HRV* 6: 29–31. My emphasis.

28 *Launceston Advertiser*, 10 March 1836, in Brown (ed.), *Clyde Company Papers, Vol. II*: 6–7.

Chapter 13

29 AOT CO 280/58.

30 Glenelg to Bourke, 13 April 1836, *HRV* 1: 24–6.

31 Henry Reynolds, *The Law of the Land*, 2nd edition (Melbourne: Penguin, 1992): 112–3.

32 Shaw, *Sir George Arthur Bart, 1784–1854*: 171–2.

33 This was done in the context of the request for the Aborigines of Van Diemen's Land to be transferred from Flinders Island to Port Phillip.

34 Joseph Ball to George Mercer, 18 June 1836, George Mercer Papers, SLV MS 13166.

35 AOT CO 280/58.

36 Glenelg to Bourke, 13 April 1836, *HRV* 1: 24–6.

37 James Stephen to Colonization Commissioners for South Australia, 27 October 1836, *HRV* 6: 36–9.

38 James Stephen, minute to Sir George Grey, 1 November 1838, *HRV* 2A: 346.

39 Glenelg to Bourke, 13 April 1836, *HRV* 1: 24–6.

40 Reynolds, *The Law of the Land*: 128–9.

41 Attwood, *Possession*: 86.

42 Lisa Ford, 'Before Settler Sovereignty and After Aboriginal Sovereignty: New South Wales in Global Settler Perspective 1788–1836,' in Attwood and Griffiths (eds), *Frontier, Race, Nation*: 185–209.

43 Joseph Ball to George Mercer, George Mercer Papers, 18 June 1836, SLV MS 13166.

44 Grey to Mercer, 14 April 1836, *HRV* 6: 110–11.

45 The House of Commons Select Committee on Aborigines (British Settlements) took evidence from 31 July 1835 to 19 May 1837 (with reports tabled in 1836 and 1837).

46 *Report of the Parliamentary Select Committee on Aboriginal Tribes (British Settlements).*

47 *Ibid.*: v.

48 *Ibid.*: 15.

49 *HRA* 3/9: 202–36.

50 Elizabeth Elbourne, 'Imperial Politics in the Family Way: Gender, Biography and the 1835–36 Select Committee on Aborigines,' in Attwood and Griffiths (eds), *Frontier, Race, Nation*: 111–35.

51 Reynolds, *The Law of the Land*: 99.

52 Arthur to Glenelg, 22 July 1837, *HRV* 2A: 24–7.

53 *Ibid.*

54 *Ibid.*

55 James Stephen, minute, 27 July 1837, *HRV* 2A: 27.

56 James Stephen to A.Y. Spearman, 30 August 1837, *HRV* 2A: 28–9.

57 Arthur to Glenelg, 15 Dec 1837, *HRV* 2A: 31–6.

58 J.M. Neeson, *Commoners: Common Right, Enclosure and Social Change in England 1700–1820* (Cambridge: Cambridge University Press, 1996): 1–2.

59 Bourke to Spring Rice, 11 March 1836, cited in King, *Richard Bourke*: 187.

60 Gipps to Glenelg, 6 April 1839, *HRV* 6: 261–3.

61 *Report of the Parliamentary Select Committee on Aboriginal Tribes (British Settlements).*

PART V.

Chapter 14

1 Colonial Secretary to Lonsdale, 14 September 1836, *HRV* 1: 49–54.

2 *HRV* 6: 132.

3 Arthur to Bourke, 6 October 1836, *HRV* 1: 60–1.

4 It should also be noted that while the spelling of Melbourne hasn't changed, as with Hobart and Launceston, the pronunciation has. In Melbourne's

case it used to be sounded as it was spelt. Bourke also named Williamstown, after the King who was to die a few months later. It is not clear what King William (no friend of Lord Melbourne or the Whigs), thought about having received the lesser honour.

5   Michel Foucault observed that most nineteenth-century town planning was based on the underlying principle of a military camp. Martin Sullivan, *Men and Women of Port Phillip*: 26.

6   Flannery, *The Birth of Melbourne*: 158.

7   Transcript from Bourke Papers, ML A1733, letter of 14 April 1837, cited in King, *Richard Bourke*: 189.

8   *HRV 3*: 101–17.

9   Sullivan, *Men and Women of Port Phillip*: 85.

10 Lonsdale became a director of the Union Bank in 1842, and the directors of the Port Phillip Bank included Alexander Thomson and Foster Fyans. *Kerrs Melbourne Almanac and Port Phillip Directory for 1842* (Melbourne: 1842).

11 H.F. Gisborne to his mother, 12 September 1839, *HRV 6*: 288–90.

12 *New South Wales Government Gazette*, 5 November 1836, *HRV 6*: 65–72.

13 Bourke to Glenelg, 15 November 1836, *HRV 6*: 72–3.

14 J.O. Randell (ed.), *Alexander Fullerton Mollison: An Overlanding Diary, April–December 1837 from Uriara Station on the Murrumbidgee to Port Phillip Victoria* (Melbourne: Mast Gully Press, 1980): xv–xviii.

15 *Ibid.*: 64.

16 J.M. Powell, *The Public Lands of Australia Felix* (Oxford: Oxford University Press, 1970): 12; *Hobart Town Courier*, 11 November 1838.

17 Broome, *Aboriginal Victorians*: xxiii.

18 *HRV 6*: 346–7, 373–4.

19 Broome, *Aboriginal Victorians*: 20.

20 Shaw, *A History of the Port Phillip District*, 89.

21 Richard Broome, 'Victoria,' in McGrath (ed.), *Contested Ground*: 129.

22 Gisborne to La Trobe, 29 December 1839, *HRV 6*: 298–303.

23 Bride (ed.), *Letters from Victorian Pioneers*: 5–7.

24 H.W. Haygarth, *Recollections of Bush Life in Australia* (London: J. Murray, 1850): 92.

25 John C. Weaver, 'Beyond the Fatal Shore: Pastoral Squatting and the Occupation of Australia 1826 to 1852,' *The American Historical Review*, 101.4 (October 1996): 981–1007, 993–4; Niel Black Diary, 29 February 1840, Niel Black Papers, SLV MS 6035.

26 Weaver, 'Beyond the Fatal Shore': 981–1007.

27 C.P. Hodgson, *Reminiscences of Australia* (London: W.N. Wright, 1846): 95.

28 Weaver, 'Beyond the Fatal Shore': 981–1007, 993–4; Niel Black Diary, 29 February 1840, Niel Black Papers, SLV MS 6035.

29 Powell, *The Public Lands of Australia Felix*: 18–19.

30 Weaver, 'Beyond the Fatal Shore': 996.

31 *Ibid.*: 1000.

32 J.B. Hirst, *The Strange Birth of Colonial Democracy: New South Wales 1848–1884* (Sydney: Allen and Unwin, 1988): 123–5.

33 Stephen Roberts, *The Squatting Age in Australia 1835–1847* (Melbourne: Melbourne University Press, 1964): 241.

34 Powell, *The Public Lands of Australia Felix*: 26–8.

35 W.C. Wentworth, *Sydney Morning Herald,* 10 April 1844, cited in Powell, *The Public Lands of Australia Felix*: 26.

36 Bride (ed.), *Letters from Victorian Pioneers*: 64.

37 Tony Dingle, *The Victorians: Settling* (Sydney: Fairfax, Syme and Weldon Associates, 1984): 31–2.

38 Sullivan, *Men and Women of Port Phillip*: 111.

39 Brown (ed.), *Clyde Company Papers*: 158–9, 107–8.

40 Foster Fyans to Latrobe, 18 February 1840, *HRV* 3: 402–3.

41 Glenelg to Bourke, 31 May 1837, *HRV* 6: 40–1.

42 Frank Broeze, 'Private Enterprise and the Peopling of Australasia 1831–50,' *The Economic History Review* 34.2 (May 1982): 235–53.

43 Wiedenhofer, *Garryowen's Melbourne: A Selection from the Chronicles of Early Melbourne*: 175.

44 Sullivan, *Men and Women of Port Phillip*: 112–14.

45 Grant and Serle, *The Melbourne Scene: 1803–1956*: 8.

46 McCombie, *The History of the Colony of Victoria*: 50–1.

47 Grant and Serle, *The Melbourne Scene*: 60.

48 McCombie, *The History of the Colony of Victoria*: 50–3.

49 Sullivan, *Men and Women of Port Phillip*: 28.

50 Flannery (ed.), *The Birth of Melbourne*: 351–2.

51 E.M. Curr, *Recollections of Squatting in Victoria* (Sydney: George Robertson, 1883; facsimile edition, State Library of South Australia, 1968): 3.

52 Census of 31 December 1839, *HRV* 3: 432; Flannery (ed.), *The Birth of Melbourne*: 96.

53 Curr, *Recollections of Squatting in Victoria*: 5.

54 Charles Griffiths, *The Present State and Prospects of the Port Phillip District of New South Wales* (Dublin: William Curry, Jun. and Company, 1845): 2, 5.

55 Bellich, *Replenishing the Earth*: 275–8.

56 Grant and Serle, *The Melbourne Scene*: 6–7.

57 *HRV* 6: 438.

58 Gipps to Lord John Russell, 30 June 1840, *HRV* 6: 433–4.

59 Dingle, *The Victorians: Settling*: 26–7.

CHAPTER 15

60 Orton to Wesleyan Missionary Society, *HRV* 2A: 99–101.

61 James Stephen lamented the departure of his 'intimate personal friend' whose 'real and only unfitness for public life arises from the strange incompatibility of his temper and principles with the rules of action to which we erect shrines in Downing Street.' James Stephen, letter, 12 February 1839, in C.E. Stephen and James Stephen, *The Life of the Right Honourable Sir James Stephen* (1903): 56.

62 *Report of the Aborigines Committee for the Meeting for Sufferings* (1840).

63 Mollison diary entry, 13 September 1837, in Randell (ed.), *Alexander Fullerton Mollison*: 42.

64 Lonsdale to Colonial Secretary, 11 May 1838, *HRV* 2A: 297–8.

65 Phillip G. King et al. to Gipps, 8 June 1838, *HRV* 2A: 349–51.

66 Colonial Secretary to King and other memorialists, 23 June 1838, *HRV* 6, 351–3.

67 *Ibid.*

68 The delay in publishing the protection regulations was to last for over a year. Gipps to Glenelg, 27 April 1838 and postscript of 2 May 1838, *HRV* 2A: 346–7.

69 Gipps to Glenelg, 27 April 1838, *HRV* 2A: 349.

70 Jan Critchett, *A 'Distant Field of Murder': Western District Frontier 1834–1848* (Melbourne: Melbourne University Press, 1990): 127.

71 Melbourne Court Register, 25 October 1836, *HRV* 2A: 55–61.

72 Rev. J. Orton Journal, ML A1715, cited in Critchett, *A 'Distant Field of Murder'*: 128–29.

73 Bride (ed.), *Letters from Victorian Pioneers*: 30.

74 Joan Austin Palmer (ed.), *William Moodie: A Pioneer of Western Victoria* (self published: Mortlake, Victoria, 1973): 72.

75 Clark (ed.), *The Journals of George Augustus Robinson, Vol. 1*: 132.

76 Mollison diary entry, 24 October 1837, in Randell (ed.), *Alexander Fullerton Mollison*: 53.

77 Critchett, *A 'Distant Field of Murder'*: 123.

78 C. Wedge to J.H. Wedge, 13 November 1839, British Parliamentary Papers 1844: 121–2; Critchett, *A 'Distant Field of Murder'*: 124.

79 Critchett, *A 'Distant Field of Murder'*: 137.

80 C.J. Tyers, 'Diary of trip from Geelong to Portland from October 1839 to 1840 surveying the far west of Port Phillip,' journal entry, 19 February 1840, *HRV* 6: 365.

81 Rolf Boldrewood, *Old Melbourne Memories* (New York: Macmillan, 1899): 45, 58, 66–9, 85–7.

82 Thomas Francis Bride (ed.), *Letters from Victorian Pioneers*: 33.

83 James Dawson, who had a distinguished record of courageous advocacy on behalf of Aboriginal people, took over an established run in the western districts in 1844. For an account of Dawson's work see Raymond Madden, 'James Dawson's Scrapbook: Advocacy and Antipathy in Colonial Victoria,' in Lynette Russell and John Arnold (eds), *The La Trobe Journal* 85 (May 2010): *Indigenous Victorians: Repressed, Resourceful and Respected*: 55–70.

84 *Ibid.*: 217–19.

85 Mollison diary entry, 13 September 1837, Randell (ed.), *Alexander Fullerton Mollison*: 55.

86 C.J. Tyers diary, 2 November 1839, *HRV* 6: 346–7.

87 Critchett, *A 'Distant Field of Murder'*: 66–7. James Dawson believed that the 'mounds' that dotted the landscape of western Victoria were in fact 'the debris of old residences which served as the winter home of individual families'. Madden, 'James Dawson's Scrapbook': 59–60.

88 Clark (ed.), *The Journals of George Augustus Robinson*: 132.

89 *Ibid.*, 122.

90 *Port Phillip Gazette*, 4 December 1841, cited in Henry Reynolds, *This Whispering in Our Hearts* (Sydney: Allen and Unwin, 1998): 52.

91 McCombie, *The History of the Colony of Victoria*: 89.

92 Critchett, *A Distant Field of Murder*, 129–130, 132; Mary McKinlay, *Forgotten Tasmanians* (Launceston: Foot and Playsted, 2010): 130–134. I am indebted to Mrs McKinlay for alerting me to the fact that I mistakenly attributed this incident to George Stoker in the first edition of this book. *Forgotten Tasmanians* provides further details of the court proceedings which McKinlay argues were 'fair and honest.'

93 *Kerrs Melbourne Almanac and Port Phillip Directory for 1842*. In his dispute with the squatters, Governor Grey also made the point that the revenue from pastoral licences in New South Wales was not sufficient even to cover the expenses of the border police.

94 Critchett, *A 'Distant Field of Murder'*: 23.

95 Bride (ed.), *Letters from Victorian Pioneers*: 150–4.

96 Melbourne Court Register, 14 April 1838, *HRV* 2A: 314.

97 Kenny, *The Lamb Enters the Dreaming*: 38–9.

98 Blainey, *A History of Victoria*: 16–7, 30–1.

99 Henry Gyles Turner, *A History of the Colony of Victoria: From Its Discovery to Its Absorption into the Commonwealth of Australia in Two Volumes, vol. 1. A.D 1797–1854* (Melbourne: Heritage Publications, 1973; first published

1904): 238–9. This history has a chapter devoted to the relations with the Aborigines.

100 Turner, *A History of the Colony of Victoria*: 235, my emphasis.

101 Rolf Boldrewood, 'The Truth About Aboriginal Outrages,' *Life*, 6 June 1903, cited in J.J. Healy, *Literature and the Aborigine in Australia 1770–1975* (St Lucia: University of Queensland Press, 1978): 55.

102 Bride (ed.), *Letters from Victorian Pioneers*: 150–4.

103 McCombie, *The History of the Colony of Victoria*: 89.

104 Tony Barta, '"They appear actually to vanish from the face of the earth": Aborigines and the European Project in Australia Felix,' *Journal of Genocide Research* 10.4 (2008): 528.

105 Critchett, A *'Distant Field of Murder'*: 6.

106 Ian D. Clark, 'George Augustus Robinson on Charles Joseph La Trobe: Personal Insights into a Problematical Relationship', *The La Trobe Journal* 85 (May 2010): 18,

107 *Ibid.*: 15. For an informed discussion of the fraught and convenient emphasis placed by settlers on infanticide and associated cannibalism in Port Phillip as the Aboriginal population collapsed, see Marguerita Stephens, 'White Without Soap: Philanthropy Caste and Exclusion in Colonial Victoria 1835–1888: A Political Economy of Race,' PhD thesis, University of Melbourne, 2003: 61–104.

108 Reynolds, *The Law of the Land*: 146.

109 Clark, 'George Augustus Robinson on Charles Joseph La Trobe: 16–18, 21.

110 Colonial Secretary to Lonsdale, 21 May 1838, *HRV 2A*: 99.

111 Surveyor General, S.A. Perry, to Colonial Secretary, 1 August 1839, *HRV 2A*: 132–3.

112 Colonial Secretary to S.A. Perry, 25 September 1839, *HRV 2A*: 134.

113 Foster Fyans to La Trobe, 20 October 1839, *HRV 2A*: 136.

114 Critchett, A *'Distant Field of Murder'*: 143–8.

115 Robinson journal entry for 24 April 1840, Clark (ed.), *The Journals of George Augustus Robinson*: 230.

Chapter 16

116 In January 1845 Assistant Protector Thomas noted that across both these language groups there were no children under five.

117 Colonial Secretary to Lonsdale, 14 September 1836, *HRV 1*: 49–54.

118 Colonial Secretary to Langhorne, 9 December 1836 *HRV 2A*: 161–3.

119 *HRV 2A*: 176–90.

120 Langhorne to Colonial Secretary, 31 March 1839, *HRV 2A*: 236.

121 For an account of this incident see Langhorne to Colonial Secretary, 30 April 1838, *HRV 2A*: 213–15.

122 Langhorne to Colonial Secretary, 31 May 1838, *HRV 2A*: 220–2.

123 Colonial Secretary to Langhorne, 6 July 1838, *HRV 2A*: 227.

124 Robinson journal entry, 28 March 1839, in Clark (ed.), *The Journals of George Augustus Robinson*: 21–2. Shortly afterwards, in early April 1839, Robinson arranged for Derrimut, Billibellary and other Aboriginal elders to put on another performance, this time for Lady Jane Franklin, wife of the Lieutenant Governor of Van Diemen's Land, who noted in her journal that 'About eight or nine o'clock … went out to see a Coroberry of the natives who are encamped in the outskirts … consisting of the tribes usually frequenting this port and of several more distant ones ….' Flannery (ed.), *The Birth of Melbourne*: 96; Robinson journal entry, 4 April 1839, in Clark (ed.), *The Journals of George Augustus Robinson*: 24.

125 Robinson journal entry, 19 April 1839, in Clark (ed.), *The Journals of George Augustus Robinson*: 31.

126 Robinson journal entry, 4 May 1839, in Clark (ed.), *The Journals of George Augustus Robinson*: 39.

127 *Ibid.*

128 Broome, *Aboriginal Victorians*: 26.

129 Robinson journal entry, 20 December 1839, in Clark (ed.), *The Journals of George Augustus Robinson*: 109.

130 Flannery (ed.), *The Birth of Melbourne*: 10.

131 Where Merri Creek joins the Yarra, now Yarra Bend Park, was a traditional meeting place which the Aborigines continued to visit in the early 1840s. In late 1842 Thomas built a hut there, and a school, initially supported by Billibellary, was later established. See Ian Clark and Toby Heydon, *A Bend in the Yarra: A History of the Merri Creek Protectorate Station and Merri Creek Aboriginal School 1841–1851* (Canberra: Aboriginal Studies Press, 2004).

132 Curr, *Recollections of Squatting in Victoria*: 20.

133 Broome, *Aboriginal Victorians*: 19.

134 Stephens, 'White Without Soap': 43–47, 65–6.

135 *Ibid.*: 66.

136 Robinson arranged for the employment of some of the Sydney Aborigines after Batman's death, but the future of those founding fathers of Melbourne seems to have been as bleak as that of their local brethren. Stewart was reported by Robinson to have drowned in the Yarra, drunk, in 1839. Court records from 1837–38 show that the Sydney Aborigines were put in the stocks for drunkenness on numerous occasions. Two young Tasmanian Aboriginal boys were alive on Batman's death. John Allen or Lurnerminner was still in Melbourne in 1840 when he was blamed for the death of a horse and fled to Hobart, where his fate is unknown. Rolepana, who

was the child survivor of the 1829 massacre conducted by a roving party led by Batman, was employed by George Ware at £12 a year with board on Batman's death, but what became of him after this is also unknown. Campbell, *John Batman and the Aborigines*: 231.

137 See Ian D. Clark, '"You Have All This Place No Good Have Children ..." Derrimut: Traitor, Saviour or a Man of His People', *Journal of the Royal Australian Historical Society* 91.2 (December 2005).

138 See Bruce Pascoe, 'How It Starts,' in Rachel Perkins and Marcia Langton (eds), *First Australians* (Melbourne: Miegunyah Press, 2010): 77–111.

PART VI.

CHAPTER 17

1 Broome, *Aboriginal Victorians*: 91–2.

2 Mollison diary, 4 July 1837, in Randell (ed.), *Alexander Fullerton Mollison*: 17–18.

3 Bellich, *Replenishing the Earth*: 272.

4 Gisborne to La Trobe, 29 December 1839, *HRV 6*: 298–303.

5 Orton to WMS, 18 July 1839, *HRV 2A*: 127–9.

6 Bride (ed.), *Letters from Victorian Pioneers*: 3–5.

7 *Ibid.*, 141.

8 William Adeney Diary, SLV MS 8520 Box 991/5.

9 *Report of the Parliamentary Select Committee on Aboriginal Tribes (British Settlements*: 3–4.

10 Robinson journal entry, 21 April 1839, Clark (ed.), *The Journals of George Augustus Robinson*: 32.

11 Foster Fyans to Colonial Secretary, 13 February 1838, *HRV 2A*: 198.

12 Critchett, *A 'Distant Field of Murder'*: 67.

13 G. Melvyn Howe, *Man Environment and Disease in Britain: A Medical Geography of Britain through the Ages* (New York: Barnes and Noble Books, 1972): 180.

14 Robert Kenny, *The Lamb Enters the Dreaming*: 185–6.

15 Judy Campbell, *Invisible Invaders: Smallpox and Other Diseases in Aboriginal Australia, 1780–1880* (Melbourne: Melbourne University Press, 2002); N.G. Butlin, *Our Original Aggression: Aboriginal Populations of Southeastern Australia, 1788–1850* (Sydney: Allen and Unwin, 1983).

16 This was the situation even in more densely populated New Zealand. See James Bellich, *Making Peoples: A History of the New Zealanders from Polynesian Settlement to the end of the Nineteenth Century* (London: Allen Lane, 1996): 175–6.

17 In 1803 two officers (who were members of different expeditions), James

Fleming and James Tuckey, recorded seeing Aborigines whose faces were disfigured by pockmarks. Smallpox could have been transmitted by American or other European whalers who were not, like British residents of New South Wales, necessarily inoculated.

18 Broome, *Aboriginal Victorians*: 8–9.

19 One of the few who did record observing Aborigines with pockmarks, Dr David Thomas, noted that 'all of them were rather advanced in years,' which would seem further to suggest that there had *not* been a recent epidemic. Broome, *Aboriginal Victorians*: 8–9.

20 Billot, *John Batman*: 90–1.

21 Josephine Flood, *The Original Australians: Story of the Aboriginal People* (Sydney: Allen and Unwin, 2006): 94.

22 For a useful discussion of the role of the disease thesis in global history, see Pamela Kyle Crossley, *What Is Global History?* (Cambridge: Polity Press, 2008): 74.

23 Tony Barta has argued that government awareness of the inevitable consequences of Australian land settlement policy amounted to genocide on the basis that 'a conception of genocide less determined by *intent* and more alive to *intentions* as exhibited in the pursuit of *interests* serves historical understanding better … The power of these interests was well known to the British government, and they decided to follow them rather than contain them.' Tony Barta, '"They appear actually to vanish from the face of the earth"': 519–39, 533–4. Dirk Moses also emphasises that the government was aware of the consequences of its policies, but put the colonisation project first. Moses suggests that there were 'choices open to policy-makers, choices they were not prepared to entertain because they fundamentally approved of the civilising process in which they were engaged. The fact is that they did not take their own humanitarian convictions seriously enough to implement the radical measures necessary to prevent Indigenous deaths.' Dirk Moses, 'Genocide and Settler Society in Australian History' in Moses (ed.), *Genocide and Settler Society*: 29–30. Their analysis is morally and empirically persuasive and is not only relevant to the specific question of whether government policy amounted to 'genocide' as now defined in international law.

24 Wiedenhofer, *Garryowen's Melbourne*: 121.

25 Broome, *The Victorians*: 67.

26 Turner, *A History of the Colony of Victoria*: 232, 221.

27 We know Gumm was illiterate because he did not sign his name at the public meeting of 1 June 1836. Minutes of Public Meeting of 1 June 1836, *HRV* 1: 36–8; Robyn Annear, *Bearbrass: Imagining Early Melbourne* (Melbourne: Black Inc, 2005; first published 1995): 232.

CHAPTER 18

28 Gipps to Russell, 19 December 1840, C.M.H. Clark (ed.), *Select Documents in Australian History 1788–1850*: 227–8.

29 Brown (ed.), *Clyde Company Papers, Vol. II*: 3.

30 Lines, *Taming the Great South Land*: 84.

31 A.G.L. Shaw, *A History of the Port Phillip District: Victoria before Separation* (Melbourne: Melbourne University Press, 2003; first published 1996): 143.

32 William J. Lines, *Taming the Great South Land*: 70–1.

33 Henry Reynolds, *Why Weren't We Told? A Personal Search for the Truth about Our History* (Melbourne: Penguin, 2000): 120–1.

34 *Ibid.*: 208, my emphasis. Elsewhere Reynolds does ask the question 'could it have been different?' Reynolds, *The Law of the Land*: 160–1.

35 *HRV 1*: 15–16.

36 Stuart Macintyre and Sean Scalmer (eds), *What If? Australian History As It Might Have Been* (Melbourne: Melbourne University Press, 2006).

37 Bellich, *Replenishing the Earth*. John Weaver points out that policy, environment and culture 'conditioned how land seizures were undertaken.' American squatters, for example, were mostly smallholders. Weaver, 'Beyond the Fatal Shore': 981–1007.

38 The approach being touched on here is commonly called 'counterfactual' history, and involves the exploration of 'alternative past possibilities' while staying within the constraints of probability and evidence. See J.C.D. Clark, *Our Shadowed Present: Modernism, Postmodernism and History* (New York: Atlantic Books, 2003). Clark usefully points out that it is 'the erosion of supposed past certainties … that permits a path to be cleared to an *open* future.'

39 Henry Reynolds, 'George Augustus Robinson in Van Diemen's Land: Race, Status and Religion,' in Johnston and Rolls (eds), *Reading Robinson*: 166.

40 *Report of the Parliamentary Select Committee on Aboriginal Tribes (British Settlements)*: vii.

41 Nikolas Rose suggests that the conditions 'under which that we take for truth and reality has been established' (that is, our own culture's definition of what is realistic) frame 'the horizon of what is thinkable' not only of the past, but of the future. He suggests that counterfactual history opens 'the horizon of what is thinkable' both within the political world and general society by exposing these conditions. This is discussed in Beverley Southgate, *What Is History For?* (Oxford: Routledge, 2005): 123, 131.

42 In his 2009 essay *Quarry Vision* Guy Pearse not only presents the familiar case for keeping most of what is now Australia's most profitable natural

resource, coal, safely in the ground, but asks why it seems not only 'unlikely' but 'unthinkable' that this will occur. Pearse suggests that 'quarry vision,' our inability to *imagine* effective action being taken, is blinding governments and people from making a rational choice about the future of coal. Guy Pearse, *Quarterly Essay 33, Quarry Vision: Coal, Climate Change and the End of the Resources Boom* (Melbourne: Black Inc., 2009), my emphasis.

Epilogue

43 *HRA* 1/ XVIII: xxiii.

44 R.V. Billis and A.S. Kenyon, *Pastures New: An Account of the Pastoral Occupation of Port Phillip* (Melbourne: Stockland Press, 1974; first published 1930): 1–2.

45 This is the phrase Geoffrey Blainey memorably used to describe the gold rushes and subsequent mining history.

46 Anthony Trollope, *Australia and New Zealand* (London: Chapman and Hall, 1873): 281–2.

References

Books and theses

Annear, Robyn. *Bearbrass: Imagining Early Melbourne*. Melbourne: Black Inc., 2005; first published 1995.

Atkinson, Alan. *The Europeans in Australia: A History, Vol. Two: Democracy*. Melbourne: Oxford University Press, 2004.

Attwood, Bain. *Possession: Batman's Treaty and the Matter of History*. Melbourne: Miegunyah Press, 2009.

Bartlett, Richard H. *Native Title in Australia*. Sydney: Butterworths, 2000.

Barwick, Diane. *Rebellion at Coranderrk*. Canberra: Aboriginal History Monograph 5, 1998.

Bellich, James. *Making People: A History of New Zealanders from Polynesian Settlement to the End of the Nineteenth Century*. London: Allen Lane, 1996.

Bellich, James. *Replenishing the Earth: The Settler Revolution and the Rise of the Anglo-World, 1783–1939*. Oxford: Oxford University Press, 2009.

Billot, C.P. *John Batman: The Story of John Batman and the Founding of Melbourne*. Melbourne: Hyland House, 1979.

Billot, C.P. *The Life and Times of John Pascoe Fawkner*. Melbourne: Hyland House, 1985.

Blainey, Geoffrey. *A History of Victoria*. Melbourne: Cambridge University Press, 2006; first published as *Our Side of the Country*, 1984.

Boldrewood, Rolf. *Old Melbourne Memories*. New York: Macmillan, 1899.

Bonwick, James. *John Batman: The Founder of Victoria*. Melbourne: Wren Publishing, 1973; first published 1867.

Bonwick, James. *The Wild White Man and the Blacks of Victoria*. Melbourne: Fergusson and Moore, 1863.

Boyce, James. *Van Diemen's Land*. Melbourne: Black Inc., 2008.

Broome, Richard, *Aboriginal Victorians: A History Since 1800*. Sydney: Allen and Unwin, 2005.

Butlin, N.G. *Our Original Aggression: Aboriginal Populations of Southeastern Australia, 1788–1850*. Sydney: Allen and Unwin, 1983.

References

Campbell, Alastair H. *John Batman and the Aborigines*. Malmsbury, Victoria: Kibble Books, 1987.

Campbell, Judy. *Invisible Invaders: Smallpox and Other Diseases in Aboriginal Australia, 1780–1880*. Melbourne: Melbourne University Press, 2002.

Chittleborough, Anne, Dooley, Gillian and Hosking, Rick (eds). *Alas, for the Pelicans!: Flinders, Baudin and Beyond, Essays and Poems*. Sydney: Wakefield Press, 2002.

Clark, Ian D. *Aboriginal Language Areas in Victoria: A Report for the Victorian Aboriginal Corporation for Languages*. Melbourne: Victorian Aboriginal Corporation For Languages, 1996.

Clark, Ian and Heydon, Toby. *A Bend in the Yarra: A History of the Merri Creek Protectorate Station and Merri Creek Aboriginal School 1841–1851*. Canberra: Aboriginal Studies Press, 2004.

Clark, J.C.D. *Our Shadowed Present: Modernism, Postmodernism and History*. New York: Atlantic Books, 2003.

Clendinnen, Inga. *Dancing with Strangers*. Melbourne: Text Publishing, 2003.

Critchett, Jan. *A 'Distant Field of Murder': Western District Frontier, 1834–1848*. Melbourne: Melbourne University Press, 1990.

Crossley, Pamela Kyle. *What is Global History?* Cambridge: Polity Press, 2008.

Curr, E.M. *Recollections of Squatting in Victoria*. Sydney: George Robertson, 1883; facsimile edition, State Library of South Australia, 1968.

Darwin, Charles. *The Voyage of the Beagle*. London: J.M.Dent, 1961; first published 1839.

Dingle, Tony. *The Victorians: Settling*. Sydney: Fairfax, Syme and Weldon Associates, 1984.

Elbourne, Elizabeth. *Blood Ground: Colonialism, Missions and the Contest for Christianity in the Cape Colony and Britain, 1799–1853*. Montreal: McGill-Queens Press, 2002.

Elphick, Richard and Giliomee, Hermann. *The Shaping of South African Society, 1652–1840*. Middletown, CT: Wesleyan University Press, 1989.

Fels, Marie. *Good Men and True: The Aboriginal Police of the Port Phillip District, 1837–53*. Melbourne: Melbourne University Press, 1988.

Finlayson, Geoffrey. *England in the Eighteen Thirties: Decade of Reform*. London: Edward Arnold, 1978.

Flannery, Tim (ed.). *The Birth of Melbourne*. Melbourne: Text Publishing, 2002.

Flood, Josephine. *The Original Australians*. Sydney: Allen and Unwin, 2006.

Gooch, Ruth. *Seal Rocks and Victoria's Primitive Beginnings*. Hastings, Vic: Warrangine Word, 2008.

Grant, James and Serle, Geoffrey. *The Melbourne Scene: 1803–1956*. Melbourne: Melbourne University Press, 1957.

Grant, Robert D. *Representations of British Emigration, Colonisation and Settlement: Imagining Empire, 1800–1860.* London: Palgrave Macmillan, 2005.

Gray, Marilyn and Knight, John (eds). *Flora of Melbourne: A Guide to the Indigenous Plants of the Greater Melbourne Area.* Melbourne: Hyland House, 2001.

Griffiths, Charles. *The Present State and Prospects of the Port Phillip District of New South Wales.* 1845.

Harcourt, Rex. *Southern Invasion Northern Conquest: Story of the Founding of Melbourne.* Melbourne: Golden Point Press, 2001.

Harrison, J.F.C. *The Early Victorians, 1832–1851.* London: Weidenfeld and Nicolson, 1971.

Haygarth, H.W. *Recollections of Bush Life in Australia.* London: J. Murray, 1850.

Healy, J.J. *Literature and the Aborigine in Australia, 1770–1975.* St Lucia: University of Queensland Press, 1978.

Hirst, J.B. *The Strange Birth of Colonial Democracy: New South Wales 1848–1884.* Sydney: Allen and Unwin, 1988.

Hodgson, C.P. *Reminiscences of Australia.* London: W.N Wright, 1846.

Howe, G. Melvyn. *Man, Environment and Disease in Britain: A Medical Geography of Britain through the Ages.* New York: Barnes and Noble Books, 1972.

Johnston, Anna. *Missionary Writing and Empire, 1800–1860.* Cambridge: Cambridge University Press, 2003.

Karskens, Grace. *The Colony: A History of Early Sydney.* Sydney: Allen and Unwin, 2009.

Kenny, Robert. *The Lamb Enters the Dreaming: Nathaniel Pepper and the Ruptured World.* Melbourne: Scribe, 2007.

Kenyon, A.S. *Pastures New: An Account of the Pastoral Occupation of Port Phillip.* Melbourne: Stockland Press, 1974; first published 1930.

King, Hazel. *Richard Bourke.* Melbourne: Oxford University Press, 1971.

Kociumbas, January. *The Oxford History of Australia, Vol. 2, 1770–1860: Possession.* Melbourne: Oxford University Press, 1992.

Lawson, Will. *Blue Gum Clippers and Whale Ships of Tasmania.* First published 1949; facsimile edition, Melbourne: D & C Book Distributors, 1986.

Lines, William J. *Taming the Great South Land: A History of the Conquest of Nature in Australia.* Sydney: Allen and Unwin, 1991.

Macintyre, Stuart and Scalmer, Sean (eds).*What If?: Australian History as It Might Have Been.* Melbourne: Melbourne University Press, 2006.

McCombie, Thomas. *The History of the Colony of Victoria from Its Settlement to the Death of Sir Charles Hotham.* London: Chapman and Hall, 1858.

McKinlay, Mary. *Forgotten Tasmanians.* Launceston: Foot and Playsted, 2010.

Nash, Michael. *The Bay Whalers: Tasmania's Shore-Based Whaling Industry.* Canberra: Navarine Publishing, 2003.

Neeson, J.M. *Commoners: Common Right, Enclosure and Social Change in England, 1700–1820.* Cambridge: Cambridge University Press, 1996.

Palmer, Joan Austin (ed.). *William Moodie: A Pioneer of Western Victoria.* Mortlake, Vic.: self published, 1973.

Pearse, Guy. *Quarterly Essay 33, Quarry Vision: Coal, Climate Change and the End of the Resources Boom.* Melbourne: Black Inc., 2009.

Powell, J.M. *The Public Lands of Australia Felix.* Oxford: Oxford University Press, 1970.

Presland, Gary. *First People: The Eastern Kulin of Melbourne, Port Phillip and Central Victoria.* Melbourne: Museum Victoria, 2010.

Presland, Gary. *The Place for a Village: How Nature Has Shaped the City of Melbourne.* Melbourne: Museum Victoria, 2008.

Reynolds, Henry. *Dispossession: Black Australians and White Invaders.* Sydney: Allen and Unwin, 1989.

Reynolds, Henry. *The Law of the Land*, 2nd edition. Melbourne: Penguin, 1992.

Reynolds, Henry. *This Whispering in Our Hearts.* Sydney: Allen and Unwin, 1998.

Reynolds, Henry. *Why Weren't We Told? A Personal Search for the Truth about Our History.* Melbourne: Penguin, 2000.

Roberts, Stephen. *The Squatting Age in Australia, 1835–1847.* Melbourne: Melbourne University Press, 1964.

Shaw, A.G.L. *Sir George Arthur, Bart, 1784–1854: Superintendent of British Honduras, Lieutenant-Governor of Van Diemen's Land and of Upper Canada, Governor of the Bombay Presidency.* Melbourne: Melbourne University Press, 1980.

Shaw, A.G.L. *A History of the Port Phillip District: Victoria Before Separation.* Melbourne: The Miegunyah Press, 1996.

Southgate, Beverley. *What Is History For?* Oxford: Routledge, 2005.

Sparrow, Jeff and Sparrow, Jill. *Radical Melbourne: A Secret History.* Melbourne: The Vulgar Press, 2001.

Stephen, C.E and Stephen, James. *The Life of the Right Honourable Sir James Stephen.* 1903.

Stephens, Marguerita. 'White Without Soap: Philanthropy, Caste and Exclusion in Colonial Victoria, 1835–1888: A Political Economy of Race.' PhD thesis, University of Melbourne, 2003.

Sullivan, Martin. *Men and Women of Port Phillip.* Sydney: Hale and Iremonger, 1985.

Tipping, Marjorie. *Convicts Unbound: The Story of the Calcutta Convicts and Their Settlement in Australia.* Ringwood, Victoria: Viking O'Neill, 1988.

Torrens, R. *Colonization of South Australia.* London: Longman, Rees, Orme,

Brown, Green and Longman, 1835; facsimile edition, Public Library of South Australia, 1962.

Trollope, Anthony. *Australia and New Zealand*. London: Chapman and Hall, 1873.

Turner, Henry Gyles. *A History of the Colony of Victoria: From Its Discovery to Its Absorption into the Commonwealth of Australia in Two Volumes, Vol. 1. A.D 1797–1854*. Melbourne: Heritage Publications, 1973; first published 1904.

Waterhouse, Richard. *The Vision Splendid: A Social and Cultural History of Rural Australia*. Fremantle: Curtin University Books, 2005.

Whitelock, Derek. *Adelaide, 1836–1976: A History of Difference*. St Lucia: University of Queensland Press, 1977.

Wiencke, Shirley W. *When the Wattles Bloom Again: The Life and Times of William Barak*. Melbourne: Self-published, 1984.

ARTICLES AND ESSAYS

Barta, Tony. '"They appear actually to vanish from the face of the earth." Aborigines and the European Project in Australia Felix.' *Journal of Genocide Research* 10.4, 2008.

Barwick, Diane. 'Mapping the Past: An Atlas of Victorian Clans, 1835–1904.' *Aboriginal History* 8.2, 1984.

Boyce, James. 'Canine Revolution: The Social and Environmental Impact of the Introduction of the Dog to Tasmania.' *Environmental History* 11.1, January 2006.

Broeze, Frank. 'Private Enterprise and the Peopling of Australasia 1831–50.' *The Economic History Review* 34.2, May 1982.

Broome, Richard. 'Victoria,' in Ann McGrath (ed.), *Contested Ground: Australian Aborigines under the British Crown*. Sydney: Allen and Unwin, 1995.

Clark, Ian D. 'George Augustus Robinson on Charles Joseph LaTrobe: Personal Insights into a Problematical Relationship.' *The LaTrobe Journal* 85, May 2010.

Clark, Ian D. "You Have All This Place No Good Have Children ..." Derrimut: Traitor, Saviour or a Man of His People?' *Journal of the Royal Australian Historical Society* 91.2, December 2005.

Elbourne, Elizabeth. 'Indigenous Peoples and Imperial Networks in the Early Nineteenth Century: The Politics of Knowledge,' in Phillip Buckner and R. Douglas Francis (eds), *Rediscovering the British World*. Calgary: University of Calgary Press, 2005.

Elbourne, Elizabeth. 'Between Van Diemen's Land and the Cape Colony,' in Anna Johnston and Mitchell Rolls (eds), *Reading Robinson: Companion Essays to* Friendly Mission. Hobart: Quintus Publishing, 2008.

References

Elbourne, Elizabeth. 'Imperial Politics in the Family Way: Gender, Biography and the 1835–36 Select Committee on Aborigines,' in Bain Attwood and Tom Griffiths (eds), *Frontier, Race, Nation: Henry Reynolds and Australian History*. Melbourne: Australian Scholarly Publishing, 2009.

Ford, Lisa. 'Before Settler Sovereignty and After Aboriginal Sovereignty: New South Wales in Global Settler Perspective, 1788–1836,' in Bain Attwood and Tom Griffiths (eds), *Frontier, Race, Nation: Henry Reynolds and Australian History*. Melbourne: Australian Scholarly Publishing, 2009.

Forth, Gordon. 'The Hentys, Whales and Sheep.' *Royal Historical Society of Victoria Journal* 55.4, December 1984.

Howell, P.A. 'The South Australia Act, 1834,' in Dean Jaensch (ed.), *The Flinders History of South Australia: Political History*. Adelaide: Wakefield Press, 1986.

Jones, Rhys. 'Fire-Stick Farming.' *Australian Natural History* 16, 1969.

Kociumbas, Jan. 'Genocide and Modernity in Colonial Australia, 1788–1850,' in A. Moses Dirk (ed.), *Genocide and Settler Society: Frontier Violence and Stolen Indigenous Children in Australian History*. Oxford: Berghahn Books, 2005.

Lester, Alan. 'British Settler Discourse and the Circuits of Empire.' *History Workshop Journal* 54, 2002.

Madden, Raymond. 'James Dawson's Scrapbook: Advocacy and Antipathy in Colonial Victoria,' in Lynette Russell and John Arnold (eds), *The La Trobe Journal* 85, May 2010.

Moses, Dirk. 'Genocide and Settler Society in Australian History,' in Dirk Moses (ed.), *Genocide and Settler Society: Frontier Violence and Stolen Indigenous Children in Australian History*. Oxford: Berghahn Books, 2005.

Murray-Smith, Stephen. 'Beyond the Pale: The Islander Community of Bass Strait in the 19th Century.' *THRA Papers and Proceedings* 20.4, 1973.

Pascoe, Bruce. 'How It Starts,' in Rachel Perkins and Marcia Langton (eds), *First Australians*. Melbourne: The Miegunyah Press, 2010.

Reynolds, Henry. 'George Augustus Robinson in Van Diemen's Land: Race, Status and Religion', in Anna Johnston and Mitchell Rolls (eds), *Reading Robinson: Companion Essays to* Friendly Mission. Hobart: Quintus Publishing, 2008.

Weaver, John C. 'Beyond the Fatal Shore: Pastoral Squatting and the Occupation of Australia, 1826 to 1852.' *The American Historical Review* 101.4, October 1996.

Published primary source documents

Billot C.P. (ed.). *Melbourne's Missing Chronicle: Being the Journal of Preparations for Departure to and Proceedings at Port Phillip by John Pascoe Fawkner*. Melbourne: Quartet Books, 1982.

Bride, Thomas Francis (ed.), *Letters from Victorian Pioneers*. Melbourne: Trustees of the Public Library, 1898.

Brown P.L. (ed.), *Clyde Company Papers, Vol. II: 1836–40*. Oxford: Oxford University Press, 1952.

Clark, C.M.H. *Select Documents in Australian History, 1788–1850*. Sydney: Angus and Robertson, 1950.

Clark, Ian D. (ed.). *The Journals of George Augustus Robinson, Chief Protector, Port Phillip Aboriginal Protectorate, Volume 1: 1 January 1839–30 September 1840*. Melbourne: Heritage Matters, 1998.

Historical Records of Victoria (HRV) Foundation Series, Volumes 1–3 and Volume 6. Melbourne: Public Record Office of Victoria.

Historical Records of Australia (HRA), Series 1 and Series 3. Sydney: Library Committee of the Commonwealth Parliament; and Melbourne: Melbourne University Press.

Peel Lynnette (ed.). *The Henty Journals: A Record of Farming, Whaling and Shipping at Portland Bay, 1834–1839*. Melbourne: The Miegunyah Press, 1996.

Plomley, N.J.B. (ed.). *Friendly Mission: The Tasmanian Journals of George Augustus Robinson*. Launceston: Queen Victoria Museum and Quintus Publishing, 2008.

Presland Gary (ed.). *Journals of G.A. Robinson, May to August 1841*. Report of the Victorian Archeological Survey, 1980.

Randell J.O. (ed.). *Alexander Fullerton Mollison: An Overlanding Diary, April–December 1837, from Uriara Station on the Murrumbidgee to Port Phillip, Victoria*. Melbourne: Mast Gully Press, 1980.

Shillinglaw, John J. *Historical Records of Port Phillip*. Melbourne: Government Printer, 1879.

The Todd Journal. Geelong: Geelong Historical Society, 1989.

Wiedenhofer, Margaret. *Garryowen's Melbourne: A Selection from the Chronicles of Early Melbourne, 1835 to 1852*. Melbourne: Nelson, 1967.

OTHER PRIMARY SOURCES

Archives Office of Tasmania (AOT)

    Colonial Office Papers, CO1.

    Wedge, J.H. 'Narrative of an Excursion Amongst the Natives of Port Phillip in the South Coast of New Holland, August 1835.

Kerr's Melbourne Almanac and Port Phillip Directory for 1842. Melbourne, 1842.

Mitchell Library (ML)

    Tuckey, J.M. *General Observations of Port Phillip*, 26 October 1803. Brabourne Papers, CY 1747.

Report of the Parliamentary Select Committee on Aboriginal Tribes (British Settlements). London: Reprinted with Comments by the Aborigines Protection Society, 1837.

Report of the Aborigines Committee for the Meeting for Sufferings. London, 1840.

State Library of Victoria (SLV):
Fawkner, John. 'Constitution and Form of Government'. SLV MS 13273.
George Mercer Papers. SLV MS 13166.
Henty Papers. SLV MSB 450.
Niel Black Papers. SLV MS 6035.
Port Phillip Papers. SLV MS 9142.
William Adeney Diary. SLV MS 8520 Box 991/5.
William Todd Journal. SLV MS 11243.

NEWSPAPERS
Argus
Cornwall Chronicle
Hobart Town Courier
Launceston Advertiser
Launceston Examiner
New South Wales Government Gazette
Port Phillip Gazette
Port Phillip Patriot
Sydney Gazette
Sydney Morning Herald

INDEX

The following abbreviations are used in the index: PP=Port Phillip; VDL=Van Diemen's Land